THIS IS MY STORY

Other books by Cleophus J. LaRue
from Westminster John Knox Press

The Heart of Black Preaching

*Power in the Pulpit: How America's Most Effective Black Preachers Prepare Their
Sermons*, EDITOR

THIS IS MY STORY

Testimonies and Sermons of Black Women in Ministry

Edited by

CLEOPHUS J. LARUE

WESTMINSTER
JOHN KNOX PRESS
LOUISVILLE · KENTUCKY

Unless otherwise indicated, Scripture quotations are from the New Revised Standard Version of the Bible, copyright © 1989 by the Division of Christian Education of the National Council of the Churches of Christ in the U.S.A., and are used by permission.

Scripture quotations marked NIV are from *The Holy Bible, New International Version*. Copyright © 1973, 1978, 1984 International Bible Society. Used by permission of Zondervan Bible Publishers.

Scripture quotations marked NKJV are from The New King James Version. Copyright © 1979, 1980, 1982, Thomas Nelson Inc., Publishers and are used by permission.

Scripture quotations marked TEV are from the *Good News Bible—New Testament*: Copyright © American Bible Society 1966, 1971, 1976.

Book design by Sharon Adams
Cover design by designpointinc.com

First edition
Published by Westminster John Knox Press
Louisville, Kentucky

This book is printed on acid-free paper that meets the American National Standards Institute Z39.48 standard.

PRINTED IN THE UNITED STATES OF AMERICA

05 06 07 08 09 10 11 12 13 14 — 10 9 8 7 6 5 4 3 2 1

Library of Congress Cataloging-in-Publication Data

This is my story : testimonies and sermons of Black women in ministry / Cleophus J. LaRue, editor.
    p. cm.
    ISBN 0-664-22776-7 (alk. paper)
    1. African American women clergy. 2. Sermons, American—African American authors. 3. Sermons, American—Women authors. 4. United States—Church history. 5. Black theology. 6. African Americans—Religion. I. LaRue, Cleophus James, 1953–

BR563.N4T465 2005
280′.4′092396073—dc22
[B]   2004057247

In loving memory of
Boyce Aloma Worsham Dilworth
(1924–1983)
Calvary First Baptist Church
Corpus Christi, Texas

"This woman was full of good works . . ."
(Acts 9:36 KJV)

This is my story, this is my song,
Praising my Savior all the day long;
This is my story, this is my song,
Praising my Savior all the day long.

.

CONTENTS

Acknowledgments

No work that gathers into a complete whole so many disparate parts is ever completed without the much needed aid of research assistants. In that regard, I wish to thank Audrey D. Thompson and Cedric Johnson, two very able PhD candidates at Princeton Theological Seminary, for the time and effort they put into this project. I also wish to thank my editor, Stephanie Egnotovich, who made this book better through her insightful and timely editorial comments. Finally, a word of thanks to the trailblazing women in this volume who have shared so freely the burdens and blessings of their call to ministry.

Introduction

Black Women and Ordained Christian Ministry

The twenty-first century will be the century for black women in ministry. In ever-increasing numbers they are announcing their calls to the gospel ministry and making haste to establish themselves in viable ministries throughout this country. Their presence in all levels of ordained Christian service—including preaching and pastoral ministries—promises to reshape our understanding of traditional clergy leadership roles, tilt us even more toward a neo-Pentecostal fervor in the way we have church, and provide us with new and creative ways of addressing problems within the community.

MY STORY

Despite the promises inherent in this new century, ordained ministry for black women continues to be an uphill battle. As one who grew up in a conservative black Baptist church in south Texas, I know how wrenching decisions pertaining to women in ordained ministry can be. Many of us came to faith in church environments that simply did not accept women as preachers and pastors. Not only did the ordination of women violate our sociocultural mores, it was also, we believed, clearly forbidden in Scripture. In black religious life women had their places in the pecking order of the church, but the pulpit was the God-given reserve of men. To violate that edict disrupted church life and marked the offending woman as a troublemaker.

I came to faith in a congregation where it was absolutely unacceptable for a woman to claim that she had been called by God to preach. It simply did not happen. When a woman thought she heard the call and had the guts to come forward, she was put in her place by the pastor in front of the entire congregation.

Women were not even allowed to stand behind the pulpit to so much as expound on a theme on special days or to address the congregation as a keynote speaker. They could only speak on the floor at the lectern or, in the common parlance of the black church, from the podium.

I accepted this stance toward women as gospel truth and established fact. It was the accepted worldview of my formative years. Those few women who insisted that they had been called by God to preach were thought by the rest of us to be eccentric to a fault or just downright "kooky." What woman in her right mind would knowingly subject herself to the wrath of God—we thought—and most assuredly to the wrath of the male pastors by insisting she had been called to preach?

As a young pastor in central Texas I, too, strongly discouraged any and all women who came forward claiming that God had called them to preach the gospel. When a woman minister visited our congregation for a funeral or some other special service, I joined with the deacons and other leaders of the church in preventing her from entering the pulpit. On one occasion we even threatened to call the police against a particularly outraged woman minister. I simply would not allow any woman claiming to be a preacher into the pulpit on my watch. Like the apostle Paul, I actually thought I was doing what pleased God.

When invited to sit on a Texas Baptist scholarship committee to award funds to prospective ministers, I took my prejudices against women preachers there as well. When an African American male minister was presented to the committee as being in need of financial assistance, I wholeheartedly supported his application. Few questions were asked and as much money as possible was awarded to him.

When a woman came forward saying she needed financial assistance in order to be trained as a missionary or a chaplain, I wholeheartedly supported her request. But when one came forward claiming she had been called by God to preach and therefore desired to prepare herself for ordained Christian ministry, I did all in my power to see to it that she would be denied. My negative stance toward women ministers was not the official position of the scholarship committee; I was simply acting out of my own prejudice, knowing full well I had the support of the Caucasian members of the committee who felt I knew best how to handle African American female ministerial candidates.

My Damascus road experience came one afternoon when the scholarship committee had adjourned for the day. A young woman who had been denied scholarship aid waited outside the building and confronted me as I was preparing to leave for home. She assured me that she well understood from my questioning that I was opposed to her call and goals in ministry. Though I protested to the contrary, she would have none of it.

In a calm voice devoid of any venom or mean-spiritedness she said to me, "Who are you to get in the way of what God has called me to do?" She assured me that even though she had been denied financial assistance, if God was indeed for her she would ultimately prevail. No more words were spoken between us, but I drove home that day a changed person. She had been denied the funds to further her education, but my stern opposition to women preachers had been dealt a lethal blow by the only thing that woman walked away with that day—her integrity.

My encounter left me shaken and convicted for she was right on target. I had used my influence to stop her and countless other women from receiving funds from our committee. It was simply an unspoken rule that we would vote against any woman who wanted to go into the gospel ministry. It was after seeing that woman's determination and utter trust in almighty God that I began seriously to rethink my position toward women in ministry. I, who had certainly known my share of prejudice and discrimination, was covertly involved in the very kind of prejudice I had railed against throughout my ministry. I knew that it could not continue.

After much prayer I decided to mention it to the members of my Texas congregation in a Sunday night service. I told them I could no longer maintain my diehard stance against women preachers even though it had been instilled in me from my youth. Much to my surprise some of the elders in the congregation whose judgment I feared the most were some of the first to say aloud in the service, "We were wondering when you would finally come around!"

Many of the women who openly expressed their support had given their best years in devoted service to God in secondary positions granted to them by male clergy. They turned out to be the most supportive in our efforts to think anew about women in ministry and to move forward in a more open and progressive way. Not long after that, I left the congregation for Princeton Theological Seminary and a whole new way of experiencing women in ministry.

The encounter with the young woman who had been denied financial assistance was the beginning of a complete reversal in my attitude toward women preachers. I have no idea where she is today, but when she decided to speak truth to entrenched intolerance she opened my blinded eyes that I might see. I do not know if she completed or even began her graduate education for I succeeded that day in preventing her from receiving any financial aid from people who had plenty of it to give. But she succeeded in showing me a more excellent way.

Churches that continue to resist the presence of women in positions of leadership and authority within their ordained clergy could well find themselves marginalized among the marginalized and on the decline in the coming years. Many black women who have their hearts set on ministry and who are determined to heed God's call continue to encounter stiff resistance from both men and women, yet they give no indication of backing away from what they believe to be their God-given right and undeniable destiny.

It is women in ministry, and the progressive males who welcome their presence, who have captured the imagination of a large segment of the black religious public. A new generation of African American leaders is coming to more prominent positions of authority in the black church, and any number are already showing signs of being more open to progressive styles of leadership, new ways of presenting the gospel, and most important, to allowing all of the faithful to participate and contribute to Christian ministry.

THE UPHILL CLIMB

Ordination of women in the United States dates back to the early nineteenth century.[1] While Antoinette Louisa Brown is believed to have been the first American woman ordained to full Christian ministry, black women have also been at the forefront of ordination struggles throughout American history.[2] Even in pre–Civil War years, women preachers were not unknown.[3]

The first black denomination to officially ordain women to the ministry was the African Methodist Episcopal Zion Church. In 1894 Bishop James Walker Hood ordained Julia A. Foote deacon. The following year Bishop Alexander Walters ordained Mary J. Small deacon. Small was later ordained "elder" in 1898 with Foote following in 1900. Thus Small and Foote became the first women to achieve the rights of full ordination to the ministry by any Methodist denomination, black or white.[4]

More than one hundred years have passed since the first black women were ordained to ministry and still only three of the seven major black denominations listed by C. Eric Lincoln and Lawrence Mamiya in their seminal study *The Black Church in the African American Experience* are officially on record as being supportive of women in ordained ministry: AME Zion, African Methodist Episcopal (AME), and Christian Methodist Episcopal (CME). The AME Church, at its quadrennial meeting in 2000, became the first of the big seven black denominations to break the glass ceiling of the bishopric by ordaining Vashti McKenzie as its first woman bishop.

The AME Church raised two more female bishops to the episcopacy at their quadrennial conference in 2004—Carolyn Tyler Guidry, a presiding elder from Los Angeles, and Sarah Frances Davis, a minister from San Antonio, Texas. In addition to being the first of three women in the denomination's top ranks, Bishop McKenzie accomplished another milestone by being selected to serve as president of the AME Church's Council of Bishops. Her elevation to that post made her the first woman bishop in any of the black church traditions to be the titular head of the church.[5]

While black Methodists are making huge strides in matters related to the ordination and advancement of women in ministry, the National Baptist Convention U.S.A., Inc., the National Baptist Convention of America, and the Progressive National Baptist Convention have no formal record of support for women in ordained ministry. What one finds at the national level, in many instances, is open hostility and entrenched resistance to all black female clergy. One highly respected Baptist pastor is believed to have lost his bid for his convention's presidency for merely hinting that he might be open to the possibility of ordaining women in the black Baptist convention he was seeking to lead.

The most heated resistance comes primarily from the old guard—men and women alike. The notable exception among sizable black Baptist bodies is the Full Gospel Baptist Fellowship headquartered in New Orleans, Louisiana. The Fellowship, presided over by Bishop Paul S. Morton, in its doctrinal statement under the heading of Full Gospel Distinctives says:

> We believe in Jesus Christ as the sovereign giver of Spiritual Gifts to the church. We believe that Spiritual Gifts are given for the perfecting of the Saints, for the work of ministry, and for the edifying of the body of Christ and are given without regard to ethnicity, social class or gender. (Ephesians 4:7–12, Galatians 3:26–28)[6]

Many black Baptist convention officials say that because of the congregational polity that governs their church procedures their practice has been not to interfere with the autonomy of the local congregation. Some say they are considering an up or down vote on the matter in the near future, but even with an affirmative vote the conventions could not require local churches to ordain women.

Even though there are no official pronouncements from the black Baptist denominations proper, individual churches, associations, and state conventions are on record in support of the ordination of women. While some endorse the utilization of women at all levels of ministry, others make a distinction between the preaching/teaching ministry and pastoral ministry. For some years now local Baptist pastors have licensed and ordained women and also hired them to staff the ministries of the church. In 2003, in one of the more progressive moves for black Baptists in the United States, the Baptist General Convention of Virginia elected Patricia Gould-Champ, pastor of the Faith Community Baptist Church in Richmond, Virginia, as its first female state president.

Even in denominations where women are allowed to participate in ordained ministries at every level, however, black women often get short shrift in church assignments and promotions. In connectional churches they are frequently assigned to struggling charges in the poorest parts of town with low budgets and declining memberships. Irrespective of denominational affiliation, some are sent or called to churches that are on the verge of collapse with the expectation that once in place they will either perform miracles or preside, in a dignified manner, over the church's imminent demise.

In the more conservative black churches, much is done by the leadership privately to prevent a woman from going public with her call. It is for many pastors an unsettling, contentious, gut-wrenching episode in the life of their congregation that they would simply like to avoid. But if the "unrepentant" woman insists on going forward with her call announcement, immediately on the heels of her public profession, she is asked to renounce her call and return to an acceptable position of leadership that she could fill without controversy. Those are the options: Renounce the call. Return to your station. Take a lesser, noncontroversial position. Or be asked to leave the congregation.

In those churches where the resistance is entrenched, the women who refuse to leave are ignored and shut out of every opportunity to exercise their ministerial gifts. In some cases, the pastor apparently grants permission for the public announcement of the call in order to make a public example of the offending woman to the rest of the congregation. Other women feel such hostility and wrath from church leaders, including the pastor, that they no longer feel comfortable remaining in that particular congregation. The pressure simply becomes more than they can bear so they leave in search of a more supportive environment.

While this is the case in many churches, it is also true that there are countless churches and pastors who have long opened their doors to women seeking to exercise their ministerial gifts. In cities across America churches exist that can best be described as "safe havens" for women who openly confess their call to the ministry and seek to minister in a particular community.

The male preachers who are progressive enough to open their doors to these women are frequently ostracized by their male colleagues for "letting down the bar," to allow women into the ministry. Some of the "safe haven" pastors have been known to break fellowship with their colleagues, while others try to have it both ways. They allow women to minister within the circles of the local church fellowship, but they will not go so far as to insist to other unapproving males that women be included in every sphere of ministerial activity in the life of the community.

For example, if a pastor who accepts women in ministry fellowships with a local congregation where they are not accepted, he will not force their presence on the church he is visiting. On such occasions, the women preachers are usually asked to take their seat with the rest of the membership in the pews while the male preachers enjoy all the privileges of the fellowship—the preservice visit in the pastor's office, a seat in the pulpit during worship, and a seat at the pastor's table during the after-service food and fellowship hour. Small matters indeed, but they are often used to remind women of their "place" in the male hierarchical structure. In another example, if the local ministerial alliance does not support women preachers, even some of the progressive pastors will encourage the women ministers in their church not to attend the alliance meetings so as not to stir up controversy. ⌣

When facing situations in which women are not allowed to participate in every capacity of ministerial life and fellowship, truly progressive pastors also refuse to participate. While the number of progressive male pastors is growing—especially among the seminary-trained younger pastors—opposition to women in ordained ministry is significant and deeply embedded in the customs and mores of the male clergy leadership in all too many black churches.

Even black male seminarians, supportive of women while in school, upon graduation tend to return to the all-male club of pastoral leadership, downplaying or outright forsaking the bonds forged with their women preacher friends and acquaintances while in school. Some say while they still support women, once out of school, they loosen the ties so as not to offend male colleagues who have not been exposed to women preachers in the relational settings of the seminary or who continue to resist their participation out of fear and ignorance. Others simply acknowledge that their continued support of women could hurt their own chances of receiving a call to a "major house."

The deliberate slights and intentional insults are without end even for women who are trained and ordained by denominations that fully accept their credentials. In some cases the women who are being denied admittance have more education than the males who are refusing to accept them. Keen to such pitfalls, black women preachers are always on the lookout for those occasions when they must interact with pastors throughout the city—funerals, holy day observances, the Martin Luther King Jr. holiday, citywide revivals, and other such activities.

With so many roadblocks thrown in their paths by those who hold power in the bona fide institutional settings, black women often seek affirmation and certification through formal study. Their divinity school and seminary numbers are increasing annually. According to the latest figures from *The Fact Book on Theological Education 2003–04*, black men outnumber black women in enrollment in accredited institutions by a mere 350 students (black men number 4,186 while black women number 3,834).

Yet doors continue to be closed to them. In the face of this outright repression and discrimination, some of the more obstinate denominations such as Baptists and some neo-Pentecostals are losing many talented women to the United Methodists, the United Church of Christ, the Presbyterian Church (U.S.A.), and other denominations that freely accept women and don't make it so difficult for them to become a part of their group. There is a monumental, spiritual drain going on in many traditional black churches as women are forced to leave those congregations or bow out because of the staunch resistance on the part of the black male leadership and others in positions of authority.

I am convinced that opponents of women in ministry, even those who are well intentioned, are on the wrong side of history, Scripture, Christian practice, and the unfolding revelatory will of God. The arguments pro and con are repeated *ad nauseam*. Some of the arguments are so clearly sexist that it is difficult to believe they are still being bandied about in the twenty-first century.

Opponents of women ministers contend that the demands of ministry and the peculiar demands of motherhood are mutually incompatible; it is inappropriate for a menstruating, married, or pregnant woman to preside at Communion or lead in worship; women simply do not have the emotional stability to do proper ministry; the presence of women in ministry will feminize the church and cause it to lose its masculine edge; and the ascendency of black women to the pulpit will further erode the presence of positive black male role models in a culture that is already dominated by women.[7]

Those who favor women's ordination point to the long and illustrious history of women in the mission field, noting how churches have unanimously hailed the accomplishments of such women in spreading the gospel around the world. They point to the fact that there are just as many scriptures that support women in ministry as oppose it. They argue that the New Testament is diverse and even contradictory regarding the status of women. Moreover, they are careful to note the manner in which the historical Jesus deliberately broke customs that were degrading to the self-concept of women.[8]

Arguments abound on both sides. However, when all is said and done it is simply time for black churches to wake up and see how much damage we are doing by continuing to block the opportunities available to capable and energetic women in ministry. For all of us who speak with such power and conviction about who God does and does not call to ordained ministry maybe the words of the prophet Isaiah are the words we most need to hear:

> For my thoughts are not your thoughts, nor are your ways my ways, says the LORD. For as the heavens are higher than the earth, so are my ways higher than your ways and my thoughts than your thoughts. (Isa. 55:8–9)

CONTEMPORARY WOMEN TELL THEIR STORY

This work brings together the accomplishments of a diverse group of contemporary women from a cross section of ministries throughout the country. Some are accomplished pastors, professors, and chaplains, while others are just beginning their graduate studies in seminary.

Cokiesha L. Bailey, a minister at the Concord Baptist Church in Dallas, Texas, and a student at the Beeson Divinity School of Samford University in

Birmingham, Alabama, grew up as the eldest daughter of a prominent Texas pastor who often expressed his disapproval of women in ordained ministry. Bailey's most difficult moment came when it was time to confront her father with the announcement of her own call. Her struggle proved instrumental in bringing him to a new level of understanding.

Cecelia E. Greene Barr, pastor of the Trinity AME Church in Detroit, Michigan, sensed early on that God had a special claim on her life. Initially lacking role models who could guide her along the way, Barr carved her own path in ministry through trial and error. She founded her own ministry in order to be of service to her community and eventually accepted a call to pastor her first church.

Deborah K. Blanks was nurtured in the loving environment of the AME Church. Her family's history in the Methodist church extended through several generations, and she heard the call of God while an undergraduate student in college. Blanks's ministry has taken her through ten years of chaplaincy in the United States Navy, three years at Brown University in Rhode Island, and finally to her present position as associate dean of religious life and of the chapel at Princeton University. Breaking new ground was never easy for Blanks, yet she is certain that she has been called to ministry for such a time as this.

Alyson Diane Browne, a former AME pastor and now director of ministries at the First Baptist Church of Lincoln Gardens in Somerset, New Jersey, probes the deep places of her heart as she reflects on her rich experiences in ministry. Browne tells her story of repressed childhood experiences, a failed marriage, doubts about her ministerial gifts, and her unsuccessful attempts to find happiness in others. She believes God's call to preach actually saved her life. In the acceptance of her call, she finally came to the realization that her place in life would not be determined by her might, nor her strength, but by the Lord's spirit. Browne speaks with power and conviction of her ministerial journey.

Delores Carpenter is a pastor, professor, prolific author, and an indefatigable trailblazer. Her story is one of reversal and disappointment, but also triumph and accomplishment. As pastor of the Michigan Park Christian Church in Washington, DC, and professor of religious education at Howard University's School of Divinity, Carpenter has inspired untold numbers of men and women to fight the good fight. Her story is up close and personal. She speaks candidly of her battle with cancer and the impact it had on her ministry. She ponders her failures and the manner in which they have helped her to become an even stronger minister. When one reads her story, one senses in her a determination "to run on and see what the end will bring."

Odessa Coder is a pastor in the Church of God in Christ in Lancaster, Pennsylvania. Her story is filled with all the human drama most pastors experience having served a congregation for over twenty years. In keeping with her Pentecostal heritage, Coder is not shy about her belief in the gifts of the Spirit.

She speaks boldly of how she has used those gifts to further the cause of Christ among her parishioners and community alike. She recounts miraculous healings and testifies to the power of prayer. She also speaks openly of the hurt she has been dealt at the hands of other Pentecostal women who simply could not believe that she had been called by God to preach and to pastor.

Claudette Anderson Copeland, licensed as an evangelist at the age of eighteen in the Church of God in Christ, has also served as a chaplain in the U.S. Air Force Chaplaincy. She founded C.O.P.E. professional services, a consulting agency for personal effectiveness in the public sector, and also Destiny Ministries, a national empowerment organization for women. She tells a very moving story of personal loneliness and sorrow and how those experiences helped her to give glory to God. Raised as a Pentecostal, she too trusted God for her healing when confronted with serious bouts of cancer. Hers is a story of triumph and tragedy that will surely serve as a source of encouragement to the many who have their own stories of sickness and disappointment.

LaVerne M. Gill, pastor of the Webster United Church of Christ in Dexter, Michigan, had grown accustomed to being in the driver's seat when it came to her career choices and goals. However, God's persistent call and claim on her life lifted her to a new level of dependence on a higher power, forcing her to admit that she was no longer in the driver's seat. Her greatest challenge continues to be doing it God's way and on God's time. Encouraged in her ministry by the powerful women with whom she came in contact during her student days at Howard University, Gill finally said yes to God in her early fifties and headed immediately to seminary. She excelled at Princeton Theological Seminary and upon graduation accepted her new responsibilities at Webster United Church of Christ. Gill brings the power of her positive attitude to her writing as she speaks of the setbacks and surprises of her ministry.

Alison P. Gise Johnson, assistant professor of theology and ethics at Virginia Union University's Samuel DeWitt Proctor School of Theology, tells how she left a lucrative job as a chemical engineer to enter seminary. Over the protests of her father she heeded God's call with much tension, but also without apology. Refusing to provide what she calls a "soft lens gaze" at her ministry, she chooses instead to expose her readers to the tensions, tears, and triumphs of her journey.

Cynthia L. Hale is the founding senior pastor of the Ray of Hope Christian Church in Decatur, Georgia. This remarkable woman began with four people meeting for Bible study. That number has increased to 7,500 persons over the last 17 years. Ray of Hope has an active membership of 3,500 and averages 2,000 in worship each Sunday morning. Her success in ministry has come at a price, and Hale speaks openly of the trade-off she's had to live with as a result of choices she made early on in her ministry.

Carla A. Jones, a recent seminary graduate, had to decide if she would quit her job as a schoolteacher in order to study full time for her Master of Divinity degree. This was no easy decision given the fact that Jones was a single mother who would have to move away from her extended family and bear all the responsibilities for maintaining a home and raising a young daughter. In her powerful and compelling testimony, Jones writes of the challenges of seminary and her single-parent status. She also speaks candidly of the sexual harassment she encountered while attending school and of her disappointment with those who took her complaints so lightly.

Cheryl A. Kirk-Duggan is clearly a free spirit who seeks God's counsel every step of the way. From the man she eventually married to her unexpected enrollment in seminary, Kirk-Duggan sees the hand of God in every decision. Even the disappointments were viewed by Kirk-Duggan as blessings from God. Hers is a faith journey, and she writes of that journey in a powerful and convincing way.

Charlotte McSwine-Harris knows all too well the highs and lows of ministry. Turned off in her youth by the old ways of having church, she experienced new highs in ministry when she relocated to the Midwest in search of employment. Her positive experiences at the progressive church she attended helped her to hear and heed her own call. The church fight that came to her in later years wounded her spirit and discouraged her heart but made her stronger and even more determined to stand her ground. Hers is a candid look at the ups and downs of pastoral ministry.

Having the thirteen women in this volume tell their story is intended to serve as an inspiration for all women who have made great strides and advances in spite of the many obstacles that have been placed before them. For the women who have made it, telling their story of how they have been able to overcome should be a source of much encouragement for those who are just starting out, or who find their way being blocked by outmoded customs and traditions.

While some of the writers are well established in their ministerial careers, others are at the preparatory stages. Some have found their voices in institutional settings, while others have felt led to pursue specialized ministries. But they all have a story. Their stories and the sermons that accompany them are reflective of the reservoir of talent and potential that reside in so many women who have heard and heeded the call of God on their lives. A sermon from each woman is included in this volume, because preaching inevitably reflects where we are in our worldview and how we have come to that place.

Moreover, male clergy, detractors and supporters alike, need to hear their stories in order to be reminded of the vast potential and gains of so many women when the household of God accepts them for who they are and what God has called them to be. The church can only be strengthened when women are no longer hindered by the constraints of outmoded customs, poorly constructed theologies, and indefensible, literal biblical translations.

Finally, the stories of these women, and countless others just like them, need to be told in seminaries and divinity schools across the country as a way of informing students and professors of the many possibilities that await women who are in preparation for ministry. I hope that this work will add to the growing body of womanist literature already on the market that provides ample testimony of the courage, fortitude, and determination of women who have heard the call of God and are determined to heed it at any price.

NOTES

1. Ordination is practiced and delineated in a variety of ways in different denominational traditions. Different denominations have different levels of ordination. There is ordination to deacons' orders; ordination to lay leadership; ordination to sacramental authority, without full standing or access to denominational decision making; ordination with full membership in conference or diocesan structures. In its fullest sense ordination is intended to confer upon one the most complete and unrestricted set of functions relating to the ministry of the gospel, administering the Word and sacrament, or carrying out the office of pastor or priest in the church. See Barbara Zikmund, Adair Lummis, and Patricia Chang, *Clergy Women: An Uphill Calling* (Louisville, KY: Westminster John Knox Press, 1998), 3.
2. See Delores C. Carpenter, *A Time for Honor: A Portrait of African American Women Clergy* (St. Louis: Chalice Press, 2001), 1–23; and Nancy A. Hardesty, *Women Called to Witness: Evangelical Feminism in the 19th Century* (Nashville: Abingdon Press, 1984), 97. Brown was ordained on September 15, 1853, by the First Congregational Church of Butler and Savannah, Wayne County, New York. The service was an ecumenical one—held in the Baptist church because it was larger, with the sermon given by Wesleyan Methodist Luther Lee and the charge delivered by Presbyterian Gerrit Smith.
3. Early in the twentieth century a number of denominations began ordaining women. Among them: the Apostolic Overcoming Holy Church of God (1916), Assemblies of God (1914), Church of the Nazarene (1908), Free Methodist Church (1911), General Conference Mennonite Church (1911), General Association of General Baptists (ca. 1925), and International Foursquare Gospel (1927). In the 1950s and '60s a number of churches began ordaining women, including the precursors of the United Methodist Church and the Presbyterian Church (U.S.A.) in 1956, the Church of the Brethren (1958), Latvian Evangelical Lutheran Church in America (1960), Apostolic Faith Mission Church of God (1963), and Bible Church of Christ (1964). The 1970s and '80s saw an even more rapid increase in the number of churches moving to include women within the ranks of their ordained clergy. Included among them were the Lutheran Church in America (1970), Moravian Church in America (1970), Mennonite Church (1973), Association of Evangelical Lutheran Churches (1976), Reformed Church in America (1981), and the Reorganized Church of Jesus Christ of Latter Day Saints (1984). J. Gordon Melton, *Women's Ordination: Offi-*

cial Statements from Religious Bodies and Ecumenical Organizations (Detroit: Gale Research Inc., 1991), 6–7.

4. C. Eric Lincoln and Lawrence Mamiya, *The Black Church in the African American Experience* (Durham, NC: Duke University Press, 1990), 285.

5. John M. Buchanan, "AME Church Elects More Women Bishops," *The Christian Century* (July 27, 2004): 18–19.

6. This doctrinal statement can be found under Full Gospel Distinctives at the Web site of the Full Gospel Baptist Church Fellowship. Included among the gifts listed in Ephesians 4:7–12 are apostles, prophets, evangelists, pastors, and teachers.

7. Biblical texts that supposedly argue against the ordination of women:

    (1) Genesis 2:18–23—Then the LORD God said, "It is not good that the man should be alone: I will make him a helper as his partner." . . . so the LORD God caused a deep sleep to fall upon the man, and he slept; then he took one of his ribs and closed up its place with flesh. And the rib that the LORD God had taken from the man he made into a woman and brought her to the man.

    (2) Mark 3:13–19:
    He went up the mountain and called to him those whom he wanted, and they came to him. And he appointed twelve, whom he also named apostles, to be with him, and to be sent out to proclaim the message, and to have authority to cast out demons. So he appointed the twelve: Simon (to whom he gave the name Peter); James son of Zebedee and John the brother of James (to whom he gave the name Boanerges, that is, Sons of Thunder); and Andrew, and Philip, and Bartholomew, and Matthew, and Thomas, and James son of Alphaeus, and Thaddaeus, and Simon the Cananaean, and Judas Iscariot, who betrayed him.

    (3) 1 Corinthians 11:3–9:
    But I want you to understand that Christ is the head of every man, and the husband is the head of his wife, and God is the head of Christ. Any man who prays or prophesies with something on his head disgraces his head, but any woman who prays or prophesies with her head unveiled disgraces her head—it is one and the same thing as having her head shaved. . . . Indeed, man was not made from woman, but woman from man. Neither was man created for the sake of woman, but woman for the sake of man.

    (4) 1 Corinthians 14:34–35:
    Women should be silent in the churches. For they are not permitted to speak, but should be subordinate, as the law also says. If there is anything they desire to know, let them ask their husbands at home. For it is shameful for a woman to speak in church.

    (5) 1 Timothy 2:11–15:
    Let a woman learn in silence with full submission. I permit no woman to teach or to have authority over a man; she is to keep silent. For Adam was formed first, then Eve; and Adam was not deceived, but the woman was deceived and became a transgressor. Yet she will be saved through childbearing, provided they continue in faith and love and holiness, with modesty.

    (6) Ephesians 5:22–24:
    Wives, be subject to your husbands as you are to the Lord. For the husband is the head of the wife just as Christ is the head of the church, the body of which he is the Savior. Just as the church is subject to Christ, so also wives ought to be, in everything, to their husbands.

(7) Titus 2:1–5:

But as for you, teach what is consistent with sound doctrine. Tell the older men to be temperate, serious, prudent, and sound in faith, in love, and in endurance. Likewise, tell the older women to be reverent in behavior, not to be slanderers or slaves to drink; they are to teach what is good, so that they may encourage the young women to love their husbands, to love their children, to be self-controlled, chaste, good managers of the household, kind, being submissive to their husbands, so that the word of God may not be discredited.

(8) 1 Peter 3:1–6:

Wives, in the same way, accept the authority of your husbands, so that, even if some of them do not obey the word, they may be won over with-out a word by their wives' conduct . . . Thus Sarah obeyed Abraham and called him lord. You have become her daughters as long as you do what is good and never let fears alarm you.

Those opposed to the ordination of women will vary in their interpretation of these scriptural texts. For example, some will emphasize the matter of wifely submission and secondary status. Others say that it is not that women are infe-rior or unequal, but that they simply have different roles to play. Opponents of women's ordination contend that the fact men cannot give birth and women cannot be priests are not value judgments, but merely the way creation has been ordered. See Melton, *A Survey of the Women's Ordination Issue*, pp. 6–7; and Alvera Mickelsen, ed., *Women, Authority and the Bible* (Downers Grove, IL: InterVarsity Press, 1986), 74–75.

8. Proponents argue that the attitude of Jesus toward women in the four canoni-cal Gospels is different from that of his contemporaries, whether Greek or Jew-ish. The wisdom of the ancients about women is totally absent from the traditions about Jesus. Jesus was perfectly at ease in the company of women since for him equality between the sexes was not so much a distant legislative goal as a rather self-evident fact. Jesus had women followers who learned from him, traveled with him at times, and supported him financially (Luke 8:2–3; see also Mark 15:41). He frequently ministered to women: he healed Peter's mother-in-law (Mark 1:29–31); he exorcised a demon from the daughter of a Syrophoenician woman (Mark 7:24–30; Matt. 15:21–30); he raised Jairus's daughter from the dead (Mark 9:20–22); he raised a widow's son at Nain (Luke 7:11–17); he taught Mary and Martha in their home at Bethany (Luke 10:38–42); and he healed a crippled woman in a synagogue. Moreover, Jesus gave women an uncommon degree of regard and responsibility, including them among his band of followers (e.g., Luke 8:2–3). As the first witnesses to the res-urrection, the women were advised to "Go and tell" (Matt. 28:7). Just because Jesus did not include a woman among the twelve disciples is no reason to exclude women from the ordained ministry. After all, Jesus did not include a Gentile, or for that matter, an African American male among the original dis-ciples, either. Proponents argue that the story of Mary and Martha indicates that women should participate in spiritual matters rather than just busy them-selves with household concerns. Melton, *A Survey of the Women's Ordination Issue*, and Virginia Ramey Mollenkott, *Women, Men, and the Bible* (New York: Crossroad Publishing Company, 1989), 4–5.

Contributors

Cokiesha Lashon Bailey, minister at Concord Baptist Church, Dallas, TX, and M.Div. student at Beeson Divinity School at Samford University in Birmingham, AL

Cecelia E. Greene Barr, pastor of Trinity African Methodist Episcopal Church and founder of Sharing Faith Ministries in Detroit, MI

Deborah K. Blanks, associate dean of religious life and of the chapel at Princeton University in Princeton, NJ

Alyson Diane Browne, director of ministries at the First Baptist Church of Lincoln Gardens in Somerset, NJ

Delores Carpenter, professor of religious education at Howard University School of Divinity and senior pastor of Michigan Park Christian Church in Washington, DC

Odessa Coder, pastor of St. Paul's Church of God in Christ, Lancaster, PA.

Claudette Anderson Copeland, pastor and cofounder of New Christian Fellowship and Destiny Ministries in San Antonio, TX

LaVerne M. Gill, pastor of the Webster United Church of Christ in Dexter, MI

Alison P. Gise Johnson, assistant professor of theology and ethics at the Samuel DeWitt Proctor School of Theology, Virginia Union University, Richmond, VA

Cynthia L. Hale, founder and senior pastor of the Ray of Hope Christian Church in Decatur, GA

Carla A. Jones, assistant minister of the Bright Hope Missionary Baptist Church in Philadelphia and a recent graduate of Princeton Theological Seminary, Princeton, NJ

Cheryl A. Kirk-Duggan, professor of theology and women's studies, director of women's studies, Shaw University Divinity School in Raliegh, NC,
  and ordained minister, Christian Methodist Episcopal Church
Charlotte McSwine-Harris, pastor of Charles City Community Church in
  Charles City, VA

1

The Testimony
of a Butterfly

CokIESHA LASHON BAILEY

I have been called to preach the gospel of Jesus Christ, not to bring glory to myself, but because it is a burden that has been placed upon me, so woe unto me if I preach not the gospel.

As children we were awestruck by the mystique and majesty of the butterfly. It didn't matter if we spotted one resting on a flower, flying around a garden, or preserved in a jar at school. Its life cycle always kept us amazed and bewildered. I found myself asking a series of questions as a young girl: "Why does something so beautiful have to go through so many ugly stages in life?" "Why does it take all of that for this sought-out creature to finally spread its wings?" Soon I began reading about the butterfly, its functions, how it is formed, and how long it takes to complete all of its stages. I found that without the egg, there would be no caterpillar; without the caterpillar, there would be no cocoon; and without the cocoon, there would be no butterfly.

Parallels can be drawn between our lives and the life of the brilliant butterfly. We cannot and must not dwell too long in one stage of life. Our graduation from one level to the next does not happen overnight but is a season that produces patience and builds character. We cannot spread our wings until our will, fleshy desires, and arrogant attitudes have been broken. It is in these various stages that we learn to understand that we cannot control life but that we can control how we react to our life circumstances. Furthermore, it is in the cocoon stage of life that we see new facets of God's character and new dimensions of his great love.

I was born to Sheila M. Smith Bailey and the late Reverend Doctor E. K. Bailey, and I grew up in the all-American city of Dallas. The lone star state has been our family's home for more than thirty years. My father, a preacher since the age of seventeen, moved from Oakland, California, to Dallas to attend Bishop College, a historically black school that prepared Christian leaders to impact the world. There he met my mother, a native of Stamford, Connecticut, who moved to Dallas to attend Bishop College as well. My father, a religion major, and my mother, a Christian education major, fell in love, married, and began their new lives as ministry partners upon graduating. My father served as a pastor for seven years before organizing Concord Missionary Baptist Church in 1975.

After trying for several years, often frustrated and tempted to give up, my parents learned that my mother was pregnant. My mother shared stories with me about the joys and challenges of being pregnant while standing by the side of a young pastor who was experiencing the highs and lows of ministry. My mother, recalling the day that I was born, said, "Initially, I was shocked at the time of your birth. It was eight weeks before the scheduled date. I was afraid that there could have been a problem, but afterwards I was so happy that you were alive, well, and beautiful."

I cherish many memories of my immediate family (which included my parents; my younger sister, Shenikwa; my god-brother, A.B.; my cousin and "brother in-love," Stuart; and my youngest brother, Emon). Other special times were spent with our beloved church members. In fact, members of the Concord church became surrogate aunts, uncles, brothers, and sisters. There were not many memories over the years that I can recall that did not include fellowshipping with our church family. For my parents and me, Concord was more than our church family; it was an extension of our community and an extension of our hearts.

One of my favorite times at church each week was in our children's church. In my opinion, our children's church was the best thing going. We had our own tailor-made service, which included our special songs, prayers, and exciting messages preached on our level. Our children's pastor was Rev. Charles C. Martin, who was a young, prolific, up-and-coming minister and musician. We were amazed at how he could preach powerfully to our parents in what we called "big church" on some Sundays and then could turn around on other Sundays and preach on our level in children's church. For years, after graduating into the youth ministry, my peers and I remembered Pastor Martin and his wife, Earlene Martin, fondly because they loved us enough that they took the time to make the Bible clear to those of us in the first through the sixth grades. It was fun, interesting, and most of all, the foundation of our spiritual journey.

Around the age of eight, I recall asking Jesus to come into my heart in children's church. I knew that he saved me, but I couldn't grasp his unconditional love and grace. So, I asked my mother at home one night if she could help me to make sure that I was a Christian. She explained 1 John to me in a way that helped me to understand God's love for me and his saving power. I was convinced after we prayed that night that I was in God's capable care and that my salvation and eternal life need not ever be questioned again.

I was a shy little girl—painfully shy. I still can't believe how difficult it was for me to simply say hello to people at times. I remember relying a lot on my siblings and my closest friends to be my mouthpiece. Although I didn't talk in public much, I really enjoyed being around so many talkative people at church. In fact, I drew from their outgoing and courageous spirits, and I dreamed that I could grow into a young lady who was poised, confident, and able to speak up.

Years rolled by swiftly. Church remained the cornerstone of our family and my heart's delight. I was very enthusiastic about attending church services, not only because I had an opportunity to worship and fellowship, but also because I loved watching my father in the pulpit. He was the world's handsomest pastor in my book. He was strong, compassionate, as gentle as a lamb and as stern as a lion. He was also the most generous individual I have ever known. He was my best friend. When my siblings and I would tell it, he had to be the most gifted preacher/pastor in the world. We were just proud to be his children. I marveled at how loving he was at home and how he made time for each one of us.

I know that it was only God's favor that allowed him to have the strength to nurture us, while maintaining a healthy relationship with my mother and a caring relationship with his twenty-plus member staff, his two hundred-plus sons in the ministry, and anyone else who needed his time, his ear, or his resources. During my teenaged years, I remember him flying all over the world preaching at revivals, crusades, conferences, and so forth.

My mother, a beautiful Christian woman, has been used by God as a national speaker. She served at our church for a season as the director of christian education. She worked over time creating and developing church curricula that would assist my father and his team in building healthy spiritual leaders. I am amazed at how she found the time not only to be a family woman, but to work as a full-time church staff member, while preparing speeches and information to encourage ministers' wives throughout the country.

Needless to say, my parents had a lifestyle that included ministry, marriage, and family. They made it clear that we were blessed not because of who we were, but because of who God is. Even when people began referring to Concord as "one of the nation's fastest-growing churches," our parents always reminded us that God was the author and orchestrator. As my father became more seasoned and sought out, I recognized that the Lord was showering our family with favor. My parents were being asked to speak throughout the United States and abroad. My father's vision of starting a nonprofit organization that would prepare pastors and preachers to impart the Word to impact the world was suddenly becoming a reality. I knew that there was something special that God wanted my father and mother to accomplish together in ministry. I was just happy to be along for the ride.

By the time I graduated from high school and entered college, I had become somewhat burned out by church. Being involved in the various ministries and representing our family at numerous functions began to take its toll on me. I loved God and my parents very much, but the pressures of being a preacher's kid were beginning to suffocate me. I remember arriving on the campus of Fisk University with mixed emotions. I was sad about the idea of being away from my parents and about being in a new city, but I can also recall the excitement of leaving Dallas, the place where everyone referred to me as "Pastor Bailey's daughter." At Fisk I was free to become an independent adult woman. But most of all, no one would care that my dad was a preacher—or so I thought.

My heart smiles at the memories that were created at Fisk. That was a time in my life that I will always hold dear to my heart. Although I had been raised in the church, my college experience was the time that God used the church to grow up in me. One of the first student ministries that I was introduced to was the Baptist Student Union (BSU). Chris Jackson, a very caring and compassionate minister who has been a lifelong mentor, was in charge of the BSU. He displayed a heart for students and for the Word of God, and he pushed our potential with his prayerful support. I attribute a great deal of my spiritual growth and character building to him.

Under his leadership I began cultivating a friendship with God. My parents had led us in family devotions throughout my childhood, and I had enjoyed memorizing Scripture and learning how to apply the Bible to my daily life. As an adult, the Baptist Student Union gave me an opportunity to rediscover the God that my parents had introduced me to at an early age. By developing a more intimate relationship with God, I experienced God's fresh presence like never before.

I leaped at the opportunity to worship him and I found myself daily indulging in meditation time with him. At times, I was very confused about how on one day I would enjoy basking in God's presence and how I could, at the blink of an eye, act or react in a way that was contradictory. As a young adult still uncertain about my life calling and the plan that God had for me, I found myself playing tug of war with the flesh and the Spirit. I wanted to please God, but I so desperately wanted to please myself as well. My life seemed so inconsistent.

As a campus student leader, I hoped to live the life that I taught other people, but as a vulnerable and insecure young woman, I struggled with being disciplined both spiritually and personally. I kept serving, I kept witnessing, and yet I kept wondering, "How in the world can God use me?" Me? The oldest child of a prominent black Baptist preacher who would rather see her parents work in ministry while rooting for them on the sidelines? Me? The girl who was so shy that she had to practice saying "hello." The one who had to rehearse asking people, "How are you?" Me? The one who struggled in math and Spanish classes? Me? The one who envied her siblings for being so outspoken because she never had the courage to speak her mind. Me? The one who was so afraid of the public that she sang her first solo with her eyes closed? How could God use me?

To add fuel to the fire, our campus chaplain, Chestina Archibald, kept telling me that she believed that I was called to be a minister. How could she see that? I wondered. "I don't want to be a preacher, my dad is the preacher," I said to myself. "I want to work in radio or newspaper, and there is no way that my parents' hard-earned money is going to be wasted. That's the whole reason I came to Fisk, so that I can learn how to be an effective communicator." Preaching was the furthest thing from my mind. In fact, when I heard about a woman being called to preach I laughed to myself. "Why does she have to call herself a preacher? My mother and other mentors are great speakers, why can't she just be a speaker?" I kept asking myself.

Besides, our church at home hadn't had women preachers in nearly twenty years. I remembered us having them when I was a child, but in an attempt to assert their gifts, they had angered my father. He stopped allowing them to be recognized from the pulpit, and he put an end to them exercising their preaching gifts at Concord. Furthermore, he was not quiet about his position on women preachers and resisted women who desired to function in that capacity. So if Rev. Archibald thought that I was called to be a preacher, she couldn't still believe that knowing how my father felt about women preachers. My father was one of my best friends. He was my mentor and hero. The thought of doing anything that he disapproved of would break my heart. So instead of sharing with my father what Rev. Archibald and others believed, I laughed at it and pressed harder to prove them wrong.

Now, recognizing my internal struggle and my desire to work in journalism, I ran from Rev. Archibald almost every time I spotted her. I loved her big voice, her spirited personality, and her humor, but I resented the fact that she saw something in me that I didn't want anyone ever to see. I wanted her and others to encourage me to work in the field of communications. I went to Fisk on two scholarships. One was provided by my beloved sisters of Delta Sigma Theta sorority. The other was given by the members of the Dallas–Ft. Worth Association for Black Communicators (DFW/ABC), an organization committed to preparing students who have a passion for journalism. Jumping ship on my "professional plan" would not have made sense. So, I passionately pursued radio after college and enjoyed learning at WRR radio in Dallas and at the Radio Advertising Bureau in Irving, Texas. I considered myself to be a young, up-and-coming black woman with a plan to succeed. Little did I know that God was working behind the scenes to abort my plan so that I could surrender to his perfect plan for my life.

Even after graduating from college and working in radio for several years, I felt God tugging at my heart. But this was different. In college, I felt that he was tugging at me so that I could be more disciplined and consistent. This time, I felt him nudging me to abandon my professional plans and to enter the ministry full time. Before I knew it, I watched God begin to do a metamorphosis in my life. I literally watched him begin to reveal to me how complacent I had become as a caterpillar and how comfortable I had become in the cocoon of life.

I stood in awe as I watched God take my shy personality and transform me into a woman who would never meet a stranger. I was amazed at how God kept being faithful to me even when I was unfaithful to him. I couldn't believe that God could take my weakness, my fears, and insecurities and transform my life into a screen that could display his glory. I am speechless when I consider how he has created me in his image. I am dumbfounded by how he has clothed me in his righteousness. I am overwhelmed by how much he loves me and how he has equipped me for what he has called me to do.

God began to reveal to me his plan, and I recall a series of incidents that led to my surrendering. I can still remember how often I'd hear the Lord whispering softly and continually, "I will equip you. Do not be afraid." I could hear him asking me consistently and lovingly, "Will you trust me?" I felt as though I had a front-row seat to the heart of God. I experienced his mercy, his forgiveness, his power, and his patience. I experienced his nurturing side and his side that corrects, disciplines, and instructs. I learned how to put the Bible into action with my words, my attitude, and my actions.

The job in radio that I once loved soon became something that I did just to collect a paycheck. I began to lose my zeal and passion for selling radio and writing radio success stories. I remember images playing in my mind like a movie. While working I would see visions of myself in a pulpit preaching and praying for women. Sometimes in these dreams I would be dressed in a robe and would reach over the pulpit to touch the women who were hurting. Other times I would simply see images of myself teaching the Word of God and crying as I exhausted myself giving hopeless people the hope of Jesus Christ. These visions terrified me! I thought, "Why do I see these things in my mind's eye?"

I so desperately wanted God to take those thoughts out of my head. I recognized that God was sovereign, but I thought he must have been mistaken this time. So, I'd close my eyes and take a break just in case I was conjuring up this "silly scene" in my head. Then, I'd return to my desk and resume working. This happened on numerous occasions. Finally, I e-mailed a dear sister in Christ, who has been a friend of mine since childhood. I said to her, "Meiki, I am having the weirdest dreams. I keep seeing myself preaching from a pulpit and wearing a robe. It is beginning to frighten me because the dreams are so real. I don't want to be a preacher and you know my father wouldn't go for that anyway." I sighed with a sense of relief because I knew that I had at least admitted to someone how I felt.

Then, I waited anxiously for her response. I knew that I could count on her to e-mail me with words that would convince me that this was far-fetched and the idea of it was something to which I should not give any more thought. To my utter amazement, she responded immediately, but it was not the response that I was hoping to see. She wrote, "Well, I don't know what this means, but I do hope that you are open to what God has said for you to do." She concluded by saying, "Whatever you do, I will support you."

That blew me away. This meant that even she was beginning to look at things differently. For over twenty years, she and I had experienced almost an identical lifestyle. Both of our fathers were preachers who believed the Bible and lived by it. Both of us had loving families, and both of us believed that women should not preach and should keep their place outside of the pulpit. How could she change her mind? She had no idea that I had been struggling with this. I knew she wasn't just siding with me because of our friendship. I knew it had to be the Lord encouraging her to encourage me.

I think the Lord knew that I would need even more confirmation, so he turned up the heat a bit more. For several weeks I was restless at night. I would be awakened each night between 2:00 a.m. and 4:00 a.m. I remember wondering why I couldn't sleep. I began to pray for other people and even for God to comfort me, as I was unaware of what he was trying to tell me. After nights of feeling burdened, I remember walking through the living room of my apartment and saying, "Lord, I am tired. Please tell me what you want me to do." I felt helpless and eager to hear from the Lord. He kept saying to me, "Will you trust me?" I answered, "Lord, yes I will trust you, but what will I be trusting you with?"

I felt as though the Lord made me answer him before he gave me the question. Then, for several days I felt as though the Lord was silent. I prayed more. I begged him and I felt that he remained silent because he knew that I would grow in patience and be totally vulnerable at his feet. Then, driving home one evening I heard God's voice: "I want you to minister to my people. I want you to take my Word to the hurting. I want you to make yourself available to be a trailblazer for other women who desire to make my name known. Cokiesha, I want you to be more concerned about obeying me than pleasing your earthly father. I will work on him, but you will have to trust me to be your personal counselor, companion, and friend."

Wow! Finally, the Lord spelled it out for me. I was so overwhelmed that hearing from him forced me to burst into tears. I drove and cried and cried and cried some more. I said out loud to the Lord, "I'll do it! God, I promise that I will do it. I don't know if it will happen. You know how my dad feels about women ministers. You know how shy I am at times, and you know that I have no formal theological training. You know how much I wanted to work in radio and you know that I have no desire to be in front of people, but if you will give me the strength and the courage, I will tell the world about you."

After the Lord and I had our special time together in the car, I remember feeling physically tired. I had spent so much time crying that I had become worn out physically, but then I felt revitalized spiritually because the burden had been lifted. Day by day I waited for the Lord to give me specific instructions. He made me feel as though we were holding hands daily. As much as I loved my earthly father, I learned how to rely more on my Heavenly Father. He was going to give me a plan of action. First, the Lord told me that it would be important to not speak out of turn regarding this issue. He said that approaching my father at the wrong time could ruin the opportunity for me and other women. Second, he told me to invest more in my prayer life. He said that only through communing in prayer would I receive the strength that I needed to endure.

Needless to say, the Lord honored his Word. Although I became discouraged at times, God kept reminding me that he would not leave me or forsake me. He told me that it was time for me to become "a big girl of faith" and that it would entail abandoning my "people-pleasing personality." So in this same year, which was 1998, I approached my father and I shared with him that I would like to leave my job in radio and apply for a position at our church. My father and my mother were a bit caught off guard. They responded as any caring parent would, I'm sure.

They said, "You worked long and hard at Fisk. We paid good money for you to learn there. Why give it all up to become a church secretary? You are loved at your job. You've received promotions. What is the problem?" I responded, "Because the Lord wants me at the church and I am willing to have a decreased salary and to work in a position that may not be deemed as prestigious and popular in order to please the Lord." After weeks of contemplation, my dad interviewed me and prayed with me as he did all potential staff members. Weeks later, he shared with me that he thought that I had several gifts that could enhance the staff and he was sure that there were things I could learn by joining the staff full time. I was ecstatic. Finally, I could be in a position that pleased the Lord. God assured me that my position was just a part of the plan. I still had to keep my promise of waiting on God to tell me the appropriate time for the long-awaited conversation of my calling into the ministry.

In the meantime, God opened up doors for me to speak at our church on several occasions. I was honored to be the 1999 Prayer Breakfast Speaker, the 2000 Women's Day Speaker, and the speaker for our senior center's Christmas banquet. I could tell that my parents were proud that the Lord was using me. They were present every time that I spoke, and they encouraged me as I studied and prepared. I even had a friend say to me, "When you spoke at the banquet, your father said to me, 'That's not teaching—she is preaching!'" I smiled, but I couldn't believe that he would be feeling that way because he had never voiced it to me.

One day, my dad and I were in the church's lounge, meeting about business, and before I left his presence I simply said, "Daddy, do you think I have been called to preach?" He looked back at me and said, "Yes." I laughed and said, "Why haven't you said anything to me about it?" He said, "Because I am still dealing with it." I smiled and said, "I love you," and we adjourned. More time passed. I began to receive invitations from other churches to speak. I couldn't believe it. God sent all these opportunities, and I was excited and humbled by every one of them.

Then, one church invitation seemed very different. A friend invited me to speak at his church for a women's conference. After several of us had spoken, someone stood up and said, "I think the time has come for us to stop keeping women from spreading the gospel." He continued, "Someone here today is struggling with their decision to preach and God wants you to trust him and to do what he wants you to do." Tears began to roll down my face as I received this message from the Lord.

I returned home and saw my dad sitting at the kitchen table. I joined him and we began to talk about our day. He asked me how it went at the conference, and I knew that I had to tell him what my heart was feeling. I caught my breath and I said, "Well, I have to tell you something." He said, "Sure, anything." His dark brown eyes always warmed my heart. He looked concerned as he always did when I had to talk to him about something serious. I said, "Daddy, I have been called." He said, "To do what?" I said, "To be a mouthpiece."

I thought he would remember that day in the church lounge when he admitted to me that he knew that I was struggling with my call. Apparently, that day had been placed in his "selective memory file." He replied, "Called to be what type of mouthpiece?" I said, "Well, you know." He responded, "No, you tell me." My eyes began to fill with tears and I heard the Lord whispering to me, "Are you more concerned about what I think of you or what your dad thinks of you?" I knew I had to show the Lord that his opinion of me mattered more. So, I replied, "Daddy, I love you so much. I would never want to do anything that would change our relationship. I would never want to do anything that would hinder your ministry. I have to acknowledge to you that I have been called to preach the gospel. I recognize how you feel about women preachers so you never have to tell Concord or your preaching peers. I just had to tell you so that I could be free."

He looked at me as though he were hearing this for the first time. He looked over his glasses and said, "Thank you for telling me. I will get back with you." I thought to myself, "That's it? 'I'll get back with you?'" I left the table with a smile on my face, but my heart was shattered. I wanted him to hug me and to say to me how proud he was that I confronted my fears. Most of all, I wanted him to tell me he supported me.

I felt the Lord holding me and whispering to me, "I told you I'd be with you. Don't be anxious. Wait on me." Knowing that God would do much more than I could imagine, I relaxed and decided that this may be a long road, but one that would be full of peace because I had God's promise.

I felt that God gave me what I needed to keep quiet. Three years passed by as I waited for my dad to "get back with me." We maintained our loving relationship as father and daughter and as employer and employee. To my surprise, he began talking to me about his reservations about women in ministry, and about his disappointments regarding past experiences with women ministers, and he shared with me preaching gifts that he believed that I had. Soon thereafter, he began asking me to learn more about notable female ministers such as Rev. Renita Weems. He reminded me about the women he watched as they walked strong in their purpose at United Theological Seminary. Among those women were his classmates Susan Newman, Joan Wharton, Cynthia Hale, and Bishop Vashti McKenzie. I got excited as he initiated conversations on women in ministry. He began to ask me to read books about women preachers with him and our assistant pastor at the time, Rev. Bryon Carter. I couldn't believe it. What God had promised was coming to pass.

In July 2003, during our Sunday morning worship, my father addressed the congregation before church adjourned. He asked for my mother to join him. He acknowledged that he had shared his opposition to women preachers over the last twenty or so years. He admitted that he had preached a position that was not biblically based but one that was promoted by his own personal biases. He stated that God had to call someone in his own house in order to get his attention. He shared with us that he searched the Scriptures and that God changed his view. He voiced his new position that women are being called by God and that no one has the right to stop what God is doing.

Moreover, he said that he witnessed God working in my life and that other people could see the hand of God on my life. He said, "If Cokiesha were my son I would have acknowledged her calling in the ministry years ago, but since she is a woman, I just decided to ignore it." He continued, "I can't ignore it any longer. I don't want to hinder what God wants to do in her life. She has chosen to enter Beeson Divinity School in the fall and she is going to go with our blessing." As he concluded he said, "We support her and she is going to preach her first sermon before she leaves. Not only that, we are going to give other women an opportunity to preach and utilize their gifts because this is the direction that God is taking us." I will never forget the joy that flooded my soul.

He asked me to join him and my mother as the church celebrated his decision. I was so happy. Although the road for me had been long, I knew the road for other female preachers around the world had been longer. I thank God for all of the dynamic trailblazers who went before me and even suffered so that other women could have an opportunity in years to come. I praise God for keeping his word to me and for cradling me in his arms when I felt abandoned and unaware of my purpose. He has proven to be more than a supreme God, but my faithful friend, my fortress, my shield and buckler, my covering, counselor, and the lover of my soul.[1]

I will forever be grateful to my church staff team, church family, and mentors who labored with me during my days of preparation for divinity school. The greatest testimony for me of how a church family will surround their pastor and family during their time of need occurred on the day that I relocated to Beeson Divinity School in Alabama. My father was too ill to make the trip and Mother wanted to stay in Dallas in order to be close to his bedside. Sensing a need to serve as my "covering," three of our members who are close to my heart moved me to my new abode. For escorting me into the new place that God had for me, I am eternally grateful to Alvin Marshall, Melba Smith, and Felix Spencer. [2]

I praise God for a rich spiritual legacy. I hope to continue embracing the Christian principles that have been instilled in me by my fore-parents and spiritual parents. I stand in awe at the ministerial legacy that has been passed down in our family. I honor the preachers and teachers who have paved the way for us, and I thank God for the godly example of my grandparents who have joined the cloud of witnesses: Rev. V. M. Bailey, Mrs. Victoria Curtis, Mr. Daniel Curtis, Mr. Joseph Smith, Mrs. Lucy Smith, and Pastor and Mrs. W. K. and Eula Jackson. Finally, I am particularly grateful to my parents, aunts, uncles, extended family, and godparents, Dr. and Mrs. Melvin Von, and Jacquie G. Wade, Mr. and Mrs. Herbert, and Gwen Odom, who loved me and mirrored for me the character of Christ.

I am now entering my second year at Beeson Divinity School at Samford University. I am excited about the things that God will lead me toward in the future. As a writer, encourager, teacher, and minister, I pray that my life and my witness will bring the Word of God to life. My life mission statement is found in Psalm 101 and I truly desire to "worship God with my life while escorting the wicked out of the city." My father wrote me a note in his book,

Preaching in Black and White, before he passed away. It is something that I will cherish for all of the days of my life. I think it allows me to hear my father's voice from heaven even today. Because of God's blessing and my father's validation of my ministry, I feel liberated as a woman, as a leader, and as a minister of the gospel. It reads:

"Cokiesha, I loved you as a baby, as a child and I love you more as an adult as I watch you walk in your God given purpose. The path you have chosen is not an easy one, but it is one that will bring glory to God. So, get out of the boat of self comfort and walk on the water of impossibility because God said it shall be done!"

Sermon: *"Dispatched to Die—Predestined to Live"*
Philippians 3:10

Cokiesha Lashon Bailey

I smile as I reflect upon the words shared with me by one of my mentors and spiritual fathers, Rev. Thurman Fry. He shared with me a military motto that he adopted when he became a United States Marine. Little did he know that I would eventually adopt it as a life purpose statement. Although he lives with the Lord today, I can hear the thunder in his voice as he shared with me this rich motto that changed my life. He said to me, "It's not yours to ask when or why, but it's yours to do or die." Well-known and respected martyr Dietrich Bonhoeffer, in *The Cost of Discipleship*, declared that the call to follow Jesus is the call to die. He suggests to us that to follow Christ involved becoming a walking dead person or even signing a death warrant. My father, and our own senior pastor, Dr. E. K. Bailey, has reminded us on many occasions of this: "We cannot be used greatly until we have been hurt significantly." You may also remember Pastor Bailey saying to us, "Grapes cannot be drunk, they must first be crushed." Most of us are familiar with classic phrases masterfully penned by William Penn. His powerful words continue to echo throughout history: "No cross, no crown, no gall, no glory, no thorn, no throne."

As I have studied the thoughts of each of these spiritual legends, I marvel at how each is distinctively different in personality and even in his life's purpose, but here, Fry, Bonhoeffer, Bailey, and Penn have a commonality that has united their hearts and minds. I believe all of them would confirm that rewards are rare without risk. I am sure they would agree that stability and strength do not come without suffering. Each of them committed their lives to encouraging others to let go so that they could hold on. They admonished others to become weak, so that they may become strong. Their timeless quotes are merely warnings to us to stop if we want to go and to sit down if we want to stand up. Ultimately, they suggested that we abandon our plans so that we may surrender to God's perfect plan for our lives.

In our text Paul makes a personal declaration that he is willing for his very life to be terminated so that he can gain Christ.

Now, in order for us to really understand what a testimony it is for Paul to say, "to live is Christ and to die is gain," we have to understand who Paul was and what he had been delivered from. So, please allow me to contemporize the transformation of Saul to Paul. Saul was an educated, respected, well rounded, well versed, professional man. In modern times, he could have been a lawyer, a professor, or a businessman of some sort.

But Saul had a dark side, another lifestyle. We can consider him to have been a "hitman." He took the lives of Christians at the request of mobs. He delighted in derailing Christians from their destiny. He desperately wanted to destroy believers and to stop them from spreading the news of Jesus. Well, one day, Saul headed out on the Damascus Road. In my sanctified imagination I can see him popping in his favorite music CDs. Imagine him in a Lincoln Navigator listening to Fabolous, 50 Cent, or Tupac. The song that really made him excited, however, was probably "Act a Fool" by Ludacris. As he drove and danced to the music, I can see his car beginning to shake. Then, suddenly he is ejected from the car and lying out there in the street wondering what happened to him.

Let's imagine a bright light shining in his face and Jesus saying, "Saul, you will never win when you are fighting with me. Now go and live a life that pleases me." Then, Saul thanked God for sparing his life and promised to live in such a way that all would know about the transforming power of God. Saul's name was changed to Paul because God often changes a person's name after he changes their nature. Further into the text, we see Paul at the end of his life, having been thrown into prison. He is writing his home church, the church of Philippi. He is encouraging each member in their faith and asking them to not worry about him because he remains strong in his faith. Finally, he makes a personal declaration to his friends that reveals to them how serious he is about standing up for God. He gives us a glimpse of his heart's cry by suggesting that if he lives he will be fine because Christ is with him and if he dies he will gain even more because he will reign with him.

"For me" in the Greek suggests that this is a personal plea. This is not for you or anyone else. The flavor of that word is what Joshua meant when he said, "as for me and my house." The word "live" suggests that the first breath I draw in the morning is directed toward doing something for Christ. Paul suggests that the actual moment after he dies is his gain because he will know Christ fully. He rejoices because in death he is freed completely from the power of sin, delivered from suffering and transported into the presence of

God. As we ponder how God has called each of us to "die" so that we may live, there are three things the Word suggests that we should do in order to fulfill God's plan: (1) Heed the call instantly; (2) defuse our fears frequently; and (3) surrender to God's plan continually.

What is God calling you to do for him? Do you remember Aubrey Hawkins, the Irving, Texas, police officer who was gunned down at a sporting goods store? He answered the call that came in reporting that "the Texas Seven" had been found. He answered the call, not knowing that it would be his final call. Cassie Burnell, a victim of the Columbine school shooting, was asked by the gunman, "Are you a Christian?" Cassie answered, "Yes," because she understood Paul's plea, "to live is Christ and to die is gain." Noah heeded the call when God asked him to build a boat. Moses heeded the call when God asked him to set his people free in Egypt. What is God calling you to do for him?

God is also calling us to defuse our fears frequently. What is a fear? Fears are the "negatives" that are developed in the "darkroom of life." They are the phobias that stop us in our tracks and prevent us from living healthy lives. So we are often being tempted by the enemy to snuff out God's will for our lives. All of us are afraid of something. Some people are afraid of birds, others of spiders or frogs. Some people are afraid of being in the public, while others are afraid of failure or rejection. In Psalm 79 we see a clear picture of fear paralyzing God's people. The soldiers were dressed in their armor, they were mounted on their horses, and when the time of war had come, they ran in the other direction. God is calling us to put his Word into action. He says in Psalm 56:11, "In God I trust; I am not afraid. What can a mere mortal do to me?" I believe Chuck Swindoll said it best when he proclaimed, "This is not the time for spiritual wimps!"

Finally, we are encouraged to surrender to God's sovereignty continually. Surrendering involves yielding to the power of another. Surrendering isn't always easy. I know that full well.

A few summers ago my good friends and I went jet skiing in Mexico. Inexperienced and unassuming, my friend Alicia and I began racing on the skis. In a matter of minutes we were forced into the water after a wrong turn. After plunging into the water, Alicia bravely climbed back on the boat with the assistance of a lifeguard. I was left in the water panicking due to my life vest coming apart when the boat turned over. The lifeguard said, "Ma'am, I cannot save you until you listen to me and calm down." I kept fighting the water and screaming. I just knew sharks were after me. He said, "I know this water and I know how to help you, but you have to listen to me." So I calmed down, but I didn't have any strength to pull myself back onto the water vehicle. The lifeguard assured me. He said, "If you will just hold on to the back of the boat, I promise to get you back to shore safely." I must admit that he kept his promise to me. I held on as he accelerated and delivered me safely back to dry land.

That's the same thing that God does for us. He insists that we calm down when we have fallen off our "jet ski" of life. He reminds us in his Word that we have to take our eyes off our problem and place them on our Problem Solver. He admonishes us to trust his ability to get us safely back to "dry land." Whatever your problem, I encourage you to hold on and watch God accelerate and accelerate until you are safe again. Don't take my word for it. Follow Jesus' example.

He did it in the Garden of Gethsemane. He prayed and asked God to take the bitter cup from him. Then, he surrendered to God's sovereignty by saying, "but not my will, thy will be done." It wasn't easy to surrender. It wasn't comfortable to surrender, but it was worth it. He let himself be taken to the cross. He hung his head for us and died. Now we can sing with the hymnists Philip Bliss and James McGranahan as they prepared the words and music to this timeless hymn "On the Cruel Cross He Suffered" (1869):

> I will sing of my redeemer,
> And His wondrous love to me;
> On the cruel cross He suffered,
> From the curse to set me free.

NOTES

1. I thank God for so many people who have shaped my life and character including: Pastor and Mrs. Johnnie Green, Pastor and Mrs. Lawrence Aker, Dr. Phillip Williams, Mrs. Marci Hailey and the late McKinley Hailey, Mrs. Billie Fry, the late Rev. Thurman Fry, Mrs. Robbie Byrd, Rev. and Mrs. Darnell and Edna Pemperton, Mrs. Dixie Daughtry, and Mr. and Mrs. Hansel Cunningham. Thank you also to longtime mentors Dr. Sharon Patterson, Mrs. Wanda B. Davis, and Dr. and Mrs. Major Jemison for being umbrellas when I needed to be reassured. I am grateful to Pastor and Mrs. Bryon Carter, Pastor and Mrs. Rodney Stodghill, Pastor and Mrs. G. Laine Robinson, Pastor S. Micheal Greene, Rev. Stuart Bailey, and all of the Concord Church pastors and wives who served as brothers and sisters of encouragement during this season of transition. I thank God for Rev. Rick Jordan, Dr. Robert Smith, Dr. Charles Martin, Dr. Melvin Wade, and Pastor Lawrence Aker, who allowed me to "drink from their cup" during the week of my first sermon. I am appreciative to Dr. Alvin Edwards, Dr. Chestina Archibald, Pastor and Mrs. Dwight McKissic, Bishop Joseph W. Walker III, Drs. Chris and Coreen Jackson, Bishop and Mrs. Michael Graves, and Rev. Lorenza Edwards for prayerfully maximizing my spiritual and personal growth.
2. Equally important, I couldn't imagine life without the support of my sister, Mrs. Shenikwa Cager; my brother-in-law, Mr. Stephen Cager; and my brother, Rev. Emon Kendrick Bailey, who have been loyal to me in all of my pursuits.

Special thanks to some dear "family" members for holding up my arms as I waited for God to bring forth his vision: Dr. Pamela Norwood, Ms. Shelley Thrash, Ms. Racquel Washington, Mrs. Alicia Young, Ms. Rhonda McGruder, Mrs. Meikel Cobb, Mrs. Yomica Edwards, Ms. Tangerla Mayhew, Mrs. Cheryl Thompson, Ms. Angel Hernandez, Mrs. Katina Potts, Ms. Sondra Gay, Minister Rhonda Russell, Minister Gwen O. Langley, Ms. Jacquie Hampton, and Ms. Jennifer Jerkins.

2

From the Pew to the Pulpit

CECELIA E. GREENE BARR

I was twenty-one years old, career minded, independent, and thoroughly enjoying the hope of my future when I found myself evolving into a new life. The change was difficult to describe. There was an inner urge for more than a career as an engineer who worked during the week and socialized on the weekend. I was beginning to sense an air of seriousness pouncing upon me that had more to do with my spiritual life than my imagination had room to conceive. This seriousness also clawed its way into my professional endeavors. The career path I'd planned did not have room for the changes that waited ahead. Little did I know at the time that my career would completely change my identity each time my spiritual understanding reached a new level of maturity. The road, which began as a youthful baptism, included many twists and turns before I could stand in the role of preacher. This is my story from the pew to the pulpit.

Every testimony begins someplace significant to the teller, and for me it starts with my family's connection with the church. The formative years of my life were spent in the Baptist tradition. It was here that I saw my paternal grandfather sit in the pulpit as an ordained minister. Rev. Ulysses Grant Greene died when I was eleven years old, and although I do not remember the contents of his sermons, I do remember the image of him in the pulpit. My maternal grandparents were equally involved in the Baptist tradition. At Haw River Baptist Church they faithfully served as the chairman of the Deacon

---

* Parts of this testimony are included in the doctoral dissertation titled *Mentoring—The Critical Link in Clergy Development: Effective Practices of Identifying, Mentoring and Elevating Clergy Apprentices into Transformational Leadership.*

Board and supervisor of the Sunday school. Church was part spiritual, part community, and part family existence. It was in this holistic environment that I responded to the gospel message by accepting the salvation God makes available through Jesus Christ. It was also here that I became quietly conditioned to accept ministry as gender exclusive. And it was also in this tradition that I first wrestled with God's call upon my life.

Females were conditioned to perceive church leadership as a male responsibility. I witnessed that in my home church and in congregations that my college choir visited. The lessons of exclusion were taught each time a man was invited into the pulpit, yet the evangelists, who were always women, were restricted from entering that raised platform. I learned these lessons well, to the point that like the male population, I too emotionally disregarded women who were living out their life of ministry. Even now, when I hear women disdain other women for preaching the gospel and serving in the role of pastor, I know by experience that they are simply responding out of a conditioned error.

In this era, almost every auxiliary in church carries the title of "ministry," but when I began to embrace the ministry I understood it as preaching the gospel message and being a pastor to God's people. From the first unction I knew God's call upon my life was to a different expression of ministry than what I had traditionally seen or accepted as normal. Today some refer to me as a trailblazer, but during those early revelations God described me as a pastor's pastor. I did not comprehend what it meant to be a pastor's pastor, but I did know it would not be business as usual. However, my life in ministry faced two formidable challenges: the status quo and my reluctance to defy it. It was the status quo that had quietly conditioned me to view my participation in the church as anything other than a leadership role. And it was my socialized desire to be accepted that made me reluctant to defy the norm.

Everything in my social and spiritual context communicated that I had erred in discerning God's call upon my life. By virtue of gender alone I was perceived as not qualified to participate fully in God's redemptive plan for humanity. Furthermore, if I insisted on continuing along this path of service I need not anticipate the attention and regard of pioneering clergy for guidance and development. Ultimately, the unspoken message was clear: I would be on my own to succeed or fail, preferably to fail and disappear from the arena of church leadership. Against these odds I stepped out in obedience and faith to follow the path of ministry that God had ordained for my life.

The beginning of my journey toward ministry started with a spiritual awakening and with my hearing the voice of God speak directly to me. At that time I was still fully entrenched in the Baptist church and ignorant of the fact that God communicates directly with believers in addition to communicating by the written biblical word. Instead of responding like Simon and Andrew (Matt. 4:18–20) when Jesus called them into service, I reacted much like Samuel (1 Sam. 3:5), wondering who it was who had called my name and surprised by what was being asked of me. The voice of God was exceptionally clear in proclaiming that I had been called to preach the gospel. Specifically, God said, "Feed my sheep and take your time with the meal."

My life in ministry has been a succession of epiphanies, most exceptionally when I received the call to ministry. The first instruction from God was for me to prepare myself academically. Fortified with excitement, I searched within my congregational context for someone in spiritual authority to share this revelation and receive instruction on how to proceed, but all I found were disinterested leaders who discounted my testimony as the words of a zealous young female. The only authority figure who did listen was an administrator at a local Bible college, who quickly informed me that I was wrong to determine that God had called me to preach. In that person's estimation God did not use women as preachers of the gospel, handlers of the sacraments, or administrators of congregational resources. But if I were interested in missionary work or Christian education, they would gladly provide intense training. Lacking confidence in my supernatural encounters with God, and without a mentor modeled after Jesus' example to help me navigate the waters of sexism in the church, I left that conversation confused and discouraged. I like to think of myself as resilient, but this would be the first of many detractors to ministry.

Years later God placed me in the African Methodist Episcopal church. After that first experience it was ten years before I dared to tell another person in authority that God had called me to preach the gospel. I felt encouraged that my testimony would not be discounted based on my gender because in this congregation the assistant pastor was female; however, I faced isolation of a different kind. In this new community, although my gender was not an issue, the size of our overwhelmingly large congregation hindered any opportunity for me to receive ministerial training. Our congregation was comparatively large and growing rapidly each month. With such an impressive growth rate, obtaining an appointment to meet with the pastor or assistant pastor for the purpose of discussing a call to ministry was generally not permitted. Instead, the pastor would hold occasional informational sessions for anyone in the congregation interested in ministry.

During these sessions the pastor succinctly explained the denominational requirements for ordination and the overall atmosphere within our congregation. I attended the session once and departed with a clear understanding that I would not be able to live a life of ministry in this congregation. Surprisingly, I was not saddened by this new information. I knew I would gladly forego a life in ministry in order to remain a member of that congregation. I loved my pastors and the maturity I had gained under their leadership. Leaving that congregation, even for ministry, just did not seem reasonable to me.

One Sunday morning as I arose to prepare for worship, God confronted my reasoning with specific instructions. In a few words, the Lord spoke the name of a church for me to find and join. I immediately objected. I did not know the address of the church, only the city where it was located. I did not know the pastor or any member of the congregation. My strongest objections had little to do with the lack of directions for finding the church or my lack of familiarity with its leadership. My resistance was based solely on a desire to remain with my current church family. My mind changed when the Lord said to me that my current pastors were doing what God had instructed them to do, but if I refused to comply with the instructions received that day I would no longer be following God, but I would from that point forward be following my pastors. Idolatry was not a part of my spiritual aspirations; therefore on that day I found my new church home.

In this new context, as in my previous church, the assistant pastor was also the pastor's wife. In both contexts these clergywomen were impressive and respected for their spiritual acumen. In what turned out to be our one and only true conversation, my new assistant advised me to remove any hindrances that a lack of theological training might erect. Following her advice, I enrolled in seminary and began the process of preparing for a task that I had yet to understand. I knew God had instructed me to prepare, but why full-time seminary instead of a few courses? I spent many days and nights in reflective speculation as to why I was even in seminary or what I would do with my training upon completion. I was able to read Scripture and glean what it meant to be a male servant during the time of Jesus, but what would it mean for me to be a servant in my period of Christian history?

I was faced with more questions than I had answers to and no one in authority to help me navigate the waters of leadership development. Naturally I began to speculate about my own experience of hearing God's call because the realities of my experiences were inconsistent with the teachings that I had received. After all, according to former teachings on spiritual authority and pastoral leadership, if God's hand was upon my life for ministry why had my former pastors not seen it? If God's call was upon my life why were experienced leaders not interested in helping me fulfill my kingdom destiny? If God's call was upon my life and I really possessed the gifts and graces for leadership, why was I being spiritually and pastorally mismanaged instead of nurtured for effectiveness? I later learned that in many instances leadership had discerned God's anointing on my life but their responses were tempered. I could not understand how I was being so thoughtlessly dismissed.

Many of these questions arose from my naive thinking that all pastors are interested in sponsoring the development of the next generation of leaders. If I had stopped here, I would not have been the first person to turn away from God's call. I would have been one among many frustrated preachers just sitting in the pew. But I did not stop during those horrendous years, because God sent help—in the form of a mentor. My uncharted path in ministry found direction through the God-ordained tutelage I received from the late Rev. Dr. Samuel DeWitt Proctor. Dr. Proctor entered my life during a time when I was experiencing unusually oppressive events and people who were suppressive in their dealings with me.

One of the lesser incidents involved the opportunity for full-time ministry. On this occasion a full-time salaried ministerial position became vacant at the church where I had voluntarily served for a couple of years. Based on the job description I met all requirements. When I approached the pastor I was told that the committee was not ready to fill the position and that I would be informed and given an opportunity to compete as soon as they were ready to proceed. Furthermore, there would not be any need to repeatedly inquire. Imagine my dismay when I was told by another source that I would never be considered for the position because I was female. Apparently, contrary to what he had told me, the pastor believed that males should hold leadership positions of that nature. As it turned out, the position was held vacant for an extended period until a "suitable" male candidate was identified. When I asked why I was not given consideration, the pastor said that he had forgotten that I had expressed interest in the position. Experiences like this can potentially harden the soul of a preacher. My mentor's teachings helped me rally from this rejection and to maintain love in my heart for this leader who so grievously offended me.

Dr. Proctor was a respected churchman but he was not an African Methodist. Although he could not help me navigate the politics of my denomination, he was responsible for broadening my concept of the kingdom and my potential participation in it. This was demonstrated toward the end of seminary when I considered enrolling in law school. My mind was changed, however, when Dr. Proctor stated that to do so would mean turning my back on the prophetic call God placed on my life. When I heard these words, I relinquished the thought of law school and focused my determination on the gospel.

These early years were a refining period in which my determination, motives, and skills were cultivated. The path of spontaneous acceptance would not have developed fortitude. Instead, each time someone hindered my path I deepened my resolve. For every time I was prejudged, the result was a greater dependence on God. Whereas I do not believe that every opportunity is an actual blessing for me, I shudder at the cruelty in which the "no" has sometimes been packaged.

Twenty years after first hearing God's call upon my life, I am now an ordained itinerant elder in the African Methodist Episcopal Church. For many years prior to receiving a pastoral appointment, I volunteered my services and gained experience in the duties of the pastorate. I also served as the chief of staff for Rev. Albert D. Tyson III, and in that capacity I had the responsibility of working directly with the ministerial team for training and organizational purposes.

In these years I have also established a not-for-profit ministry that is independent of the AME Church. It is a cross-denominational, Christ-centered ministry called Sharing Faith Ministries (SFM), and in it I seek to utilize my gifts and talents across cultures and denominations. It is through SFM that I implement my passions for ministry, which include preaching, teaching, and clergy mentoring. SFM is a virtual congregation in that we have a fluid group of people across the country, who receive ministry via newsletters, taped sermons, workshops, Bible courses, and leadership training. Our Web site makes it possible to enter locations otherwise closed to us.

There are those who scoff at the work I do through SFM, but God has responded by giving me favor with respected pastors and bishops both within and outside the African Methodist tradition. As a result, each year I have the blessing of traveling the country and addressing congregations as a guest preacher as well as instructing preachers during leadership training sessions. The 501(c)3 ministry model for SFM is not business as usual. Instead we strive to pass through denominational barriers in order to assist believers in walking more maturely with Christ.

I have labored faithfully with SFM over these years, and I know the Lord has been pleased with my commitment to the call. Consistent with God's nature to "perfect that which concerns me" (Ps. 138:8 NKJV), on March 26, 2004, the Lord moved again with an unprecedented blessing. To my complete surprise and delight, I was assigned a pastoral appointment to Trinity African Methodist Episcopal Church in Detroit, Michigan, by the Right Rev. Philip R. Cousin Sr.

Each Sunday morning approximately seventy members are present to worship God and hear what thus saith the Lord through his servant. Our Bible study attendance has more than tripled in four short months. But most important, the members proclaim that under my leadership they are now on fire for knowledge and revelation. In the grandest of colloquial phrases, I told Bishop Cousin that he "hooked a sister up!" Yet even this blessing was not without obstacles. Just like Jesse presented all of his older sons to the prophet Samuel and never considered his son David, there were those who presented other candidates before the bishop in lieu of me. But, God said my name to the bishop and laid me on his heart.

I thank God that deposits were made in my spirit that taught me how to continue to press forward with my calling. I recognize that what I have attained is the result of an affirming spiritual apprenticeship even though the duration was very short. Given the obstacles I faced both prior to Dr. Proctor's tutelage and subsequent to that time, I would not have been able to confidently proceed in the path God was directing if a clergy mentor had not invested ministerial wisdom into my life. Dr. Proctor's mentoring had the most significant impact on my life. Since his death God has also placed other clergy leaders in my path who have made positive contributions. Out of these vital relationships has come an interest in helping other clergy benefit from mentoring. The vision is called the *Clergy Mentoring Institute (CMI)*.

The objectives of the CMI include resolution to the problem of finding a sponsor. When there is no clear system or structure for entering and learning the fine elements of ministry beyond the inadequate seminary and denominational models of ordination, people need another route. Those called to ministry with gifts and graces also have many questions that mentors could help answer. CMI seeks to find and develop clergy mentors who have an interest in the next generation. The reason is basic to human behavior: Political preoccupation with personal advancement and survival accompanied by time management problems, rather than investing in the next generation that may "replace" them causes some clergy to disregard those young in ministry. Most important, the sense of marginalization, especially for those called who are without power, network, heritage, or even an understanding of the significance of these issues, needs to be addressed. Overall, CMI wants to attack the feeling of isolation in ministry. The heart of CMI beats with the needs of those who have yearned for a mentoring process based on relationship.

This has been my story from the pew to the pulpit. I have changed dramatically over the years. Once I was a relatively shy young girl who faithfully attended worship. Now I have emerged persistent in the pursuit of my calling. Every career experience now plays a vital role in my holistic vision of ministry. My years as an engineer allowed me to hone my skills as a strategist for large projects. Working as a public-school teacher awakened the educator within me. And years as a professional sales representative equipped me with the dexterity necessary to market a model of ministry that represents a different paradigm.

Some describe me as a trailblazer, but I like to think of myself as traveling the trails that God blazes ahead of me. I am also a wife and mother of two very young children, and this is where I derive my encouragement. Where some preachers have lost families as a result of ministry, God gave me an incredibly supportive husband after I had already become a minister. His confidence in

God's anointing on my life fuels me when others laugh behind my back. Before becoming my husband he was first my friend. I firmly believe that every woman in ministry needs a few solid friends whom she respects and who respect her. Those friends will pray for her, rejoice with her, correct her errors, support her mission, and celebrate her vision. I thank God for my friends; those who have been with me throughout this entire journey and the ones who have passed into eternity. Without them ministry would have been a lonely road.

Sermon: "Say My Name!"
1 Samuel 16:1–12

CECELIA E. GREENE BARR

Have you ever wanted to be selected for a team? When I was in grade school our physical education classes always involved team sport participation. The teacher selected a captain for each team, and then the captains selected from among the class which players to include on their respective teams. Regardless of the sport, invariably the smallest, least athletic-looking person would be the last one selected. The team stuck with that particular player seldom hesitated in expressing their discontent with being forced to accept this last-resort recruit. Ministry is like a sport that utilizes a similar selection process: God as teacher, ecclesiastical or congregational leadership as team captains, and believers in the role of hopeful candidates. How do you become fortunate enough to be selected for the team? No matter the sport or circumstances, somebody must say your name.

When this Scripture opens, Samuel is lamenting over God's rejection of Saul as king of Israel. Events have caused God to select another king of Israel, and it falls upon Samuel to perform the anointing ceremony precisely as God commands. Hesitation is in Samuel's voice because Israel's relationship with kings is relatively new and Saul is still alive. A remarkable difference exists between Israel's first and second kings. Saul is described as the king Israel has chosen for themselves (1 Sam. 8:18), whereas David is described as the king God has provided for himself (1 Sam. 16:1).

God has a rich history of being a provider. Abraham was in the process of offering Isaac as a sacrifice, but God provided a ram as a substitute (Gen. 22:1–14). When Jacob's family was suffering during a famine, God provided sustenance through Joseph (Gen. 45:3–8). When the Israelites cried for deliverance, God provided Moses (Exod. 3:7–10). When Barak warred against Sisera for Israel's freedom, God provided the prophetess Deborah to lead the way (Judg. 4:4–9). Whenever the enemy encamps around you, God provides angels for protection (Ps. 91:11). When your journey seems dark and uncertain, God provides himself as a lamp for your pathway (Ps. 27:1). Job questioned God and God provided a response (Job 38–40). The curse of sin was broken because God provided Jesus. The disciples needed direction, and God provided Mary Magdalene along with other women to proclaim the gospel (Mark 16:1–8). When Jesus ascended to heaven, God provided the Holy Spirit to dwell in believers (Luke 24:49–53). Rest assured that in all times and circumstances, of God's own choosing, God will provide.

Upon his arrival Samuel sanctifies Jesse and his sons, then invites them to the sacrifice. Although Jesse and the city elders did not know that Samuel came to anoint a new king, Samuel was internally clear about his assignment. Leadership was changing hands. With just one word from God, a changing of the guard was about to take place. Samuel invites Jesse and his sons, but Jesse chooses to exclude David from consideration. We don't know for certain why Jesse excluded David; we just know that he did. Yes, David was tending the sheep but surely the other brothers were also busy with family chores as well, yet they were invited. Whatever the reason, David was left out of the process.

When it comes to preparing for service in God's kingdom my experiences have trained me to conceive of it as a process. The process of selection—we are shaped by it, trained through it, frustrated because of it, and if mishandled while in its midst, we end up resenting it. No matter how anointed or spiritually mature, you are expected to go through the process, step by step. No one is ordained unless a pastor makes a recommendation. No one is appointed to the pastorate unless someone vouches for that person to the leadership. Church structure dictates the process and rarely is there any deviation.

Sanctification was a step along the usual process toward service in God's kingdom, yet even though Jesse excluded David, God did not exclude him from his destiny. I'm convinced that even today there are those who operate out of a "spirit of Jesse." For less than obvious reasons, when God sends out the invitation for Christian service, the "spirit of Jesse," for no valid reason, will choose to exclude. Exclusion based on personal preference, family pedigree, perceived worthiness, gender, age, life circumstances, background, body composition, dialect of speech, or anything else is but a small obstacle when God has decided to say your name. Jesse may want to keep you in the fields tending sheep, but when God decides to say your name no one will sit down until you are brought into the room and included in the process. Jesse might forget that you exist. You may even think Jesse is looking out for your best interests, but what you really need is for God to say your name.

Preparation is also necessary when one seeks to be used in God's service. As a hopeful and sanctified candidate, you may have years of academic preparation. You may have fine-tuned your interpersonal skills, sharpened your networking abilities, applied practical wisdom, and embraced the disciplines of spiritual formation. Even with this impressive arsenal, someone must be in the room, the place of decision, that is interested in saying your name. I propose that instead of depending on Jesse you need to depend on God.

Why does it matters who says your name, just so long as your name is called? The first benefit of God, instead of Jesse, saying your name is described as divine selection. When the "spirit of Jesse" says your name, there is usually a price tag attached—that is, favors to be repaid, homage to be expressed, praise to be given, worship to be extolled, and allegiance to be shown to Jesse for what he has done on your behalf. When God speaks, your selection is divine and debt free. When God speaks your name, it is crystal clear that you are the one for the task. With divine selection you are not beholding to anyone except God; therefore, your integrity remains intact. You do not become an idol worshiper because God alone receives the praise for your accomplishments. Divine selection means that if necessary, God will redirect circumstances if the normal process becomes a hindrance to your progress. It means that God has placed confidence in you and that God's hand is upon you. Divine selection means that others may fall at the hurdles of mediocrity, weak judgment, and complacency but that these will not hinder you. Instead, yours will be the long jump of consistency and integrity.

When God says your name, there is divine provision. God will not call you to a work without providing for accomplishment. In this day, ministry has refocused from a constant gaze on otherworldly expectations to present-day victory. Effective servants need God to provide spiritual weaponry for defeating the enemies of God's kingdom. Spiritual weaponry such as the supernatural manifestations of the Holy Spirit is the difference between being empowered and overpowered. Divine provision also moves a servant into his or her divine destiny.

While conversing with a preacher, I listened as he recalled his ministerial journey. Now that he had more than eighty years of life behind him, this servant could reflect on his past with clarity and brutal honesty. Along with his many successes he told me about the time in which he also failed to be effective. Moving through the denominational process, he had gained the attention of several presiding elders who took personal delight in recommending him for a promotion. It was this promotion that proved to be the worse move of his pastoral career. Thinking retrospectively, he warned that sometimes people can think more of you than what you are capable of achieving. In short, he had been promoted to his level of incompetence. When God says your name, you can rest assured that your destiny is within your competencies.

Jesse made seven of his sons pass before Samuel, and Samuel said to Jesse, "The Lord has not chosen any of these. Are all of your sons here?" Even as the Spirit of God ministers this Word to you today, committee chairpersons, search committees, conference coordinators, book publishers, bishops, district superintendents, and keepers of all kinds of gates are asking the "spirit of Jesse" the same question. Are all your candidates here? The answer is "no" because you are not present, at least not yet! I want to leave you with this final prophetic instruction.

In 1 Chronicles 4:10 a short history is recorded in which Jabez prayed asking God to bless him, enlarge his borders, that God's hand may be upon him and to keep Jabez from hurt or harm. The same verse declares that God granted him what he asked. If you have been excluded like David, I prophetically instruct you to pray your own prayer much like Jabez's. Pray asking God to say your name!

> Say my name, God, when the system, that is, the "spirit of Jesse," would seek to exclude me from participation. Say my name when servants are being considered for selection as pastors, conference participants, promotion, and leadership on various levels. Say my name, God, when my identity is obscured from their memory. Say my name, God, when my anointing is ignored and my abilities are rejected. Say my name, God, when others are trying to promote their own agenda and your will is no longer resting in their hearts. Say my name, God, so no one else can claim your glory or sit in the seat of your wisdom. Thank you, God, for saying my name.

3

For Such a Time as This

DEBORAH K. BLANKS

I was only nineteen years old when I accepted the unmistakable call of God to preach the gospel of Jesus Christ. All I knew was that I felt a deep unrelenting and irresistible urge to represent God in the world. To say that I had any idea as to what this human *yes* to a divine call would mean for my life is to suggest that I was light years ahead of my chronological age.

At nineteen I was a junior in college trying to figure out if my political science major would lead me to law school and a lucrative career as an attorney exercising skills of elocution in the halls of justice. What I realized as I sought God in moments of silence and times of much praying was that there were more questions than answers to what this particular call would mean for my life. I inquired of preachers and sainted men and women of faith of how one really knew that they were called of God to preach—to ministry. No one gave a satisfactory answer to my query. People would only say that when one was called that one would definitively know it.

It was some years later when I read about the call of the Rev. Dr. Martin Luther King Jr., and learned how he described his call as a process, that I realized that my call experience was just that—there was no blinding light, no voice summoning me from slumber, no grand emotional overture, but just an unmistakable, unrelenting reality that God was calling me to do something that transcended my human understanding. I was female, a teenager, African American, and deeply rooted in a rich African American church tradition. Why was God calling me? What would God do with me or through me?

When I spoke with my grandparents about the call to ministry they appeared neither surprised nor dismayed. My grandmother, Mamie Blanks, a

stalwart soldier of the cross, encouraged me to do that which God was ordaining for my life, while my dear grandfather, Samuel Blanks, a very traditional
man in his thinking on most gender-specific matters, did not allow any semblance of sexism to cloud our conversation. He affirmed my call, and said to
me, "If God has called you, then God will equip you for the work." My grandparents taught me that faith has the final word when God has initiated the
divine dialogue.

From my earliest pew-sitting days in what I now know was a Pentecostal
church in my birthplace of Mount Vernon, New York, I witnessed my first
woman preacher in the pulpit. We addressed her as Mother Richardson. She
preached almost every Sunday, and would frequently raise the same rhetorical
question when preaching about the unsearchable riches of Christ: "Didn't he
do it?" Mother Richardson was a very tall woman with a deep resonant voice
that thundered forth the message of God with a power that stirred something
in those who heard her. During those formative years, I listened to that woman
of God whose stature made me look heavenward, and whose voice sounded
like the rushing of many waters. Her strong, passionate preaching captivated
me as a little girl and made me believe.

Those early years of being under the watchful eyes and prayers of those
warriors of the faith fortified me for the journey ahead. When I was eight years
old my family moved to Newark, New Jersey, and I began attending Saint
James African Methodist Episcopal Church, and once again was privileged to
be in a church where two women—the Reverends Mary White Williams and
Betty Wilkins—were on the ministerial staff and preached every month on the
second and fourth Sundays at the 7:30 a.m. service. They were ordained itinerant elders in the denomination, which is the highest ordination that one can
receive. Both women brought to the pulpit their tremendous gifts and graces,
and were full participants in the ministry of the church. Seeing them in the
pulpit on a regular basis made me fully aware that there were no limitations
on where one could serve in the kingdom of God.

It was in Saint James Church—the church of my childhood—that the seeds
of faith and love for God were nurtured. The gothic edifice, Tiffany stained-
glass windows, raised mahogany pulpit, rare Skinner pipe organ, and the amazing people from every walk of life provided a sanctuary within a sanctuary. My
pastor was the Rev. Dr. D. McNeil Owens. Rev. Owens was an impressive
southern gentleman of distinction. He was brilliant, articulate, seminary educated, and a preacher whose sermons whet the intellectual appetite. Long
before the "shout of rejoicing" reached the feet or hands ascended in praise,
his poignant sermons had a way of reaching the inner court of the mind, caus-
ing the heart to respond to the deep mysteries of God. It was Rev. Owens who
first announced from the pulpit that he sensed that God was calling me to

preach. I could not believe it when he actually expressed this belief from the pulpit. I was on speaking terms with God, but God had not informed me about this; thus, I did not readily believe that God had let him in on such highly classified information.

I was a committed young person in the church serving as choir member, usher, and an active member of the Young People's Department. Often I was asked to offer the altar call prayer at our Youth Day Sunday services, which were held on the third Sunday of every month. During those times, something transcendent seemed to happen to me during the prayer. Many times I felt that it was not me praying at all, and that I was transported to another realm even though I had never left the sanctuary of Saint James. When Rev. Owens first spoke the words from the pulpit that God had God's hand upon my life and was calling me to ministry, I vividly recall literally going under the pew, because I could not imagine that I was being called out from among my peers and from the life that I envisioned for myself. Ministry was without a doubt a high and holy reality, but it scared the "Bee-Jesus" out me as I wrestled with what it would mean to be God's servant in the world.

It took some time for me to grasp God's reality for my life, but when it happened there was never a doubt in my mind. As the saints of old would say, "knee bent and body bowed," in a college dorm room, I said yes to the Lord, and began the journey that would forever change and challenge my life. My pastor during those college years at Rutgers University, Douglass College, was the Reverend Henry A. Hildebrand. Rev. Hildebrand served as pastor of the Mount Zion AME Church in New Brunswick, New Jersey. He was a pastor par excellence, an incredible mentor and role model to both me and a college classmate of mine, the Rev. Dietra C. Bell of Atlantic City, New Jersey. We were both young women responding to a call in our lives, and this amazing pastor embraced us and taught us much about ministry in the life of the church.

In the late 1970s, before praise teams were as popular in the church as they are nowadays, we were up front at Mount Zion Church trying to get the saints revved up in their praise of God. Our youthful zeal was encouraged and validated by our college pastor and friend. Never once did Rev. Hildebrand ever discourage us from being the people that God called us to be. In fact, he took the two of us under his pastoral wings and "godfathered" us through the process toward ordination. In June 2001, Rev. Hildebrand retired from active service as an AME pastor, and stepped down as the shepherd of Mount Zion Church after thirty-seven years. I received an unexpected telephone call from him requesting that I offer the invocation at the service celebrating his long and distinguished ministry.

Upon graduation from college I headed off to Atlanta, Georgia, to attend the Interdenominational Theological Center. I was one of three women in the entering class of the Turner Theological Seminary of the ITC, which is the African Methodist Episcopal Seminary. The Rev. Marla Coulter McDonald of Little Rock, Arkansas, and my college classmate, the Rev. Dietra Bell, were the two other women in the class. Very early in our seminary career we were introduced to the scholar preachers, the Rev. Dr. Jacquelyn Grant and the Rev. Dr. Carolyn McCrary, who were both professors at the seminary and also ordained clergy within the AME Church. Both of these women were wonderful mentors and invaluable resources.

Rev. Grant introduced us to womanist theology and recruited us to be a part of her new and exciting brainchild *Black Women in Church and Society*, a program at the ITC in Atlanta, which raised the consciousness and profile of the significant contribution of women to the church and larger world. And Rev. McCrary opened our eyes to the human anguish endured by saints and sinners alike, and enlightened us about pastoral care and counseling as one of the many gateways to deliverance and salvation.

My most dramatic memory of *womanist* anything happened on my first Sunday in Atlanta at the Flipper Temple AME Church when my new seminary sisters and I attended church together. The Rev. Dr. Grant was the preacher for the annual Woman's Day service. Before beginning the sermon, she asked us to bow our heads in prayer and began praying, "Mother-Father God." Our eyes were closed and heads bowed, but in one sweeping movement or so it seemed, we lifted our heads, opened our eyes, and looked at one another in total disbelief. We had never heard anyone in our churches back home or anywhere else invoke the Divine in that way. That was the beginning of a new way of imaging and envisioning God that transformed my thinking and my life.

My time at the Interdenominational Theological Center were the best years of my life. ITC was holy ground. Whether in the classroom, library, cafeteria, or the "Waldorf Astoria" efficiency apartments nestled on the outer edge of campus, I knew without a doubt that I was in a community that honored my humanity and celebrated my intellectual ability. In the classroom we were challenged to think about God and the Word of God much more broadly and encouraged to ask honest, and sometimes hard, questions about Scripture, faith, and the church. Professors dared us to move from the zones of Christian comfortability and grapple with the realities of evil, suffering, and blatant injustice in the world and the church.

I often wondered during those first two years at ITC if my faith would survive the relocation of my mind and thinking about God and God-related matters. The question that often visited me during the seminary years was, "Would my faith be deepened or diminished by the time of graduation?" In hindsight, I know that the three-year journey at ITC liberated me as a preacher of the gospel and grounded me as a woman of faith to be a radical representative for the kingdom's sake in the world.

I am a living witness with the testimony that my faith plumbed the unfathomable depths and reemerged deepened, strengthened, and stretched beyond what I could have hoped or imagined. I was no longer a person inclined just to believe for the sake of believing, but to believe in a God who reveals the divine self in silence and speaking; in humanity and creation; in scripture, ritual, and tradition; in times of great faith and in seasons of doubt. ITC forced me to consider how my faith informs my whole life—the seminary experience breathed new life into my being.

The pilgrimage at ITC readied me for ministry, but the question that loomed large as I approached the end of my time there was, "What ministry is God leading me to, and where will that ministry be carried out?" Forasmuch as I loved the church and pondered the possibility of making a lifelong contribution in a conventional setting, I did not feel led to serve in a traditional pastorate. As I thought about different venues where I could serve, the military chaplaincy came to the fore as a viable option. The initial commitment was three years and provided the chance to serve a diverse group of people in unique locations.

The U.S. Navy offered me the opportunity to explore the full range of sea service offerings: ships, overseas assignments, submarines (at least a visit), as well as the possibility to serve with Marines and the Coast Guard. The more I prayed, the more I knew that the military chaplaincy was the place that I would begin ministry as a woman of the cloth. I began the tedious paperwork process and was accepted as an officer in the Navy to serve as an active-duty chaplain. My first official duty station of my new career was the Navy Chaplains School in Newport, Rhode Island, with nineteen others. I was one of three African Americans and the only female in a class of nineteen.

If the African American church of my upbringing and the community of faith during the seminary years was a safe haven that nurtured and nourished the life in me, then the Navy Chaplain Corps was the antithesis, and my firsthand introduction to the double-edged sword of racism and sexism. I had been raised to believe that people were innately good and would generally treat you with respect and goodwill. It would be safe to say that those who had charge over me at the Chaplains School were people who upheld the ethical tenets of the Navy; however, in the class were chaplains who wore the cross on the collar, but were unashamedly racist and sexist and made no private bones about it. The only reason I believe that I survived the indoctrination period was because of the unwavering support of the African American brothers. I was young and naive about so many things, and was simply trying to get my Navy sea legs so that I could stand in the midst of any storm.

I made it through the seven long weeks, and successfully graduated and received orders to report to the Naval Hospital, Portsmouth, Virginia. Once again, I was the only female and person of color on a staff of about ten. All of my colleagues were middle- to upper-aged white men. Although we all wore the same uniform and the cross on the collar, I realized very early on that those who were charged to provide mentorship and guidance of me were only interested in short-circuiting my potential naval career.

The very first fitness report that I received after only six months on the job indicated that I was performing my duties in a satisfactory manner and that I had potential to grow. Now "satisfactory" anything in an evaluative report about professional performance in the Navy of that period was the kiss of death. Fitness reports for the male chaplains used language like "superior," "extraordinary," "head and shoulders above their peers," "promote early," and on and on. When I questioned my senior chaplain about the report and its impact upon my future, I was told that it was important to show growth for one as junior as I.

On one occasion I requested to see my fitness reports so that I would know exactly what was in the record. The senior chaplain told me in no uncertain terms that I had to sit in the secretary's office and could not photocopy anything from the record. He was in a meeting and allegedly could not be disturbed; hence, I sat in the office and perused the record. As I reviewed what was in the fitness report, I decided that I should take some notes and secured a tablet to do so. I was writing down a few things when the secretary got up from behind her desk and entered the senior chaplain's office to inform him that I was writing something down. He came storming out of the office, snatched the pad from me, and accused me of disobeying a direct order. He had said there would be no copying, which I knew meant that I could not photocopy anything; never did he indicate that I could not take notes from my own record.

I remember this experience like it was yesterday; the chaplain was livid, angry, enraged, and breathing threats, which made me nervous but did not shake me. He said in a pejorative tone, "Are you finished?" I answered quietly, "No, I am not." He informed me that I had five minutes to finish reviewing the record. I never understood how someone who wore the same cross that I wore on the collar, and professed a faith akin to mine, could so effortlessly crucify me just because I happened to be of another race and gender. That chaplain would have never admitted that his actions were racist or sexist, but the denigrating and despicable behavior toward me was a manifestation of deeper issues.

Each duty station brought with it new challenges and the challenges were always with the chaplains in charge. While serving at the Recruit Training Chapel in Orlando, Florida, I was given responsibility to lead an early morning worship service. When I took over the service, the attendance was approximately seventy-five people. I hired a young white man who had deep roots in the Assembly of God Church to serve as the musician. Together we created an extraordinary worship experience with liturgy, music, and dynamic preaching by three white colleagues and I that stirred the hearts of all. The service grew from the seventy-five to over twelve hundred young people filling that chapel.

Most people would say that this was definitely a success story, and that everyone should be proud. However, in a staff meeting, the senior chaplain in charge questioned whether the service was more "racial than religious." I found that question troubling since the musician was white, the three chaplains who served with me were white, and I was the lone woman of color. What the chaplain was not able or willing to articulate aloud was that he was upset that this small, insignificant service in the minds of some had grown so large. The service was now in direct competition with another worship service, which was the poster service of the Chaplain Corps at that time.

While I thought that the goal of ministry was to provide a sacred space in which those young people could come to sing and sway, cry and rejoice, and give glory and praise to God, I was called on the carpet to address whether a worship service was more "racial than religious." During my decade of service I encountered similar experiences played out in various ways with different chaplains, and often felt that the reason that the dishonorable conduct of some was not addressed or reprimanded had to do with the fact that the "senior" wielded the evil ax of power without apology or accountability. Unfortunately, what I endured during this particular season of my life is a reality that many women have to face daily in the church and world to varying degrees.

I was honorably discharged from the United States Navy Chaplain Corps after ten years of active-duty service. The move from military life to the civilian sector was a smooth transition. As I thought about my next placement in ministry, I considered accepting an offer to serve as executive minister at my home church where I grew up. The church continued its relevant and important ministry in an urban community, and was shepherded by the progressive pastor-scholar, the Rev. Dr. William D. Watley. After prayerful consideration of this particular vocational opportunity, I felt led once again to explore ministry in an institutional setting. The hunger within to pursue ministry beyond the hallowed walls of the church called out to me. I realized that my calling was to embody the presence of the sacred in a secular setting.

Through a Navy Chaplain colleague, I learned of a job opening at Brown University in Providence, Rhode Island, for an assistant university chaplain. This opportunity seemed designed and ordered by God for my life. Although the military and university worlds are vastly different, they had some unique commonalities. Both the military and university serve a racially, ethnically, educationally, and religiously pluralistic population. In each of these communities people were at the beginning of their academic or professional journeys (at least undergraduates and new recruits). What was most evident to me was that my skills were transferable in the higher education venue.

When I applied for the job at Brown, the search committee had already interviewed the first candidate. I was the last candidate out of a field of seven to interview for the post, and I got it. My getting the job at Brown convinced me that what God has for you you will get. To say that the position at Brown was ideal and definitely a good fit is an understatement. My boss was a woman, the Rev. Janet Cooper Nelson, University Chaplain. Rev. Cooper Nelson embodied the essence of excellence as a pastor on a university campus, and became the perfect role model and mentor for my next chapter of pastoral ministry.

People often ask me, "What is the job of a chaplain within the university context?" My response is simply, "Ordained clergy who work in the academy serve as pastor to faculty, students, and staff of the university." The "person of the cloth" is charged with the responsibility of strengthening, deepening, and broadening the spiritual and ethical life of the university through the liturgical, sacramental, and pastoral acts of ministry. Those fortunate enough to labor in the academy have the authentic privilege to be a prophetic voice and conscience for the university as well as shepherd the lives of young people who will be leaders in the nation and the world.

I served at Brown for three years. My choice to leave Brown was more personal than professional. I wanted to return to New Jersey to live and work. The position of Assistant Dean of Religious Life and of the Chapel at Princeton University providentially opened up, and once again I competed successfully and got this second opportunity of a lifetime to work as a pastor within the Ivy League. Princeton has afforded me the high honor to be the third African American clergyperson to serve as a Dean of Religious Life and of the Chapel and to be the first woman of the African Diaspora to hold this prestigious post.

As in the church of my childhood, I worship and preach in a magnificent gothic cathedral, appointed with Tiffany stained-glass windows, an elevated mahogany pulpit, and a rare (Skinner-Mander) pipe organ. God must have a great sense of humor, and a sovereign hand on the life of the young teenager who attempted to go under a pew upon hearing that God might be able to use a finite life for the good and glory of the kingdom of God on Earth. Often I ask myself, "Who would have thunk it?"

I know that the journey that began as a child is an ever-unfolding reality. Only God could call a shy, quiet teenager and raise her up to be a voice in the church, military chaplaincy, and academy for such a time as this. I was young and now I am older, and I know unequivocally that God is gender inclusive and opens doors and makes ways for the life that is surrendered to God.

Sermon: "Telling God Where It Hurts"
Mark 5:25–35

DEBORAH K. BLANKS

The New Testament is replete with stories that capture our imagination and captivate our attention. Each gospel is filled with narratives that cause us to sit on the edge of our seats as we ponder the outcome even though we may already know the ending. The conversation that takes place at Jacob's well between the status quo–breaking, dialogue-detaining, life-changing, Rabbi Jesus and the unnamed woman makes us long for just a sip of that life-giving water he talks about to quench the thirst of our lives. The encounter at Simon the leper's house that causes a woman to break an alabaster jar containing an expensive fragrance and anoint him from head to toe and then bathe his feet with her hair makes us long to linger in the presence of such an audacious love. The exchange that happens between the Syrophonecian woman who is persistent in faith in the face of an arbitrary "dissing" in order to receive *deliverance crumbs* from the table of Jesus makes us aware that daring faith gets the attention of God.

Mark records the story of another unnamed woman whose life account brings us front and center with some real issues. This story is also found in Matthew and in Luke. Interestingly enough, not one of the versions of this story tells us her name. She has no identity. She has no renown. She has no name. We do not have any background information on her. We do not know anything about her family tree. We do not know whether at one time she was the Martha Stewart of the region or the Jerusalem Idol competing for national fame and acclaim. We do not know if she was ever the center of attention or someone who was never noticed. The facts are straightforward: she had suffered for twelve years; she was bleeding to be exact; she had exhausted her HMO plan and could not obtain another referral; some of the physicians she had seen had taken advantage of her; her prognosis was not good, because the Scripture says that, "she was no better but rather grew worse."

She was hurting. She was hoping against hope. She was believing against all odds. Yet something occurred and when it happened we do not know or how it happened we have no clue about. For even though she had suffered from an extremely personal disease, something within her causes her to dare to appear in public and seek out the help that she needs. This unnamed and unknown woman of the Scriptures makes a *"by any means necessary"* move. One might say that by her radical act, she in essence is "Telling God Where It Hurts."

What about us? How many of us feel safe enough to tell God where it hurts? Do we feel comfortable enough to share with God those things that are so profoundly personal? Are we able to share the details of our thought life and the throbbing realities of what's really in our hearts? Are we willing to be vulnerable enough with God to speak the truth of our lives to the Trusted One? Have we come to a place where we can be honest with the Sovereign about the secrets of our souls? Can we share the upsetting, the seemingly unforgivable, the things that hurt us so deeply that it causes an unrelenting ache in our souls? How many of us feel safe enough to tell God where it hurts, even though God already knows everything about us? The ancient prophet Jeremiah posed the question, "Is there anything too hard for God?" In other words, "Are there hurts beyond healing? Is there brokenness beyond repair? Is there misery beyond a miracle? The answer to these questions and others is a resounding "no"! For the text suggests that faith that presses its way will find the miracle in an unexpected place.

Our sister of the text had gone everywhere and tried everything. Her *situation* had stigmatized her social standing in the community. The Levitical laws rendered her ritually unclean, which meant that she could not associate with family or friends. She was bleeding! She could not join other women around Jacob's well to discuss the happenings of the day. She was bleeding! She could not sit in the congregation and hear the Shammah from the Torah read, "Hear O Israel, the Lord is one!" She was bleeding! She was cut off from her community, excommunicated from her ethnic heritage, and separated from her spiritual birthright. She was bleeding! Imagine the isolation. Visualize the victimization. Picture the pain.

People of color do not have to dig too deep to understand what the unnamed sister might have been experiencing. We know what it is like to be treated differently just because we have more melanin in our skin—that is to say, that our tan is naturally browner. We know the struggles of working inside the big house of corporate structures, and yet relegated outside the inner circle of power. We know what it's like to be stopped on the major thoroughfares of our nation, just because we are driving while black or brown. We know what it's like to be eyed suspiciously while shopping in places of business. We know what it's like to be the last hired and first fired. We know what it's like to deal with people who treat us unkindly and heartlessly just because they have the power to do so. We know what it is like to have people who look like us work to make our condition worse rather than better. Bleeding! There is a bleeding in our society.

> There's bleeding because a black person is murdered in the United States every forty-two minutes.
> There's bleeding because the FBI Uniform Crime Report indicates that blacks, 12 percent of the population, account for half of all the murder victims (with 95 percent being killed by other blacks).
> There's bleeding because the number of black males killed every year is higher than the total number of black soldiers killed during the bloodiest decade of the Vietnam War.
> There's bleeding because in some of our communities the destructive dealings that take place is as dangerous as Osama bin Laden's Al-Qaeda network and more deadly than Sadaam Hussein's alleged weapons of mass destruction. There is a bleeding in our world.
> 840 million people in the world are hungry.
> 34 million people in America, including 12.1 million children live below the poverty line.
> 43 million people in the United States do not have health care coverage.
> 1400 women a year die as a result of domestic violence.
> 2000-plus military members and counting have died in the war in Iraq.

Bleeding! What can we do to stop the bleeding? What should we do to halt the hemorrhage? What can we do to heal the hurt? Well, I asked our sister of the text. I sought her expertise on the matter, because she is a living example of survival. She said, "I had exhausted all of my resources. There were not many folk I could be near, but through a few contacts I heard reports about a man who was working miracles. I knew because of my unclean status that I would not be able to come out publicly and state my condition like other folk. So I decided that the best thing for me to do was to get in the flow of the crowd. The man made a stop in my town and multitudes gathered around him. I didn't want to be noticed; I just wanted to be in the crowd."

She was in the crowd that day. She came up behind him and touched the hem of his garment; for she said, if only I may touch his clothes, I shall be made well. Now in her touch she was telling God where it hurt. Perchance there's somebody in this house who has been bleeding.

> Bleeding because of a rebellious child
> Bleeding because of a substance-addicted family member
> Bleeding because of a loss of employment
> Bleeding because a loved one has died
> Bleeding because of deferred dreams and unfulfilled hopes
> Bleeding because of childhood scars and adult wounds
> Bleeding because of the void, emptiness, and hollowness of your life

When I was a just little girl and didn't feel well, my grandmother would come to me and she would say, "Tell me where it hurts." Like the woman of Scripture, we must tell God where it hurts. There's no indication that she had ever met Jesus before. There's no indication that she had even been a passing acquaintance. There's no indication that she had ever seen him perform a miracle. There's no indication that she had firsthand knowledge of his healing powers. But she had heard reports about him. I wonder whether you have heard any reports about Jesus. Have you heard about what he has done? Have you heard about what he will do? Have you heard about what he can do?

There's a story told about a young child and an old man who were seated together on a fishing dock. They were talking about many things: why the sunset is sometimes red; why the rain falls; why some creatures live in water and others require air. As the old man was baiting the child's hook, the youngster looked up at him and asked, "Does anyone ever see God?" The old man reflected a moment as he looked out across the sylvan lake and the lush foliage surrounding it and answered: "Dear, we can't see God, but we can see where God's been." This woman must have heard where Jesus had just been. She must have heard that he had just delivered the demoniac. She must have heard that he had just spoken the words "Peace be still" and caused a cosmic *chill out* of the contrary wind and misbehaving sea. She must have heard that he had just touched the mother-in-law of Peter and her fever had left her. She must have heard that he only spoke the word and the servant of the centurion was healed.

The Scriptures do not tell us what, but we do know that something within her reached out in faith to receive the cure for her condition, the deliverance of her disease, the panacea for her pain, and the healing for her hurt.

> She did not let the culture confine her.
> She did not let the gender ground her.
> She did not let the pain paralyze her.
> She did not let the patriarchy pulverize her.
> She did not let the severity of the situation suppress her.
> She did not let the identity question render her invisible.
> *She pressed through the sweat.*
> *She pressed through the smell.*
> *She pressed through the uncleanness.*
> *She pressed through the embarrassment.*

Her faith and hope were pressing through the crowd. She didn't want to touch Jesus physically—just the hem of his garment. Every devout Jew wore an outer robe with four tassels on it, one at each corner. The tassels were worn in obedience to the command in Numbers 15, and to signify to others, and to remind the man himself, that the wearer was a member of the chosen peo-

ple of God. They were the badge of the devout Jew. It was one of these tassels that the woman slipped through the crowd and touched; and having
touched it, she found herself cured. When she touched Jesus a transfusion of
power, of healing, and deliverance went out of him to her, and he asked,
"Who touched me?" He knew that somebody had "pressed" their way
through and received the virtue of God.

Another important point in this story is that Jesus was already on his way
to perform a miracle for Jairus, the ruler of the synagogue.

> Jairus, the named, needed a miracle from the Messiah for his daughter.
> Jairus, the known, needed a wonder wrought by the Wonder Worker.
> Jairus, the renowned, needed the One who embodied life to restore life to
> his dying daughter.

This woman pressed through the crowd even though Jesus was on his way
somewhere else to bless somebody else. What is the word for us speaking
across the centuries, "Tell God where it hurts!"

> God has a miracle for the somebody and the nobody.
> God has miracle for the learned and the unlearned.
> God has a miracle for the pulpit and the pew.
> God has a miracle for the single one and the married couple.
> God has a miracle for the man and the woman.
> God has a miracle for the corporate executive and the cleaning lady.
> God has a miracle for the African and the European.

Jesus looked and saw this no-name woman, and called her "daughter."
That designation signifies kinship, relationship, and lineage. Her touch of the
hem of his garment healed her bleeding. His words healed her soul. If we
want the bleeding to stop, we must tell God where it hurts.

And if you tell God where it hurts, heaven and earth will exchange a holy
kiss. If you tell God where it hurts, divinity will perform a dance on the stage
of eternity. If you tell God where it hurts, grace and mercy will give thunder-
ous applause.

4

Not by Might, Nor by Power . . .

ALYSON DIANE BROWNE

I spent my formative years from age three to thirteen as a member of the New Jerusalem Apostolic Church. My great aunts, Willie and Mary Smith, were charter members. It was at New Jerusalem that I came to believe God existed, God intervened in the affairs of humankind, and God wanted to be in relationship with us. In retrospect, my early perception of God was that God was judgmental and loved conditionally. The teachings of the church informed my perception; the rules and customs reinforced it. Obeying the rules was paramount. Restrictions were placed on attire; makeup and jewelry were discouraged. Certain activities, such as card playing, moviegoing, dancing, and a host of others were considered sinful and therefore frowned upon. If you engaged in the "restricted" behavior, the church labeled you a sinner or a backslider, and you felt the chill of judgment and ostracism.

I gave my life to God at an early age. I thought that being a Christian was the best thing one could be. I was afraid of going to hell and I wanted to be accepted into the church culture. Those members who were saved in the church were, in my mind, treated differently from those who weren't. I wanted to belong. I adhered to the rules. I prayed and read the Bible regularly. I believed that my relationship with God was black and white. As long as I kept the rules I was acceptable in the eyes of God and New Jerusalem. This perception would haunt me and distort my relationship with God even after I was no longer a member.

When I entered junior high school, I wanted to be like my peers. My junior high and high school years were spent enjoying teen life. Still, I knew the day would come when God would confront me. I believed God had plans for me that would not be put off by my detour. In my last year of high school, the parties, drugs, and drinking lost their attraction. I had a sense of foreboding in my spirit, and I knew a change was imminent. I promised God that after the prom, graduation, and one final night of partying, I would commit my life to God. This wasn't a bargain; it was a vow. A vow I kept. The Friday after graduation I went to church. I don't remember the preacher or the sermon. When the invitation was extended, I went immediately to the altar. I knelt and asked God's forgiveness for my sins. With resolve I committed the rest of my life to God.

Two months later while my cousins and I were having a prayer meeting, I suddenly fell to the floor, motionless and oblivious to my surroundings. I heard God's voice, audible only to my spirit's ears, saying, "You will be my minister. You will preach or die." My "Yes, Lord" was immediate. I knew that I could not turn away from God again and live. I was eighteen. At the time I was attending St. Paul's Seventh Day Christian Church, pastored by my late uncle the Rev. Deforest B. Soaries Sr. There were no women preachers in the small denomination, and I had no delusions about being the first. I had to find a denomination that affirmed women in ministry. Never did I doubt that God called me. Although I have often wondered *why* God called me, I have never wondered *whether* God called me, a woman.

Preaching women had been a part of my life as far back as I could remember. I have a vivid image of my brother and me standing in the front of the sanctuary singing. I was three and my brother was five. My aunt, the late Rev. Gladys G. Browne, was the pastor of the church located in South East Washington, DC. Years later I learned about my great aunt, Evangelist Mattie Browne Stewart, whose "Yes" to God in the early 1900s was the genesis of the preaching lineage in the Browne family.

Further exposure to women preachers occurred as a result of membership in the Woman's National Evangelistic and Missionary Conference, Inc. In 1911, the founder was directed by God in a vision to start the organization. The purpose of the Conference was to bring Christian women together and provide the freedom to preach, evangelize, engage in missionary endeavors, and exercise their God-given gifts and graces. The Conference was a form of protest against many of the mainline denominations that did not permit women to preach. Women of all denominations were invited to join, but men could hold only honorary membership. Women denied the right to preach in their own denominations maintained loyalty to their churches yet found liberty in the Conference.

As I look back, I realize that I was privy to a sisterhood that transcended familial connections. At the time of its inception, most of the Conference sisters were domestic workers. Meetings were held on Thursday because it was the traditional "day off." In addition to worship and fellowship, friendships and support systems resulted that strengthened women in all aspects of their lives.

The Conference provided spiritual nurture for me in my youth and young adulthood. Many of the sisters became my "spiritual mothers." When I began preaching they gave me occasion to do so in their meetings and always encouraged me to "stay with the Lord." I learned from them as they conducted business meetings, held elections, and made decisions for the good of the Conference. I held office in the Young People's Department, the New Jersey Branch, and the Parent Body. I heard countless sermons by women, and my belief that God called women to preach, pastor, and hold leadership positions was reinforced.

When God called me to preach, I knew that I had to find a church that was receptive of women preachers. In September 1970 a friend invited me to Bethel African Methodist Episcopal Church (AME) in Arverne, New York, to preach for youth day. I attended Bethel for two years before joining. In my study of AME history, I learned that the denomination began as a protest against racial discrimination. I was impressed by the fact that women were ordained and given pastoral appointments.

I was engaged to my childhood sweetheart, whom I met in the Woman's National Evangelistic and Missionary Conference. He was Baptist and I told him emphatically that I would not join his church because women preachers were neither accepted nor ordained. He had not asked me to join his church, but I had answered the question nonetheless.

When I entered the ministerial process the bishop asked if I were married. I told him I was engaged, and he asked how my fiancé felt about my being in ministry. I answered, "My fiancé has no problem with my being in ministry." Later it occurred to me that none of the men were asked how their spouses or fiancées felt about them being in ministry. In the 1980s when I served on the Board of Examiners and later became the first woman appointed Dean of the Newark–New Brunswick Ministerial Institute of the New Jersey Annual Conference, women were still being asked the same question by some of the older ministers, men of course. I took great delight in asking the same question of the men. On several occasions, one or two of the sisters and I would wink on the sly.

I was ordained an itinerant deacon in 1975 and an itinerant elder in 1977. Even after my last ordination I never envisioned myself in the pastorate. I observed firsthand the obstacles women faced regarding pastoral appointments and positions of leadership in the New York Annual Conference. The few women serving as pastors were much older than me. Their congregations were very small, and year after year the Bishop reassigned them to the same congregations. There were no female presiding elders, no female bishops. The leading pastors, synonymous with leaders of the New York Annual Conference, were all men. Women were not programmed during the official Annual

Conference worship services. The Department of Evangelism and the Women's Missionary Society constituted the women's sphere. On their respective Annual days, held prior to the official opening of the Annual Conference, women had the opportunity to preach and lead in worship. It was painfully clear to me that the Annual Conference structure was closed to women and that opportunities for significant pastoral appointments were nonexistent.

When I served on the ministerial staff of the Allen AME, Jamaica, New York, with Dr. Jacquelyn Grant it became apparent that AME liturgy was just as exclusive as AMEC polity. Dr. Grant's pioneering work in the area of womanist theology, and that of other scholars, continues to inform my reading of Scripture, my proclamation of the gospel, and my commitment to do justice on behalf of all people in general and women in particular.

When reading the Decalogue, Jackie would say, "Thou shalt not covet thy neighbor's wife," adding "Thou shalt not covet thy neighbor's husband." I sensed the collective cringe of the congregation and silently applauded her daring. I confess, however, that when it was my turn to read the Decalogue I didn't follow suit. Nonetheless, Jackie's actions enlightened me to the power of language and further raised my consciousness regarding the disparities that women faced in the church, community, and the world.

Jackie delivered a position paper detailing the status of women at the 1976 General Conference in Atlanta, Georgia. Her paper and the subsequent response led to a meeting with the Council of Bishops in 1977. Because of our Allen AME connection, Jackie invited me to attend the meeting. In addition to Jackie and myself, the Reverends Mary Ann Bellinger, Nurjhan Govan, and Jeane B. Williams were in attendance. Following the meeting the Council of Bishops agreed to the formation of an ad hoc committee to conduct research on the "herstory" of women in ministry in the AME. The efforts of the ad hoc committee led to the establishment of the Commission on Women in Ministry in 1989. In 1992, the resolution to admit the Commission on Women in Ministry to the Connectional Church was accepted by the General Conference. I was privileged to serve on the ad hoc committee and the steering committee. In the connectional organization of African Methodist Episcopal Women in Ministry (AME/WIM) I served as vice president and general secretary, and edited *Bricks Without Straw*, the AME/WIM newsletter. These early efforts helped pave the way for the election of the first female bishop in the AMEC in 2000.

My marriage to my childhood sweetheart didn't last long. We had the usual problems newlyweds encounter. I was an introvert and he was an extrovert. He was a gifted singer, pianist, and organist and played for several church choirs. When I accompanied him to rehearsals and to the churches where he was employed, I felt like, and allowed myself to be treated as, an appendage. I became pregnant two months after our wedding, placing further stress on our marriage. Our daughter Joyelle was born a month before our first annive ....y. We were unable to surmount our problems. My husband moved out, leaving me hurt, confused, and vulnerable.

In 1977, Bishop Hildebrand assigned me to the pastorate of Mt. Olive AME in Port Washington, Long Island. I lived and worked in New Jersey and commuted to the church several times weekly. During a brief reconciliation, I became pregnant with our son Justin. Full-time employment, single parenting, commuting to New York, and pastoring were demanding. I know God gave me the strength to do so for four years. The congregation was receptive to me, their first female pastor, and their love and support intensified during and after my pregnancy.

I moved to New York for our third and final reconciliation, hoping our marriage would be stronger and last forever. I slipped back into my former "keep the rules" mentality. If I were a good wife, God would turn our marriage around. This distorted perception of God led me to accept some things that no woman should have to live with.

I thank God for the day I realized that I was dying inside. It was slow and painful, but I was dying nonetheless. I had tried unsuccessfully to compartmentalize my pain. This slow death affected every area of my life: motherhood, relationships, and the pastorate. Even more important, it eroded the core of my being. On that day I also realized that I wanted to live. My present life was a far cry from God's destiny for me. I understood that being the best me had nothing to do with keeping the rules but had everything to do with what God would do in and through me. I began to define *my* faith, *my* understanding of God apart from what I had been taught and told, apart from the church traditions and customs of my youth. Time and experience were the most profound of my instructors. Through them I received the grace of God and knew it. What I had been taught about God and how I experienced God were intensely distinct. My relationship with God is not predicated upon whether or not I "toe the line" but is grounded in God's unconditional, immeasurable love.

Bishop Hildebrand knew that my husband and I were planning to divorce. I will never forget his words: "I'm going to send you home and put you in a church with a parsonage so that your children will be provided for." Going home meant returning to New Jersey. In 1982, I was transferred to the New Jersey Annual Conference and assigned to St. Mark AME in Cranford. There were rumors that the church would be padlocked on my first Sunday. Preachers in the New Jersey Conference wondered who I was and why I had been assigned a Class-A Charge—that is, a church with a parsonage and the ability to support a full-time pastor. No other woman in the First Episcopal District had a similar appointment. Bishop Hildebrand made a bold and unprecedented appointment.

I remained in Cranford for eleven years. Surprisingly, mine was the longest tenure of any pastor in St. Mark history. After a fire nearly destroyed the building, the church voted to rebuild rather than renovate. I made a commitment to stay until the completion of construction. None of us knew that it would take five years. Disgruntled members who wanted to renovate rather than rebuild left the church and wrote the Bishop asking for my removal. One member said, "We will starve you out." It was a time of great challenge filled with unremitting financial anxieties and construction delays. A miracle-working God and loyal, hardworking, and praying members made the new church a reality. Several members loaned thousands of dollars so the project could be completed. I was not starved out. The new building was dedicated in November 1993. I am the only woman in the First Episcopal District to complete construction of a new church. However, my greatest challenge was imminent.

I was forty-two years old and there were times when I would cry for no apparent reason. Significant portions of my childhood were gone from my memory. I knew that something was radically wrong, and I had a suspicion as to what it was. The flashbacks were my final evidence that I had been molested as a child. The rage I felt is indescribable. At the same time, the reality of what happened to me answered so many questions about what had shaped me subconsciously. The experience accounted for my shyness, my inordinate self-consciousness, and my inability to trust. Further, it explained why my voice had been buried along with my childhood innocence. Very rarely did I express my opinions or share my feelings. I didn't think anyone cared to hear them. Silence was my way of being in the world. My feelings, my opinions, and my voice shared a desolate grave.

I am convinced that God's calling me to preach saved my life. God's directive to preach resurrected my voice, saving it from an unwarranted grave. In the preaching moment, the Alyson who was forced into silence emerges. Preaching affords me the freedom of expression and movement stolen from me as a child. In the preaching space, I am neither shy nor self-conscious. I have something to say that people want to hear. I am clear that what I have to say is God inspired and no one can rob me of this gift. Preaching gave my life focus and meaning. When God said, "You will preach or die," I believed God was saying that if I refused to preach God would take my life. I now understand that God was saying, "Preach; it will save your life." When I preach I am keenly aware of my connection to God. The fusion of God's divinity with my humanity is overwhelming.

My gift for preaching has opened doors of opportunity for me. In the First Episcopal District of the AMEC, I was the first woman to preach the opening day sermon of the New Jersey Annual Conference, and I was the first woman to preach the Communion Meditation at the AMEC Missionary Quadrennial in Georgia. I served on various committees in the New Jersey Annual Conference. I have advocated for the full inclusion and participation of women in every aspect of denominational life. Every position I held in the AMEC enabled me to do so.

I was assigned to Quinn Chapel, Atlantic Highlands, New Jersey, in April 1994. It was a welcome respite from the rigors of the building project. My daughter Joyelle directed the Youth Choir, and my son Justin played the drums. My most unforgettable memory is the initial sermon and licensing of my son and my son in the ministry, Ryan Buckland. The fourth generation of preachers in the Browne family began with my son's "Yes" to God.

I began assessing my life in 1998, my fourth year at Quinn. I was thinking about where I wanted to be in the year 2003. The probability was quite high that I would still be pastoring Quinn Chapel. I wanted more. I had dreams of returning to school and obtaining the PhD degree. I wanted to continue in ministry, but I no longer wanted to pastor; after twenty-one years I took a leave. I presently serve as the Director of Ministries at the First Baptist Church of Lincoln Gardens, Somerset, New Jersey. My cousin, the Rev. Dr. Deforest B. Soaries Jr., is the pastor. I returned to seminary and am presently a candidate for the ThM Degree at Princeton Theological Seminary, Princeton, New Jersey. I elected this route on my journey toward the PhD degree because I have been out of seminary for so long and needed to be reintroduced to the rigors of academia.

My childhood church introduced me to God and planted an embryonic seed that refused to die; membership and service in other churches watered this seed. Before I was ordained the Woman's National Evangelistic and Missionary Conference nurtured me and affirmed my call. The African Methodist Episcopal Church equipped, ordained, and entrusted me with three congregations. God, the designer of my destiny, gave the increase.

Family and friends were God's gifts in my life and ministry. What I thought held permanence proved to be temporary. What I never envisioned God brought into existence. The divine architect has always been present.

"Not by might nor by power, but by my Spirit, says the Lord of Hosts." These words have prefaced my sermons for thirty-three years and are the inspiration for my spiritual journey.

Sermon: *"Straighten Up"*
Luke 13:10–17

ALYSON DIANE BROWNE

On a Sabbath Jesus was teaching in one of the synagogues, and a woman was there who had been crippled by a spirit for eighteen years. She was bent over and could not straighten up at all. When Jesus saw her he called her forward and said to her, "Woman, you are free from your infirmity." Then he put his hands on her, and immediately she straightened up and praised God.

I have no name in this story. I am given no personal identity that would indicate that I was born into a family, that I have a mother and a father. There is no mention of my lineage, nothing that would attest to the fact that I belong to someone somewhere. Luke, the physician and writer of this story, describes me as the "bent over woman." This is certainly my condition. It is a condition that I have suffered with for eighteen years.

Can you imagine being bent over, shoulders hunched and neck bent? Can you imagine living like I have for eighteen years? My worldview is restricted to that which my eyes can encompass on the ground. My world, my life, my days are filled with dirt, rocks, paths, and feet. There are no smiling faces and no twinkling eyes in my world. By the same token, I am spared the looks of pity and scorn. You see, illness is believed to be a curse or the result of a sin committed. The bottom line is that folk don't want to be around me.

In the last eighteen years I have been unable to look up and capture the dawning of a new day. I have not seen the sun rise and kiss the morning dew with its bright rays. At dusk I cannot see the moon slowly bid the sun goodnight and begin its nocturnal watch. I am no longer able to take an evening stroll and gaze with wonder at the stars in their heavenly residence.

I never really see anyone's face. Oh, I hear the rude comments, the whispering, the name calling, and the laughter. I don't see the faces, but I can hear. I know people by their feet and sandals. I can distinguish who is wealthy by the soft supple leather of their sandals. The sandals of the wealthy are skill-fully designed with careful attention to every detail. The sandals of the work-ing class are crafted from a lesser-quality leather. There is nothing unique about their design. Those who are poor have no sandals at all. You can tell a lot about people by looking at their feet and their sandals. Each tells a story about the individual's life and lifestyle. I can tell how old you are by looking at your feet.

My condition and therefore my presence is an embarrassment to folk. My presence is tolerated and endured, but I know people would be more com-fortable if I just stayed at home. My condition has not altered my faith. I am a devout Jew. I attend Sabbath services regularly. So much of my life has been altered by my condition, that my faith and church are the only things that make life bearable for me.

Even though I have to sit in the segregated section of the temple reserved for women, even though I cannot read from the Holy Scriptures or engage in dialogue with the rabbis, I still go to church. When I am in church I feel in a profound way the presence of the living God. When I'm in church, I don't feel defined by my condition but I feel connected to the God who created all people in God's own image and likeness. When I'm in church I feel a deep sense of kinship with the God who is nearer than my breath and closer than my hands and feet.

I am devalued by my condition. I have lost relationships and ties to my community. But in church I have peace. Worship has sustained me through my illness. You have an idea of how important church is to me. And so as this particular Sabbath day began it was no different from any other. I arose early. Whenever I'm going out I have to get up very early because it takes me so long to get ready. Laboriously, I prepared my breakfast. I pulled my shapeless dress over my deformed body and made my way to the temple. As I walked, the dirt, stones, and the beaten path were my old friends.

Arriving at the temple, I made my way to the woman's section and took my usual seat. A visiting rabbi was preaching. I later learned that his name is Jesus. His message and his demeanor captivated me. The power and author-ity of his words were unlike any other rabbi I had heard before. I was com-pletely focused on Jesus' words and then it happened. I thought I heard someone speaking to me. I thought to myself, this can't be right—no one would speak directly to me in the sanctuary. I heard his voice, but of course I couldn't see his face. Was the rabbi calling me? Out loud and in public. It is against the law for a man to speak openly to a woman in public.

He was indeed speaking to me. Not only was he speaking to me, he was bidding me come to the main area of the sanctuary. Surely, there must be some mistake. Doesn't he know that I am the hunchback, the bent-over woman? Doesn't he know that my condition has marginalized me? Doesn't he realize I am ridiculed and scorned by the people who attend this very church?

Despite my reservations and the questions racing through my mind, I knew he was waiting for me to come forward. Awkwardly I rose from my seat, shuffling slowly in the direction of his voice. I could sense every eye on me. My condition has rendered me anonymous, but in that moment, I could feel some vestige of personhood returning. Bowed and burdened by the weight of my infirmity, I stood in front of him. I could only see his feet. He wore the sandals of the working class. I wondered what his face looked like. His voice had brought a hush over the church, and everyone was waiting to see what would happen next—including me.

He spoke directly to me, "Woman, you are loosed from your infirmity." And then he touched me. His words and his touch reached a place in my soul that had been thirsting for a long time. His words and his touch loosened the bone and tissue that had turned in upon my body. I could feel my back begin to straighten up. I hadn't gone to church looking for a miracle, but the miracle worker came looking for me.

Every eye in the temple was upon me. Silenced by the miracle unfolding before their eyes, they were waiting for my response. When my eyes met the eyes of Jesus, I knew the source of my healing and my salvation. I couldn't process all that had just occurred, and I was a bit unsteady on my feet. My body ached because it was compelled to straighten up. Oh, but the joy that I felt could not be contained. I broke out into spontaneous praise and worship.

You would think that my former friends and neighbors, my church family, would rejoice with me. You would think that my "sisters" would have come running from their section of the temple to join with me in praise. I already knew people didn't want to be bothered with you if you're sick, and I learned on that Sabbath day that people are not happy when you get well. The CEO of the temple became indignant. He had the nerve to question the appropriateness of Jesus healing on the Sabbath. I bet if he'd been bent over for eighteen years and Jesus healed him he would not have been concerned about what day of the week it was.

But Jesus had a word for the brother: "You take care of your oxen and donkeys on the Sabbath. Shouldn't this daughter of Abraham be released from eighteen years of bondage?" Jesus called me a daughter of Abraham, a designation that any Jew would covet. Jesus included me in the community of the faithful and registered my name in the lamb's book of life.

I know that some of you are bent over. Your condition may not be physical as mine was, but you are bent over nonetheless. You are bent over due to mistreatment and abuse. Some of you are bent over by the unexpected and inevitable realities of life. Many of you are bowed by circumstances you did not cause and do not deserve. Some of you are bent over because a relationship has ended or never began. Some of you are bent over by a community that excludes you because you are a woman. Many of you are bent over from the weight of low self-esteem. I've got news for you: no one can ride your back unless you bend it.

I know what it's like to be bent over. I know what it feels like when you are powerless to change your situation. I know a man named Jesus who is still in the miracle-working business. One touch, one encounter and you will straighten up. All that your condition has robbed you of can be restored. It's time. You've been bent over long enough. You've got divine permission to straighten up!

5

The Journey
I Have Known

DELORES CARPENTER

My quest for truth, a rather ordinary one, parallels all of humanity's search for identity, purpose, and meaning. I have always felt that my future was linked to God in some way. The consciousness of a call to ministry came at an early age, and I have tried to discover effective ways to be faithful to that call. This has not been an easy task. Nor have I taken a direct route. Rather, it has been a circuitous one—a mosaic of many fragments.

In spite of its scenic contours, I am convinced that my search for clarity and integrity in handling the Word of God has been my life's anchor. The good news of the gospel is the most important sustaining and nurturing force in the world. It is important to me that its message never be muted or muffled. Its own nature is audacious and bold. And though these traits do not come naturally for me, I have felt their security, while shaking in my shoes with uncertainty and paradox.

For example, I am convinced of divine intervention on my behalf in 1983 when I battled with cancer. And I proclaim with all certainty that God is a healer, despite numerous other persons' death after much prayer. This is paradoxical and begs to reverse my own testimony. But instead, I attribute such seeming contradictions to something I call "the divine consideration."

It is always reserved as God's prerogative to heal in dramatic ways. Yet, everyday men and women, young and old, are restored to wholeness in small, wonderful ways. So I am encouraged to continue in faith, knowing that there is a Higher Power—a Creative Force which desires to move human existence from brokenness to a new sense of wholeness and well-being. God is a God of love and life. Yet it seems inevitable that all are broken on the wheel of life at some point. What sustains us is our belief that there is a heart of kindness at the center of the universe.

It was not easy to entertain what God could possibly do with a young girl of humble origins, whose family lacked education, money, or exposure to more sophisticated settings. When I was a child my family of origin was not long off the farm, and not far from a sharecropping existence. School was a delight. I ventured into a world of reading and learning as a means of bettering my life. My segregated colored neighborhood was full of relatives who taught in the school and protective friends who lived all along the walk to school. You were never out of sight of some caring adult, who felt responsibility for your proper conduct. It was that kind of world, full of dangerous consequences for colored people who stepped out of line.

The religious faith of my grandmother and mother was the most positive experience in my home environment. It brought many happy moments of travel, church attendance, and visitors to the house to discuss the Bible, to pray, and to preach. My grandmother erected a tent on the vacant lot next door for one whole summer and hosted one preacher and singing group after another until Hurricane Hazel blew down the tent.

When baptized, I took the gospel message seriously to heart. In my thirteen-year-old naïveté, I dedicated my life to walk the paths where God would lead.

The gospel taught me that God distributed gifts to men and women. It taught me that everyone has at least one talent and that if one is faithful in using that one talent, it can be multiplied into others. These were words of purpose and identity to a marginalized young woman who witnessed the confusion of racial segregation and the casualties of school integration in the mid-1950s in Baltimore.

I never knew or had a conversation with my father. My mother told me that God was my father. I believed it implicitly. That began a lifelong relationship, in which I tired to please God in every way possible and I was empowered by the knowledge that he was watching out for me. There's never been a day that I have not felt that God was with me in some way. I did not always have a clear direction. I groped for God with heart and mind. Yet, I believed that God was never far away, though hidden. I felt forsaken at times, without definitive answers, without a road map or a blueprint. I felt like I was sat down in a wilderness with no path, only thicket and underbrush, dust and barrenness.

However, God always puts encouragers in my life at critical points of decision. I came to learn that it was all right for women to realize that they had power—personal power and God-given power. But to have authority over other than children and other women was unheard of. To try to speak on behalf of God or religious tradition and, "God forbid," the religious community, was

perceived by many men and women as a mockery before God. Others believed
that women could preach but not pastor. I kept hitting those glass ceilings,
those limitations, even in God's house and within a theology that stressed freedom and equality. This was the greatest paradox of all for me.

It is most unsettling when someone challenges your essential identity. Since
I was fourteen years old, my journey toward a ministerial career was discouraged and marred by blatant denial and refutation. A full account of my call story
appears in William Rogers's *Irresistible Urge to Preach*. I was licensed to preach
at sixteen. At the age of eighteen I became the first woman ever ordained in the
Progressive Freewill Baptist Conference of Baltimore. I preached much and
extensively. All the while, I sat through sermons and listened to religious broad-
casts that admonished me. But the Holy Spirit, working in me, led me to continue in the ministry. Others said that I had no right to be what I was. But thanks
to Deutero-Isaiah, I grasped the full import of God as Creator of all the world,
the Lord of all nature, and the director of all history.

It was clear that God always had the prerogative to do a new thing, even
things not thought of before. To be Creator is to be free to act and to design.
It is the freedom or free will of God with which the human spirit is indelibly
marked. And if God's image is in all men and women, I believe that with this
image comes the capacity to know God and to know God is calling each and
every one to glorify him. And when men and women strive to be free, this desire
is inspired by God. Such a longing led my black ancestors to sing, "Before I'll
be a slave, I'll be buried in my grave, and go home to my Lord to be free."

So I trusted in my experience of God and the ministry God established in
me. I saw many people come to Christ in my early days of preaching Sunday
after Sunday in many different kinds of churches. I saw people's lives changed
for the better in my neighborhood, in my church, and among those I coun-
seled. The fruits of my labors were an encouragement.

Having graduated summa cum laude and fifth in the 1966 class of Morgan
State College, I had other opportunities in sociology and social work. My decision instead to go to seminary further testified to my conviction that God had
called me and to my irresistible urge to preach. Undertaking graduate theological study was my response to my desire to be as prepared as I possibly could
be. But I had absolutely no idea what I would do with such an education, except
better serve God in a freelance fashion, speaking occasionally here and there.
For many years I worked diligently in social service, community organization,
and higher education settings. I fleetingly longed to fulfill my adolescent desire
to become a minister in a more institutional way.

I had married a minister and left seminary with the thought that I would
enable my husband's ministry. This proved less than satisfactory within a few
years. By that time, however, I threw my life energy into other work and the

raising of two delightful, fun-to-be-with daughters. I never regretted this in any way. However, there was a self I wanted to be that had not yet matured. There was a spiritual and spirited foundation that I cherished but had not yet recaptured. My husband and I achieved the educational, materialistic, and family goals to which we aspired in our early thirties. We both had to ask the question, what else is there? I knew I had unfinished business of a ministerial, church-related nature. He wanted different professional and career-enhancing experiences, which would better enable him to support his young family, so we both went on a search, which in some ways would lead us apart.

It took me twenty years to conceptualize and concretize the possibility of working in a church-related setting. I received my first invitation to candidate as pastor of a medium-sized Disciples church in Cincinnati, Ohio, in 1980. I stared at the letter in utter disbelief. Was the church finally going to take women pastors seriously? Shortly after, I was interviewed by the search committee of a Congregational church in Long Island, New York. Such possibilities astounded me. I prayed to God that if given an opportunity, I would take on this new calling—to be a pastor. In 1985, this became a reality.

Prior to 1985, for approximately six years, I spent considerable time serving in various regional and national capacities of the Christian Church (Disciples of Christ).

I transferred my ministerial standing from the Freewill Baptists to the Disciples in 1973, primarily because of marriage. After preaching "The Hunger of Eve" at a national convention in 1976, I was catapulted into the national life of the church. Before becoming a pastor, I served on the highest national boards and consultations. Bob Lynn, then vice president of the Lilly Endowment, observed that I served on more Lilly religion projects than anyone else in the country. He later hired me as an evaluation coordinator. I worked part-time for the Lilly Endowment for three years.

During this time I was hard at full-time work in the community college movement at Essex County College in Newark, where I served as Dean and Assistant to the President. This was a ministry to the underemployed and the undereducated. I experienced much career advancement and positive results in this arena. But as I seemed to move further away from the development of people, my attention turned toward the center of the church. I intentionally prepared to teach in graduate theological education by completing a doctorate in education from Rutgers University. It has been a great blessing to have taught as Professor of Religious Education at Howard University School of Divinity for the past twenty-two years.

When I first came to Howard in 1982, I also accepted an interim pastorate of five months. After my last Sunday at Heritage Christian Church, a predominately white congregation, I sat on the side of my bed. I realized how deeply I had bonded with the parishioners and how much I had enjoyed this experience. I said that day, "I might like to try this again." And so I did in 1985 when I became pastor of Michigan Park Christian Church (MPCC) in Washington, DC. I never thought I'd stay eighteen years, but the joy I feel toward pastoring has not diminished. I especially love the teaching and preaching of the Word. My message is largely one of encouragement.

When my husband, now a Navy chaplain, was being stationed eight hours away, there were twenty outspoken, longtime leaders in my congregation who were unhappy with some of the changes I had initiated. A fuller treatment of the revitalization of MPCC is written as a case study in two books by Chris Hobgood—*The Once and Future Pastor* and *Welcoming Resistance*, both published by the Alban Institute in Washington, DC. I took a sabbatical leave from both the church and the university. I was on an emotional roller coaster for three months, trying to decide what to do. Would I relocate with my husband, return to the church and the university, or return to the university alone?

Persons of the academy and academic guilds insisted that I could not be a pastor/professor. When I pointed to many outstanding religious leaders who had done the same, one gentleman told me that I was not like them. Colleagues plagued me with comments such as no one could do both well. Fortunately, laity and clergy from other churches throughout the Washington, DC area and across the nation encouraged me to return to the church. You might well imagine that on any given day, depending on which side of the bed I rolled out of, I would vacillate back and forth. I sought God for direction. I desperately needed a word from the Lord. If I was willing to risk my marriage for the sake of this calling in my life, I certainly wanted to have a meaningful foundation on which to stand. In the midst of much prayer and reflection, I received two messages from God. The first was, "You are a beautiful person and you have a beautiful life. Enjoy it." This sentiment has sustained me through many self-doubts and has reassured me and encouraged me to laugh and savor each happy moment of every day.

The second word from the Lord was, "Do not try to overcontrol situations." This was a little tougher, but it taught me not to feel responsible for every detail of church and family life. I have come to a much more patient stance with people who seem to be moving slowly, or whose views are different and unintelligible to me. I know that God is in control and I no longer worry about those who disagree with me or do not affirm me. I also do not worry when I hear comments from others who do not understand the big picture of my life. I have learned to work as hard and as well as I can, and not to worry about what others think I should or should not be doing. Learning to let God control the situation and putting anxiety behind us frees us to focus more intently upon those things that we are committed to achieving. These two words from the Lord have become a part of my philosophy for living.

Why did God spare my life when others around me were dying? When I was diagnosed with stage three out of four breast cancer, I was prepared for living terminally. I confronted death squarely. I worried most about my children, who were seven and twelve years old. But I readily knew that my husband and mother would care for them, without any doubt. I was saddened to have to imagine what it would be like for them not to have a mother. Yet, I was ready to leave this earthly existence and move to eternal life with all the rewards and joys of being closer to God's presence. If I had died then, all would have been well. Of this I am confident.

On the other side of survival, as I watched others die, I was to encounter some tough questions and problems. Before cancer survival, I was invincible. After it, I became more vulnerable. My first reaction was to do more than live a comfortable, detached professor's life. It seemed too easy. I asked God for a harder assignment as a way of expressing my gratitude for his divine mercy and grace. I had a new lease on life, a second chance, a life chosen by me, in which to try and glorify God. God took me at my word and toughened me in ways for which I was not prepared. The pastorate challenged me. While the most loving at times, it's the hardest job I've ever had. Yet under this tough exterior, there is still a childlike faith and joyous resilience.

Sometimes the difficulties of life have led me to question the wisdom of choosing life in 1983. Wouldn't it have been better for me to die in peace, undisturbed by additional struggles? It is true that at times, it is easier to give up than to be encouraged to go on. But the key to a meaningful life never consists in what is happening in one's own life at any given time. Your own life is filled with valleys and peaks, but the enfoldment of purpose must involve your service or testimony to others. I can truly be sensitive and walk with others on their spiritual journey, because I have endured and will endure in the future my own trials and triumphs.

After surviving breast cancer, my next greatest struggle was surviving a divorce after thirty years of marriage. Struggles like these make us strong and toughen us for more difficult assignments of leadership and caring. These things help us to connect with others in special ways. One of my greatest developing edges is in the relational area. Before, I felt more individualistic, more self-sufficient. After all I've been through, I realize a need to connect with people for nurture and support. This leads me to understand better the revelation of God as relational. God's creation of the world and human beings and his love for them speaks of relationship. I'm glad I suffered enough to know that I am becoming a broader, more open person because I can no longer walk through life alone, "my Lord and I."

The legacy I seek to leave behind goes beyond what I have already discussed. I hope to have strengthened the music ministry within the Black Church through the *African American Heritage Hymnal*, a project on which I served as visionary and general editor. Ten years of research and collaboration resulted in the publication of this hymnal. For the past three years it has been a best-seller. Through a rebate arrangement, hymnal sales have sponsored music scholarships for students who aim to become ministers of music in African American churches. A portion of these funds is earmarked for economic development in Africa.

"A Living Bridge to Africa" is another passion that, for the past ten years, has absorbed much of my visioning, energy, and resources.[1] Only time will measure the impact of these efforts. For a nominal salary, I serve as executive director of the African Heritage and Cultural Institute of America. Having done some serious public organizing in 1990 against homicide in the District of Columbia, I discovered that women clergy's leadership was not appreciated by many of my male colleagues. Therefore, I turned my eyes toward Africa, where there seems to be more opportunity for community development because the needs are much greater. One African proverb affirms that it does not matter who kills the snake, only that the snake is killed.

My primary research has been on black female Master of Divinity graduates, 1972–1999, and is described in my book, *A Time for Honor: A Portrait of Black Clergy Women.* Three articles on this research appear in journals and textbooks, with others in the process of being published. This book has been much quoted as one of the first baseline studies to document the plight and progress of "learned" black clergywomen during a time when they first swelled the ranks of seminary graduates.

Most recently I have begun the new adventure of teaching "Introduction to Preaching" at Howard University School of Divinity. It has the possibility of opening new vistas of significance in my spiritual journey.

God is the God of the living, and our understanding of life is fundamental to our spiritual journey. At this juncture, life is a system of connections, sometimes disconnecting and reconnecting. We first differentiate from small inner-family cells and attach ourselves to larger worlds in which to choose for ourselves who we are and who we want to be.

On this journey, we connect to God and others. Some relationships we pick up and others we let go. Eventually we reinforce and strengthen our connection with God and our Savior Jesus Christ. At the same time we renew our love of family and old friends in new ways. Now I can be devastated and hurt in a way not previously possible. It sounds like weakness, but it's really growth—I am growing as I allow myself to be loved. The word "beloved" has great meaning and I have come to realize that Jesus was right—love is the greatest commandment. Love God and love others as you love yourself. I remember the charge to keep that I have made—God to glorify, another dying soul to save and fit it for the sky.

The following Scriptures have guided me thus far on the way:

> But strive first for the kingdom of God and his righteousness, and all these things will be given to you as well. (Matt. 6:33)

> No testing has overtaken you that is not common to everyone. God is faithful, and he will not let you be tested beyond your strength, but with the testing he will also provide the way out so that you may be able to endure it. (1 Cor. 10:13)

> Because we look not at what can be seen but at what cannot be seen; for what can be seen is temporary, but what cannot be seen is eternal (2 Cor. 4:18)

> One thing have I asked of the LORD, that will I seek after: to live in the house of the LORD all the days of my life, to behold the beauty of the LORD, and to inquire in his temple. (Ps. 27:4)

> You shall love the LORD your God with all your heart, and with all your soul, and with all your might. (Deut. 6:5)

I don't focus on the afterlife much for that is in God's hands. But I sometimes keep one eye on heaven. I consider myself a spirit first. I am an eternal spirit that is trying to navigate the human experience. I am certain that the knowledge of a victorious end helps me keep going.

A key to my early spiritual development was a large picture storybook of the Bible. It set a God consciousness in motion that I cherish and use as an inner authority for my life. I seek to live an ethical life, to allow the light of the presence of Christ to ever shine through my actions and thoughts and to follow peace with all and to make myself available in service to others. I also want to love God with all my heart, to love others as I love myself, to live an honest life according to the Ten Commandments, and to practice spiritual disciplines and try and apply this same discipline to my health and stewardship. I strive to tithe and give generously to the needy and to usher in the kingdom of God, to visit the sick and those in prison, to feed the hungry, and to clothe the naked. Finally, I want to teach and preach as effectively as I can.

These fundamental building blocks were reinforced in my adolescent years through my close association with other Christian youth, such as those in the Apostolic Club at Morgan State College and in Youth in Christ, an organization that I helped to form. Speaking of that, I have been a consistent development person drawn toward putting into place what was previously not there. In doing this I believe that I am joining in with God to preserve concrete expressions of God in the world.

Presently I am in conversation with a number of people about economic development in Africa. I am called to this task of educating and putting people to work who are both persecuted or undereducated for the sake of making a better life for them and their children. Any funds from this project will go back into humanitarian efforts in Africa. If all persons of faith would attempt to improve one corner of the world, it would go a long way toward the reconciliation and reunification of the human family, thus bringing the kingdom of God to Earth.

In my recent ministry I have mentored forty new ministers outside of the classroom. Many more have told me that I have inspired them from afar, even through the radio ministry "Renew a Right Spirit."

This brings me to the subject of those who have mentored me in the ministry, sometimes unbeknownst to them. I have to stand with my mother and grandmother, Rev. Sarah Causion, then move on to my first pastor and his daughter, Rev. P. A. Hodges and Rev. Mary Johnson. At the college level were Rev. Richard McKinney and Rev. Samuel Cornish. Also during these years were Bishop Monroe Saunders Sr. and Bishop Harold I. Williams.

In seminary, Dean Samuel Gandy and Dr. Leon Wright greatly encouraged me. My former husband, Rev. Anthony Carpenter, exposed me to aspects of the body of Christ that I may never have found on my own, including bringing me into both the United Church of Christ and the Disciples of Christ. Dean Jerry Lieberman and Dean Herbert Scuorzo guided me through my Essex County College years. My pastor/professor role models and mentors were Drs. Samuel Proctor and James Scott. Rev. Bob Lynn of the Lilly Endowment and Dr. C. Eric Lincoln, the godfather of my research on black women in the ministry, and Dr. Deotis Roberts pushed me along.

I have been blessed to work with tremendous Disciples of Christ leaders such as Rev. Kenneth Telgarden, Rev. John Hambert, Dr. Duane Cummings, Rev. Bill Nichols, Rev. Chris Hobgood, Rev. John Foulkes, Dr. Darryl Trimieux, and Rev. Dr. Cynthia Hale.

Dr. James Tyms, Dean Lawrence Jones, and Samuel Gandy brought me to Howard University as a professor and nurtured me there. Dean Evans Crawford, Dr. Cain Hope Felder, Dr. Cheryl Sanders, Dr. Henry Ferry, and Dr. Kortright Davis have been nurturing colleagues. Across the street from Howard University's School of Divinity sits Michigan Park Christian Church. Never in my life had I received so much love from so many. Every chairperson, lay leader, and member of the Ministerial Team has added value to my witness in that place. The names are too numerous to be included in this essay. Although many of my mentors have died, I continue to be surrounded by a great cloud of mentors, supporters, and well-wishers. Dr. Leon Wright, my beloved New Testament professor at Howard University, was right. I was only twenty-one years old when he told me not to "hang out" with the malcontents. Therefore, when it comes to women in ministry, to those who only tear down and not build up, I send grace and mercy. After forty-four years in the ministry, understanding this magnificent obsession is ontological, epistemological, and hermeneutical. So I run on to see what the end will be.

Sermon: "What Can You Get with the Faith You've Got?" Matthew 15:28

DELORES CARPENTER

In the original language of the text, Matthew used the word "great" twenty times, but only once did he link it to faith. The word *great* is in an emphatic position, thus drawing attention to it. Two persons are praised publicly. One was the Gentile centurion at Capernaum and the other is this Canaanite woman, called Syrophoenician in Mark's account. Mark stressed the persistence and humility of the woman, while Matthew stressed her faith. In Clementine literature she was called "Justa" and her daughter was called "Bernice."

This is one of the healing stories of people outside the Israelite nation. Jesus seems to take a harsh attitude toward the suppliant woman. She is a Canaanite, descendant of Cush, the African son of Noah. This makes her a sister to African Americans. This woman lived near the cities of Tyre and Sidon, which were north of Palestine along the Mediterranean coast in what is today Lebanon.

The Jewish people believed that their religion was for them alone—not for outsiders. Non-Jews, such as the Canaanites, were referred to as wicked and godless. Thus, the disciples told Jesus, "She's one of those outsiders. Just give her what she wants so that we can get rid of her." She is presented as something of a nuisance, in that the disciples complain to Jesus about her continual shouting and Jesus said nothing to her when she addressed him directly for help. Eventually, because of her great faith, and because she was not too proud to beg, Jesus finally granted her request for the healing of her demon-possessed daughter.

Faith, in this instance, is like a commodity—something of value that can be exchanged for something that one desires. The woman had enough faith on deposit to strike a deal with Jesus. Woman, great is your faith! Let it be done for you as you wish. The woman's faith bought her daughter's deliverance. In this instance, faith served as the currency.

A Realtor in southern California relates a surprising sale he once made and a lesson he learned from it. He and another Realtor were in their office one day when a not-too-prosperous-looking Asian man came in and inquired about a rather expensive property their firm was offering. Right behind him came a married couple who were also interested in the same property. And what a contrast they were to the first guy. They had prosperity and sophistication written all over them. The senior Realtor ignored the Asian man and led the obviously affluent husband and wife into his office. The junior Realtor was left to "waste his time" with the Asian, and after letting him sit in the reception area for a while, finally had him come to his desk—clearly the only way to get rid of him, which was what he wanted to do as expeditiously as possible.

Turned out that affluent-looking couple could not qualify financially to purchase the property, but the Asian could. In fact, he had brought with him, in a cardboard carton, the total cash needed to purchase the property. That story comes to mind in looking at today's text. The Canaanite woman pestering the disciples was presumably not a "qualified believer." Not only was she a Gentile, but she was a woman. Two strikes against her in that unenlightened time. Even Jesus seemed to wonder about her. For he said to her, "I was sent only to the lost sheep of the house of Israel." But it did not take Jesus long to realize that she had sufficient faith to cover her request. She had a portfolio of faith.

When the church was struggling as to whether its kingdom message was open for both Gentiles and Jews, here comes this lonely woman from a despised race. This Canaanite stood on the exchange floor of faith and shouted out until she convinced Jesus to have mercy on the outcasts.

A commodity exchange is a place where such commodities as wheat, coffee, and cotton are bought and sold. When farmers harvest their crops, they must sell them in large quantities. The exchange is a place where the people who sell and who buy thousands of bales of grain meet. The Chicago Board of Trade is the largest commodity exchange in the United States. It was started in 1848, and some five hundred members buy and sell there. The members do their trading in "pits" on the exchange floor. These pits consist of a series of rings that rise like steps. The buyers stand on these steps where they can be seen in the pit, and make offers and purchases by signs with their hands and by *shouting*. Each step stands for a different month of delivery. There are different pits for wheat, corn, rye, cotton, oats, and soybeans.

Some twenty years ago, we played a game called P.I.T. It was a card game, in which you were dealt seven cards. On each card was the name of a grain like oats, barley, wheat, or corn. The first person to trade his or her cards in such a way as to end up with all seven cards matching—that is, being of the same grain, all oats, all barley, or all corn—won the game.

The first time I observed people playing P.I.T. was at my friend Bill Warren's home in New Jersey. I was struck by how *loud* the game was. I wondered why they had to be so loud. That was before I learned to play the game. People who wanted to get rid of unwanted cards that didn't match would *holler out* the number of matching cards they had to give away: 4, 3, 2, 1. They hoped that somebody else's 4, 3, 2, and 1 were the matching cards that they needed. It was a competitive, fast-moving game. You couldn't win unless you were willing to shout out. If you didn't grab for the cards you needed, you'd never win the game.

Likewise, when the Canaanite woman stood that day on the exchange floor of faith, she too had to shout. Where did she learn to shout like that? Where did she learn not to take no for an answer? Well, I believed that she learned it in the Lebanese marketplace, where people bought and sold. The Canaanites went from slavery to becoming some of the world's greatest traders. I asked my daughter—who taught for a year in French-speaking Gabon, Africa—who owned the shops in Gabon. Her reply was the Gabonese and the Lebanese.

Even today this woman's ancestors are still prominent in trade. The woman's people had taught her how to trade—how to get something else for what you've already got. She stood in her own culture unashamedly. She used her own cultural expression to say, "Even the dogs eat the crumbs that fall from the Master's table." There are rabbinical sayings that designated godless people and heathens as dogs. I can see the good sister now—hands on her hip, finger pointed, and head rocking—"Even the dogs eat the crumbs that fall from the Master's table."

And when she shouted out, there was more at stake than a card game. For she had a daughter back home who needed the help that only Jesus could give. She was not standing there hollering on her own behalf. She had a daughter back home in trouble. The Bible says the child was vexed in spirit. "Vexed in spirit" can mean many things. I believe I know this daughter. Perhaps the daughter had dropped out of school. Perhaps she was pregnant. Perhaps she was a victim of sexual harassment. Perhaps she was anorexic or bulimic. Perhaps she was depressed.

Perhaps she was sick with a headache and a stomachache that would not go away. Perhaps she was throwing up. Perhaps she had suffered incest or rape. Perhaps somebody told her that she was ugly. Perhaps she has a spirit of weakness and was bent over and couldn't straighten up. Perhaps she had been bleeding so long and it just wouldn't stop. Perhaps she had children who told her that they hated her. Perhaps she was menopausal and the doctors kept telling her that there was nothing they could do about it. Whatever it was, she and her mother were deeply troubled. Not only do I know this daughter, I was this daughter.

I was this daughter who was vexed with a spirit. At fourteen I sensed that God had called me to preach. Afraid that no one would believe me, I very cautiously told a woman in my church about my call. I went to her because she seemed to me to be the most saved, Holy Ghost–filled woman in the church. I thought that if anyone would understand me and believe me it was she. But she did not. She told me that the devil had spoken to me because God didn't call a woman to preach. Ironically, later in her life, she too became a preacher.

Her comments plunged me into a dark night of the soul. My deep depression lasted for two years. No one could comfort me. But like the girl in the text I had a praying mother. She became proactive on my behalf when my grades in school dropped and as I cried and cried, especially in the Lord's house. With her help and the help of my pastor and youth minister, God delivered me to stand and preach my first sermon.

We need more mothers today like the Canaanite mother; mothers who will cry out in the schools and municipalities of this land. It is still amazing how much they can accomplish on behalf of their children when they possess great faith. Because great faith moves God.

Today, what can you get with the faith you've got? The book of the Bible named Hebrews says that faith is the substance of things hoped for and the evidence of things not seen. What are you hoping for today that is not yet seen? What have you tasted and enjoyed before it has fully materialized? What can you believe in, stand up for, or shout out for? Is it a time to come when this world will not need war to settle issues of hatred, ideology, and religion? Do you have great faith to believe that we can work to provide a safety net for "the poor" who need assistance to raise their children, and get themselves up on their feet?

Great faith is exemplified in a story about greens that I first heard Rev. Jeremiah Wright tell. A young boy was out in the fields down South helping his Daddy pick cotton. When he walked back to the house to go to the bathroom, he could smell the delicious aroma of dinner that was to come. Wanting some greens for himself, he asked if he might take some of the greens back out the fields to his father, whom he alleged was getting hungry. His mother said no, because they weren't ready yet. When his mama left the kitchen, he hurriedly grabbed a dry biscuit that was left over from breakfast. He broke it apart and laid it on top of the steaming pot in which the greens were cooking. And before his mama could ask, "What you doing in that pot?" he was on his way out the door.

He wrapped the biscuit in a handkerchief. Back in the field, he gave the whole thing to his father and told him to eat it. He said, "Here's some greens." His father looked at it and said, "What kind of greens are these? There's nothing here but a sopping biscuit." But the son said, "Oh, no, there is more than a biscuit here, for if you taste it you will see that this biscuit is the substance of things hoped for and the evidence of things not seen."

Do you have great faith? Great faith to see the impossible? Great faith to get what your children need? Great faith to move mountains? Great faith to believe in a better world? What can you get with the faith you've got?

NOTES

1. "A Living Bridge to Africa" is a phrase I coined to capture my desire to facilitate contemporary interchange between Africans and African Americans.

6

Determined to
Please God

ODESSA CODER

I truly thank God for giving me the opportunity to tell my story, for doing so has brought back many memories—both good and bad—of twenty-three years of heartaches and triumphs. I have tried very hard to forget the heartaches, realizing that the triumphs only serve to show me that the Lord my God still reigns. Also, the writing of my story gives me an opportunity to encourage my sisters in the Lord, and to let them know that we need one another and that we must be supportive of one another.

The spiritual and natural worlds need to know that we, too, have a story to tell. I hope that my story will inspire my sisters, especially those who are still groping in the dark, trying to find that small ray of light at the end of the tunnel (hoping it's not a train). Almighty God, himself, has put his seal on our calling and given his stamp of approval to women all over the world so that when they *see* the light they will *know* that he is our light and our salvation. Therefore, we do not have to fear.

We give the good news when we teach or preach the Word of God, letting the whole world know that he still lives. We know that he lives, because he lives *in* us and *through* us. We can then assure the world that God has given us the authority to expound upon that good news, for I believe that if God chose a woman to *carry* the Word, then we can surely *deliver* the Word. No, it will not be easy.

There will be those who feel that not only do they know God but they also know whom he has called regardless of what God has spoken to your heart. Some feel that God would never call a woman, and certainly not to teach or preach the Word. They might say, "You misunderstood the message he gave

89

to you," but let me tell you, my sisters, you will know when he has called you, and when he calls you, he qualifies you. If he said it, that qualifies it! I am proudly a woman pastor. I did it, and you can do it, too! We are in this together, and one day I hope to read *your* story.

FAMILY AND CHURCH DYNAMICS

I am the mother of three, *two* natural sons and *one* spiritual church. Earl Douglas is my oldest son and Randall Rene is my younger son. Finally, the youngest of all my children is St. Paul's Church of God in Christ, my twenty-three year old *third* spiritual child. I had a long, hard labor with all three, having labored for twenty-three hours with Doug, fourteen hours with Randy, and feeling sometimes that I am still in labor with St. Paul's Church. As I look back on all of the difficult times I've had carrying my three, and look at how they now have grown into strong, mature, God-fearing, Holy Ghost–filled adults—and how God has brought them up out of the ashes—all of a sudden, every bit of pain I endured was worth it.

St. Paul's is in the process of buying a larger church building to handle its growth. That word seems so strange now. When I think of St. Paul's and when I look back at its birth and early years, it sometimes seems like a dream and at other times like a nightmare. St. Paul's was an independent Methodist church before being founded by this servant of God, and was then converted to the Church of God in Christ.

As I stated, this church was independent. When the pastor died, the congregation suddenly found themselves without a spiritual leader. They tried to hold the church together with whatever spiritual knowledge they possessed, but it was not enough to keep the church going. In a very short period of time they became emotionally and spiritually fragmented. The Rev. Louis Butcher Jr., now pastor of Brightside Baptist Church, the largest African American church in Lancaster, Pennsylvania, would come and help us with services.

THE BEGINNING (1980s)

Rev. Butcher's father was a pastor and my father, a deacon. Both of these men worked on the railroad in Lancaster and were friends. Of course, our families were friends also. My brother and Rev. Louis Butcher were very close friends, and if a problem arose in either family, we were there for each other. I give a lot of attention to this friendship for more than one reason—one being that I truly believe God himself has intervened in our lives to make two dreams become visions that have manifested themselves in our lives just the way the Lord God wanted them to be demonstrated. We had a lot more in common than just friendship. We also had a spiritual bond. Rev. Louis Butcher Jr. was just starting his church, and he spoke to my father about using the church in the afternoons since St. Paul's occupied the premises only in the morning.

There was no reason not to allow this to occur, so on Sunday mornings he would come to St. Paul's in place of the pastor we had lost, and he was a blessing to our church. However, he and the other ministers had their own responsibilities and the church could not expect them to sacrifice their own visions to keep St. Paul's going. We were aware that the time would come when they could no longer accommodate us. That day did eventually come.

Without a permanent pastor, the membership fell away to seven people! During this time, I was attending the Lancaster Bible College and was a member of Ray's Temple Church of God in Christ in Lancaster. St. Paul's was my childhood church and I had a strong bond with the members, especially since a large number of my family held membership there.

The membership had dropped off so drastically, with no one to guide them, that they felt I was the answer to their prayers. I would come over to teach Bible study almost daily. One day after a council meeting they asked if I would consider taking on the responsibility of the church and the challenge of becoming the new pastor. Of course, I was scared to death, but I was spiritually compelled to say "yes." So I prepared to *go back home*. I spoke to Elder Scott White, who had taken me in under "watch care." Under his guidance I became fully aware of the basic precepts of the Church of God in Christ. It was a previously unknown fact to me that women were not accepted as pastors. However, Elder White guided me through every facet of the ministry that was required.

Following my ordination, he took me to Holy Temple Church of God in Christ and before Bishop O. T. Jones Jr., Prelate of the Commonwealth of Pennsylvania Jurisdiction of the Church of God in Christ. Bishop Jones accepted my church and me without reservation and with open arms. The bishop and his entire cabinet, male and female alike, treated me with the same respect given any pastor. They were protective of me and showed concern whenever a problem arose. I was given the right hand of fellowship and taken into the Coatesville district, one of the thirteen districts of the Commonwealth of Pennsylvania.

The district superintendent, Pastor Jacob Meeks, also showed me the dignity afforded any other pastor. He and his wife, Lenora Meeks, were considerate of my church and me. On the other hand, some of the women "from the old school" did not accept me as a pastor. It appeared that they felt I should be "under the women's ministry" over which the women had charge. They were "just not gonna have," as they put it, "someone who had no experience." In their thinking I had disobeyed God and was an embarrassment to the church.

I remember the first year I took part in the Communion ceremony. We were to wear white robes and the color of the stole didn't matter. My stole happened to be red. So there I was in my first robe that my church had proudly bought just for this ceremony. In an effort to be fashionable and coordinated, I wore *red* stockings to match my stole! Needless to say, with *no* jurisdiction over a pastor, these women proceeded to lecture me, telling me how *unsaved* I was to wear *red* anything. Please understand, most of the women were excellent missionaries; they simply could not accept a woman as a pastor. According to their "old school" thinking, I was not acting in accordance with the Word of God; at least not in the way that they and many people with their thought processes saw it. In their eyes I did nothing right.

Along with all the other problems I encountered early on in my ministry, my health began to fail. You can just imagine the comments from those who felt I should not be a pastor or even a minister. Some even suggested that if I would stop trying to minister maybe I would not be sick. Over a period of time, God dealt with most of them and they changed their way of thinking. Some in time came to be at least civil in their behavior toward me.

I wish I could say that everyone accepted me a female minister; however, that would not be true. To say that I did not ever desire to leave the ministry also would not be true. Every time I reached the point where I felt I couldn't take it any longer, I would hear again God's encouragement that he, himself, had called me to this ministry and would be an ever-present help to accomplish his purposes.

I suppose I have always been a "people" person, as my mother phrased it back in 1959 when I graduated from St. Joseph Hospital as a practical nurse. I worked in the emergency room of St. Joseph's until 1961, when I went to the Veterans' Hospital in Coatesville, Pennsylvania. After two years I returned to nursing at the hospital in Lancaster. For the next sixteen years I vacillated between St. Joseph Hospital and the General Hospital. I would probably still be in nursing had I not become ill again. I found myself unable to maintain such a hectic work schedule, going to the hospital every three to five weeks for my own health needs. I had many wonderful doctors, one of whom was Dr. Harold White, who was the first to show serious interest in my health. He doggedly pursued relief for me.

I needed, and had, eleven surgeries and spent more days in the hospital than I care to count. I was found to have sickle cell anemia and had to go on Social Security disability. I finally got to the point where I felt death was the end result of my condition. I was at a place where I knew I had to make some serious spiritual changes in my life. I guess that is when I became, for lack of a better word, a spiritual person. That is when I decided to make a mark in my life. I needed to know that if I died, I had made a difference and left a mark. While I loved nursing, it did not fulfill me spiritually and the empty, hollow feeling was too much for me to handle. I needed to feel like when I got to heaven, I would hear God say: Well done, my good and faithful servant. *That* is when I heard him call me.

My husband and I were separated at this time and I was struggling to raise my sons alone with the help of my family. My father and mother took care of my older son so that I had only to care for my younger one. I was in the intensive care unit in the hospital when I had a vision of a man all dressed in white with a long white beard. He was standing next to a blackboard that was divided into two sections. On the left side there was a list and on the right another list, which was much longer. This man never spoke a word but I heard him in my head as if he'd spoken out of his mouth. He told me that the list on the left side contained the things that I had done in my life, but the list on the right (which was almost twice as long as the other) contained the things that I would do in life. When I told everyone about this vision, people just looked at each other with a pitiful little smile and patted me on my head, telling me to go back to sleep (with the help of the Demerol they were administering to me). I did just that but I knew that the Lord was telling me I had a job to do and that what I had done up to this point was all right but it wasn't enough to please God in the ministry.

THE CHURCH'S GROWTH

Within a few months after starting the church, the rest of my family joined us. My mother, who had belonged to Ebenezer Baptist Church, which she dearly loved, wanted to come and help me. Soon thereafter my brother and my older son united with us and had their first taste of what I call "spiritual prejudice." By this time, I guess I was just about used to hearing this kind of conversation. It went something like this:

"Did you hear about Earl and Aldine Stewart's daughter?"

"No, tell me what?"

"Well, she is a pastor now."

"No, you mean the one that was a nurse?"

"Yes, that nice quiet one."

"Well, I don't believe it."

"Don't she know that the Bible speaks about women, that they are not supposed to speak anything from the Bible?"

"She is going to go to hell."

"Oh, I know, but she said God called her!"

"Can you imagine that? God did not call any other women, but he called *her*."

Then the laughter would ring out like a clear sounding bell, so loud that everybody could hear. They would add their own little portion of Scripture to let me know how wrong I was and that what I was doing would not only cause *me* to go to hell, but that I would drag the whole congregation to hell right along with me!

"Then tell me, what are we supposed to call her?"

"Well, I think you call them *sister*."

All of a sudden, friends I'd known for years became strangers to me. I was a "them" since they didn't know what to call me. (Some still refuse to call me pastor even though I have my Master of Divinity degree.)

I suppose not being accepted came easier to me than for other women. When God called me he did not tell me women were not accepted as pastors in the denomination. This never did register with me because I felt then, as I do now, that if God called me he would qualify me. Need I say more? That does not mean that the mountain climb will be easy. I am still on my journey up the rough side, and every time I get disgusted and want to leave, God allows something beautiful to happen to encourage my heart.

One of these was the time I was appointed to the Women's Commission in Lancaster, for a three-year term. I was then given a full scholarship to the Leadership Lancaster Program under the direction of Nancy Neff, a very strong woman who also holds her own in a man's world. She was an inspiration to me throughout the whole program. That was in 1992, and we have remained friends ever since. I was given the Shero award from Millersville University (for community service, especially to young black women), as I had given lectures there. This was the first award of its kind, and I felt so honored to receive it. Again, I can only thank God for his goodness. So, for a little while, things seemed all right and I thought we were on our way.

Since St. Paul's is a multicultural church, it is very easy for one from another race to come and be accepted into the congregation. As a result of my being in Leadership Lancaster and Lancaster Theological Seminary, people from many different races and cultures have joined our ranks without hesitation. If they ask, "Is it all right if I come to your church?" I simply explain that I don't tolerate prejudice. You see, my husband was Caucasian and my son is mulatto—born with blond hair and blue-green eyes. His wife is Hispanic and all three of their sons are copper-colored with coal black, straight hair. So, how can I show prejudice of any kind?

I have known prejudice in the church, however. We went to Memphis on my first trip to the National Convocation of the Church of God in Christ where they were having national elections and thus seating was limited. It was on a first-come, first-served basis. We had been standing for hours, so when a seat became available I took it. As soon as I sat down, a minister came up to me screaming for me to get up out of the seat. At first, I just sat there, not believing my ears, but then he moved toward me in a menacing way and I became nervous. Looking around for someone to come to my rescue I saw no one. What I got instead were looks implying that if I wanted to be a pastor in a man's job that I should just deal with this unpleasant encounter.

Once again, however, God came to my rescue by way of Deacon Walter Jones, the brother of Bishop O. T. Jones. He was on the trustee board of the national church and saw the whole incident. Like a knight in shining armor, he came to me and told the offensive minister that I had every right to sit there, and then proceeded to tell me not to move. Of course, that was just fine until it was time for me to go to the ladies' room (smiles). I was afraid to move, but the man sitting next to me very kindly told me he would watch my seat for me. By now, I have acquired quite a few friends in Memphis and in the Church of God in Christ. I am not leaving. I love this church.

THE GIFT OF HEALING

I have been blessed with the gift of prophecy. For as long as I can remember, there were times when churches would ask me to come, but when I got there I was not allowed to speak from their pulpit. They wanted me to prophesy, not to preach. They wanted the *milk* without the *straw*. Twenty-five years ago, my mother had a brain tumor and it was so large that it caused her face to become very large on the left side. Her eye stayed teary and her hearing on that side was almost gone. She was hospitalized and the doctor was to operate the next day. They told my mother the surgery would be very severe and that they would have to cut into the bone. As a result of the surgery her face would be disfigured but she would live and the headaches would cease.

Her pain was so severe that she agreed to the surgery. My mother is a very attractive woman and the thought of her being disfigured was more than we could handle. We knew how my mother liked everything she wore to be "just right." She had no need of makeup and never wore it, for her skin was soft, black, and smooth—a beautiful woman. So, I asked my mother if she believed that God could heal her without that radical surgery and she replied, without hesitation, "Yes." Now, look at God when we trust him. I went to God with my whole heart and soul, begging him to heal my mother with *his* surgical skills, and he did just that! Within a few hours, the surgeon came back to my mother's room and announced that he had an emergency and had to leave town for the weekend, indicating that my mom could go home for two days and return on Monday for the surgery. My mother went home and never went back to that hospital!

I won't tell you that her pain went away as soon as she left the hospital. As a matter of fact, she doesn't remember how long she had to wait, but wait she did. And she trusted God for her healing and he did just that. Listen to this: the doctor said her tumor must have fallen down into her throat and dissolved in the process. That is so pathetic for a doctor to say, but we just let it alone because we know that Mom was healed through faith. Praise the Lord, my mom is now ninety-two years old and is every bit the beautiful woman she was twenty-five years ago. After this healing the Lord again moved.

My brother fell off the back of a truck on a job and broke his leg. It was swollen so badly that he had to wait until the swelling went down before they could put a cast on it. This happened on a Saturday. God woke me up on Sunday morning and told me to pray for his leg. At the hospital his leg had been wrapped with a bandage and he'd been given x-rays to bring with him when they were going to put on the cast. I called my brother and asked if he believed God could heal him without having a cast on for six weeks, and he agreed to come to church that Sunday morning.

I asked my brother to bring the x-rays with him to church and reminded him of how God had healed Mom just on faith. He, too, had the same gift of faith and believed just like Mom. God did it again, and this time we had a witness to the miracle. The guest speaker for our morning service was Elder Robert Hargrove, the assistant pastor to our then presiding Bishop O. T. Jones. He witnessed this miracle. I laid hands, and Bill and he literally ran around the whole length of the church. I wrapped his leg again with the bandage and left it on for six weeks. When we took it off his leg looked just as it would if it had been in a cast for those past six weeks and, of course, he was healed.

The job told Bill that if he did not let them cast his leg, they would not put it through their insurance, but he told them that he would just have to pay the bill himself because he was not going to go back on his testimony that Almighty God had healed him. There were other healings, too, and I did wonder why God hadn't healed me. I, too, had strong faith, and I still do, but I don't ask any more why I remain sick. There is one thing I believe, and that is, if God doesn't heal me, it is not because he is not *able*. Perhaps there is someone who is ill and they're not getting better—they need to know that God *can* and *will* use you. As long as you are willing, he will make you able.

It seems that as many people as there were who came against this ministry, there were just as many who were supportive of it. My sister-in-law, Evangelist Mae Stewart, was probably the most supportive of all, especially when we started. She was there the whole time, from the inception even unto this day. Of course, my son Randy has taken some of the pressure off both of us, and I am grateful he took hold of the vision and followed it to the letter, every step of the way. He is now chairman of the deacon board and also St. Paul's church administrator, handling all of the church finances. As for my oldest son, he does all of our computer work and, when we move into our next church, he will teach our computer class. My mother, who is my Church Mother and my sister, assists with the mother's board.

Some time ago God told me that our churches needed a logo. We had a very gifted artist in our congregation by the name of Jean Frazier, and I asked her to design it for us. I put a lot of importance on this logo because it would signify the direction in which our church is moving regarding the ongoing development of this ministry. God said that we would have four churches. When this writing is finished, we will be in our second church. The logo we finally settled on carried the no cross/no crown theme. It symbolizes that we all have a cross to bear; the clouds are representative of the times when it will not be sunny; and the birds are doves of peace. We are moving onward and upward.

Sermon: "Tell Them You're with Me"
Luke 23:39–43 (KJV)

ODESSA CODER

And one of the malefactors which were hanged railed on him, saying, If thou be Christ, save thyself and us. (v. 39)

But the other answering rebuked him, saying, Dost not thou fear God, seeing thou are in the same condemnation? (v. 40)

And we indeed justly; for we receive the due reward of our deeds: but this man hath done nothing amiss. (v. 41)

And he said unto Jesus, Lord, remember me when thou comest into thy kingdom. (v. 42)

And Jesus said unto him, Verily, I say unto thee, Today shalt thou be with me in paradise. (v. 43)

When I was young my parents were very careful about the kind of people we chose as friends. My sister, who was older, and my brother, who was younger, all had different friends. When someone new would move into our neighborhood, we heard these words constantly from our parents: "Now remember, you're judged by the company you keep." And every now and then my parents would meet one of my friends' parents and, of course, if they became friends, then they would think their children were the best for us as a friend. But this was not always so. Sometimes that children they thought so nice would turn out to be the worst people; they were simply on their best behavior when they visited our home—just like *we* were when we would visit *theirs*. I'm sure we surprised their parents with our behavior at times also.

My point is this: even though we thought we'd fooled their parents with our good behavior, we were wrong as "two left feet," and neither did my so-called friends completely fool our parents. The parents on both sides would give all of us just enough rope "to hang ourselves," as my father used to say. I never knew exactly what that meant until one night in October. It was what we called, before I knew better, "trick or treat" night. On this particular night, we would go to homes in our neighborhood and ask for candy. If they said "no," we would play a trick on the homeowner. The house we'd chosen was just two blocks from mine. We just knew we were going to get a lot of good candy at this big house.

Well, everything that *looks* good is not as good as it looks. We knocked on the door and the lady opened the door and quickly shut it in our faces without any explanation. She just shut the door on us. Needless to say we were upset and angered, so we gathered up a big bunch of leaves. Dummy me. Not knowing what was going to happen, I thought (at the most) that they were going to fill her front porch with all those leaves so that when she went out the next day, she would have a porch full of leaves. Oh, how wrong I was! Someone rang the bell and they all threw the whole pile of dirty leaves into her house, and then everyone scattered, except for me. I was so stunned I froze.

I was a chubby little girl and definitely not athletic, so I could not move quickly on a moment's notice, much less run fast, so she caught me with no trouble at all. My friends—my good friends—left me. That is when I really found out who my friends were and what it really means to be judged by the company you keep. With dustpan and broom in one hand and me in the other, the lady of the house made me clean up all those leaves in her hallway. She told me that the gang I was hanging out with had done this kind of prank before. I had no knowledge of this, so it came as quite a shock to me.

Then, to really make my life flash before my eyes, the lady told me that she knew my parents and was going to make them aware of the kind of friends their daughter traveled around with. And finally, the last straw, she said, "I always thought you were such a nice, quiet, decent girl. You seemed so sweet but I know your three friends and I am really shocked at you being with such a bad group of girls." Even after I tried to explain that I was not aware of what they were going to do, it did not help. She then spoke those old familiar words: "Don't you know you are judged by the kids you hang around with?" The words were changed a little, but the meaning was the same. I was devastated.

Individuals putting their best foot forward can sometimes cloud our judgment about the true inward nature of that person. This ability to hide one's true feelings is especially true when it comes to friends and personal relationships. In other words, there have been times when I have desired true friendship even though my better judgment warned me against the person. Feeling I could handle anything that came my way, I would move forward with the friendship only to be hurt and crushed later by that person's deceit and betrayal. My mind now wanders back to Calvary, to the cross, and how Jesus might have felt about his friends. I realize that this is really a stretch of the imagination. But go with me for just a few minutes and imagine how he must have felt about his friends. He knew what they were about. He chose them himself and taught them to love God and trust in his Word. They knew he would be there for them when they needed him. They pledged their loyalty to him and kept their pledge until that last night when he was betrayed. It was then that the reality set in that their teacher and master was going to be crucified. If they were with him, they too could conceivably be judged by the company they kept and thus killed just like him.

He was innocent but that meant nothing. He was marked for death, and someone had to pay the bill. The cost of our salvation was a price he alone could pay. He alone was willing to pay. Again, I wonder if Jesus looked out through the now thinned-out crowd to see who his friends really were. It was a small group of people. No doubt it was hard for him to focus even though they were only about twenty-five feet from the cross. He could still see the pain in his mother's eyes as she saw the agony and physical pain he was going through. Her heart ached for her child. Her baby was dying. It did not matter that he was now a grown man. He was still her baby.

What made it so heartbreaking was that she knew he had done nothing wrong. Worst of all, she could not pray to the Father for her son. She tried. She called out to the Lord, and . . . nothing. She could not understand. It is a terrible thing to call on God and not hear a sound. She and her son had followed everything the Lord had put before them. Why would he turn his back now? Jesus had prayed for people whom he did not even know. Now it was Jesus' turn. She saw how they had beaten him. She saw his friends leave him; friends who said they would be with him until the end.

Peter knew who Jesus was, because the Holy Spirit had revealed it to him. This same Peter whom Jesus had called "the rock" also walked away. They were all gone. Only she and the beloved one, John, remained faithful. This was her son, her only son, and she was losing him. She remembered how when he was a child she thought she had lost him but three days later he was found. Little did she know three days from now he'd be found again but when she looked, the friends were gone.

I suppose they thought, as I said early on in this message, "You are judged by the company you keep." When things were going well and no one was trying to challenge Jesus and his ministry—when he fed the five thousand with a few little fishes and a few loaves of bread—he was all right. And when the demon-possessed went to Jesus and God through Jesus healed and rebuked the demons, everyone there took credit right along with the master. Yet he was the one God empowered to give the blessings to the lame, the blind, and even the broken-hearted.

Oh, they were all his friends then. And how about when they were on the ship, in the storm of the century? They called to Jesus who was asleep and cried to him, "O Master, don't you care that we may perish?" He then caused the winds to cease and the waves to calm down and again, they were his friends. What went wrong with this man who could heal with just a look and who would never stop loving or caring for his sheep? This man who would never leave them found himself alone and rejected. But even then he had love and compassion in the face of death.

When we think that all that is lost and there is no hope, remember he's still there. I would like to, for just a moment, use my imagination at the cross. When the thief asked Jesus to remember him I can just imagine that thief riding the death train and then being transferred to the glory train. The thief rode on down to paradise station and got off at the pearly gates. There he sees St. Peter who was the gatekeeper for the day.

Peter is there checking off the names in the book of life. He begins to thumb through the book looking for the thief's name. Peter says to him, "I don't see your name anywhere." The thief replied, "It may not be there yet, but it's coming. I have a special pass. I just got it today. I also have a reference from the master himself. I believe you call him Jesus. I only met him today someone told me he was the Christ. He told me: if anyone asks who you're here with, tell them you're with me."

7

All Dressed Up with Nowhere to Go

CLAUDETTE ANDERSON
COPELAND

IN THE BEGINNING

I was born Claudette Anderson, on a welfare ward of the Erie County hospital in Buffalo, New York, on August 17 just after the midpoint of the twentieth century. My father was a successful gambler and man of the night; my mother was a sweet young thing from Georgia, twenty-two years his junior. I was shaped in a loving, raucous environment of gamblers, hustlers, drug dealers, thieves, loud-talking men, and beautiful worldly women.

I was the older child, having one sister eleven years my junior. I became a caretaker, a responsible child, and a surrogate parent figure very early. By the time I was eleven years old, my life was in an accordion . . . a victim of childhood sexual violation on one hand—pulled by its secret sorrows—and on the other hand indelibly loved and shaped in an environment of incredible fathering and devoted mothering. It was at the point of my father's departure from our family when I was twelve years old that I first allowed myself to feel my sorrows fully. Here too I began to sense a stirring, a hunger, a search for God.

My parents divorced in my early adolescence, as I was leaving childhood and finding my way as a young woman; it left me devastated and grieving. My mother immediately married a man who was cold and rejecting, and who made no effort to love or embrace me. She was buried in work and economic survival. I internalized my profound loneliness and my sorrows by literally trying to die: I underwent abdominal surgery and contracted tuberculosis and juvenile rheumatoid arthritis, all within a period of eighteen months. Physicians became my allies. Hospitalizations were my times of refuge.

In this season, along with sickness I began acting out—fighting, rebelling, and heading for sure destruction in the urban streets. My mother transferred me to a "white school" to get me away from the bad elements of my neighborhood. This move was to be providential, for it was here at the age of fourteen years I would meet the boy I would marry, and the friend who would introduce me to the Lord Jesus Christ.

My family had no formal religion, though my mother had had me baptized in the Methodist church at the age of five. We attended church on some special days like Easter and Mother's Day. My father disdained preachers and formal religion, though he fancied himself a man who respected and believed in a higher power. By the time I began to reach for God in some conscious way, there was no one to point the way. From the age of eleven to about fourteen, I was a little vagabond. I attached myself to any neighbor who was headed to a church. I caught the bus and went alone to the neighborhood "tent revivals" held by the sanctified people.

I joined my neighbor's gospel singing group one summer and went to all the Sunday afternoon church programs in town. I always "got happy and shouted," prompting my neighbors to declare "the Lord was dealing with me" and that "God had his hand on me." I believe I was converted during my short foray into the Calvary Baptist Church, but no one ever took the time to inquire for my belief, or to examine me for my salvation. The wandering continued. I begged to go to the summer vacation Bible school held by St. Nicholas, the remaining Catholic parish in our ghetto neighborhood. I longed to know God; I cried for God; I sought in my heart for the empty place to be filled.

I joined myself to a neighborhood community choir, which in retrospect I realize was composed mainly of adoring gay men who made me their narrator/teenaged mascot, and who deeply cared for me as a little sister. This season furthered my suspicion that I was called to preach, even if I was still altogether skeletal in my knowledge of whom I was preaching about. My time traveling with them continued to widen my exposure to the ways of worship. I just did not know how to meet this God, nor how to define that meeting if indeed God was in my life.

The Eyes of the Lord Run to and Fro

It was the invitation of another fourteen-year-old classmate who was zealous for God that brought me in. It was Mary Lewis's direct insistence and clear explanation: I needed to be *saved*, and *this* is what it meant, and this *how* I could do it. She patiently and persistently sought my soul, invited me to her small Pentecostal church, until I too surrendered my heart and life to the passion and drama of becoming "saved, sanctified, and filled with the precious Holy

Ghost." The Lord had been looking for me. Or I had been looking for the Lord. Nevertheless, now I was found.

My formative years were in the Church of God in Christ. This is a predominantly African American denomination, formed in 1904 on the basis of the belief in a second work of grace (sanctification) as distinct from conversion, and the literal infilling of the Holy Spirit according to Acts 2:4. As important as giving me definition for my beliefs, they gave me structure for my floundering life. They gave me surrogate fathers in this strongly patriarchal system. They gave me a platform for the honing of my gifts, with their strong emphasis on training youth, and insistence that gifts be utilized in practical and very public ways. The Church of God in Christ gave me back the confidence that my father had begun to build in me in childhood, my sense of worth, and a place to belong. *And they gave me my first example of women of God*, exhorting, teaching, testifying with fervent voices and fiery temperaments, about the goodness and faithfulness of God. Their God made ways out of no ways; he healed their sick bodies when they had no money for doctors; their God brought wayward children home and gave them peace with their "unsaved" husbands.

I sat as a wide-eyed girl between the knees of these women, out of earshot of the male preachers who trivialized the gathering of women and never came to these prayer gatherings. Never mind that *they said* women could not be preachers or pastors; never mind the double-speak they expected the unthinking to believe: *I knew* what I was seeing and hearing in these women. It was the power of the true and living God in operation, in small, unlikely, ignored places. The real unmistakable God operated through old sanctified mothers and sassy young missionaries with their long dresses and obscured sensuality. I devoured it all, spoken and implied. *And my spirit began to leap*. At fourteen, I submitted my whole self to the men, the women, and the ideology of this assembly.

When I turned fifteen, Missionary Ervelean McGrier escorted me into the office of our pastor Bishop L. R. Anderson, where I announced that I believed I was called to preach. He kindly reminded me that women could not preach, but he recognized the gift of God in me and assured me I would make a fine young missionary-evangelist. For the next four years I immersed myself in the doctrines of holiness, scriptural memorization, and the lessons of prayer, faith, missionary service, and sacrifice.

It was here I experienced my first personal encounter with the healing power of God. When my lungs were deteriorating with tuberculosis, after the laying on of hands, I was totally healed. I began to enjoy my first platform of ministering the word of God on youth days and missionary services and street corners and nursing homes and wherever else the older missionaries would take me. I learned early the joy and headiness of seeing people respond to this great hope, amazed that I had been a part of the transaction. It was here that I learned to manage myself as a woman in an atmosphere that smelled of maleness, sounded of maleness, and that guarded the power and privilege of maleness at all costs. I learned the dance between submission and seeing through the power grid. As a young woman, I learned that I could never reach my potential without learning to tap into the power that the brothers jealously and sometimes brutally guarded.

One of my memorable gatekeepers was my youth pastor: a kindly, big man "too-old-to-still-be-the-youth leader" type, Elder Sam Kinkle. He was a company man. He publicly held the church's line. He was one of the few formally educated elders in our jurisdiction. But in private at every single opportunity his stern admonition to me would be "Nothing ventured, nothing gained." I believe it was his cryptic way of telling a young teenager with potential, "Don't get stuck in this system like the rest of us—take a chance on what you know within yourself."

He died before I was adult enough to grasp what he was seeding into me, and many days I wish I could have gone back to say thank you. He was my first conductor on the underground railroad. He taught me to recognize early that not all men would be my oppressors, nor would all women be my champions. Little did I know that this season in the Pentecostal church would be the solid foundation that would uphold me throughout the remainder of my life.

College Days and Beyond

I headed to the University of Connecticut with the intention of becoming a physician. I had been deeply touched by those men who had cut me, excavated my body, and healed me time and again. I wanted to become them. Outside the scrutiny of my small sanctified world, I began to blossom as I felt my own genuine spiritual vitality. The college campus in all its whiteness, all its foreignness, became my proving ground for salvation and ministry formation. I feared that I would not "hold on" to my testimony, but trusted what the saints had taught me. My first week on campus, I identified an unused chapel. I promised I would meet God there every day, and for the next four years, Monday through Friday, I met the Lord on my knees in that place. It was often lonely, but it was training in walking alone with God. Later God gave me companions in prayer; from there we gave birth to other souls, and other ministries on the university campus. In an era of Black Power, cultural ferment and upheaval, and more permissive attitudes about traditional values, we were an anchor for many young brothers and sisters who came to college as nominal Christians and left as vibrant, practicing ones.

By the time I was to graduate, I knew my calling was not medicine, but I dared not believe there was an avenue for me to do ministry as a life's work. I had never seen it done. I had no models. I had not one living example up close. I had only known one or two "preacher women" in my life, and they had been so reviled, so disdained by the preaching men who led me that I had learned to discount them. I had been taught to be suspicious of any woman who called herself a preacher, to keep my distance, and to make her invisible.

The women in our denomination were allowed to minister as long as they dutifully denied any *preaching call* or leadership aspirations; that is, as long as they remained in their places as good "missionaries" or "evangelists," daring not to "usurp authority over any man." Hence, by the time my own vocational plans were taking shape, I was in a silent quandary. How could I be hearing God call me to full-time ministry in a world that did not allow women entrance?

During my senior year in college my fiancé, David, was enrolled in seminary at Colgate-Rochester Divinity School. We happened to meet a professor Leonard Lovett, PhD, the newly appointed dean of the newly created Charles Harrison Mason Theological Seminary, a part of the Interdenominational Theological Center (ITC) in Atlanta. He sat for hours with us both, casting a dream of a new day of enlightenment on the horizon for our denomination. He talked of doors that would swing open for the theologically trained and told us that we were invited to be a part of this new Camelot.

By the next fall, my fiancé (now husband) had transferred, and I had enrolled in seminary, the ITC, as a full-time student. The year was 1974 and women made up about 5 percent of my entering class. Believing that Christian education was my only "permissible" tract, I entered to pursue the master's degree in religious education. My preaching gifts were soon evident to my dean, Oliver Haney, who was the second (denominational) man in this brief journey who affirmed my whole possibility as a minister. I soon changed to the Master of Divinity degree program and was on my way to an unknown future.

The seminary experience was the best opportunity of my entire life. Seminary broadened my cultural reality: for the first time I traveled on mission journeys and became acquainted with the richness of Afro-Caribbean and African peoples. Here I developed my palate for world travel, which would call me again and again to various corners of the globe with the preached word. Seminary took me behind the pages of the very Bible that had both enlivened me and suffocated me, teased me and trapped me. It helped me to make sense of the fundamental knowing I had in my spirit (the call to preach) over against the prohibitions of my formative teachers. It taught me ways to understand and not to discard the institution and beloved saints who had taught me in their own way to love God. It came at the juncture in life where I had to choose, as Abraham Maslow said, to "go forward into growth, or step backward into safety." My church was highly suspicious of seminary. As much as I loved and adored my spiritual family of origin, the cost to abide by their counsel in this instance would have been to remain small, increasingly deformed, and eventually ossified.

All Dressed Up with Nowhere to Go

I graduated from seminary third in my class (behind two brilliant *women* graduates). I entered a year and a half of clinical pastoral education (CPE). If seminary was the best decision of my educational life, CPE was the best decision of my personal life. Here I began to examine the ways in which my *private reality* and my *public image* were at odds. I gained the tools to monitor the congruence or incongruence of these polarities, and to set out to make them one whole. I began to understand the ways that sick preachers reproduce themselves onto congregations or onto vulnerable persons who come to us for aid. I began to visualize myself as the first female African American Clinical Supervisor—or at least the second (for in the mid-1970s, racial and ethnic minorities were almost nonexistent in CPE).

However, upon completion of my clinical work, my marriage was threatening to collapse. Our finances were in shambles. Our personal realities were at odds. I chose to leave Atlanta and join my husband for his career in the Air Force chaplaincy in hopes for a new start. I suspect that if our marriage had been healthier and my personal options more clear, I would have pursued the area that had captured my passion and remained in Atlanta to study.

The years from twenty-five to twenty-eight were years of terrible wandering. I took odd jobs, tried to fit a theological degree into various secular settings, and argued with a denomination that pretended to consider ordination of women but that had no intention of either ordaining or employing any woman in ministry. I explored other denominations; I knocked on doors; I read; I visited; I wrote. I offered my services to the chapel program of my husband's Air Force base and created a Ministry of Grief and Loss for staff and patients. I sold Mary Kay Cosmetics. I sold pots and pans. I worked in Child Protective Services for the state of Illinois. And as a perpetual *ministry* outsider, I became increasingly depressed. I felt I had been tricked. Bamboozled. Hoodwinked. God had gotten me out here, and now abandoned me to flounder and drown.

I had the urge to forgo the whole ministry notion, get pregnant, and settle down into domesticity and maternity. This decision escorted me to the threshold of the next gargantuan problem: *my body did not work*. It became clear that I would not conceive without heroic and costly measures. I was not feeling heroic, and we had no money.

Still, at the bottom of a very deep, dark well, I felt the rumblings to preach the gospel every day of my life—in my kitchen; to my cat; in my shower; every place.

In an effort to hold to both marriage and ministry it seemed that the only ministry door that was viable was the military. Like a lactating mother desperate for a place to express her life milk, I needed to do ministry or I suffered. I sought and finally received ordination by a bishop in my denomination (despite its current polity) and was commissioned as a reserve officer. I later came onto active duty, and my spouse and I were moved into individual duty assignments in San Antonio, Texas. The year was 1982.

The military chaplaincy, as they advertised, was a "great place to start." There was a hunger for ethnic relevance in their chapel programs, and I was hungry to be utilized. This context gave me a field "white unto harvest"; families to shepherd, singles to pastor, souls to evangelize, and a steady stream of hurting, confused human beings to comfort and guide. It also gave me a real live dose of ministering in some new contexts where military families had never associated with any black officer, up close in *personal* life. Their surprise was sometime polite; sometime outright hostile. ("We did not expect any colored chaplain to bury our Daddy—and a lady at that!") It taught me to maneuver politically in a context that was not just male, but *white and male.*

I had no mentors, no allies, and I had to learn a game where competence and integrity were *not* the only rules. By the end of my three-year tour of duty I had earned the genuine respect of my peers and superior officers, and to some degree regretted leaving the military. It had been the first place, despite the human undercurrent, that I ministered in a context that had *rules and regulations* in place about fair and equal treatment. It also was the first place I had ever received a steady paycheck, for simply doing ministry; with no strings or shenanigans attached! I knew no other context where I had ever seen this happen, for in my background, women ministered indeed, but out of the goodness of their voluntary hearts. Gratis. Free. Happily unpaid. Amen. It was a great challenge to step again into a world of ghetto churchmen and traditional-thinking Christians, and depend on them for my livelihood.

Moving On

My spouse and I desired some permanence, some sense of rooting in our lives. We wanted to settle into community and realized that for us, the military way of life would be far too nomadic, and likely to demand many domestic separations. He wanted to give birth to his vision of a local church in the San Antonio community, and believed that together we could make a great contribution. With a following from my military congregation and from his, together we planted a nondenominational church, the New Creation Christian Fellowship, that has now flourished for almost twenty years and grown at seasons, to several thousand members strong.

During the growth of our church I became less and less apologetic about my own definition as a preacher. Not a chaplain; not a teacher; not a counselor; not a church administrator. Not just a woman "co-pastor," married to a preaching man. But first and foremost, I *am a preacher of this great gospel.* In my thirties, with a growing church as my platform and the use of technology (audiotapes, video, radio) I began to be intentional about giving voice to the fire in my belly. This primary desire to evangelize the lost and to edify the body of Christ has remained my highest aim.

One of my greatest gifts in the early years was a partner who supported and affirmed my preaching and ministerial life. I was a young evangelist when he married me. He celebrated my gifts, and we joined our hopes together under God, to try to make a difference. Eventually though, my husband suffered much from the males in our context, who were still bound to their notions of female subordination, and who goaded and questioned him constantly about this notion of having a "preaching wife."

They compared us. They put him down. They insulted him in ways that they deemed harmless. They were troubled by my gift that would not conform to their notions of what a woman should be able to do. Not just men, but later thoughtless women, who meant to celebrate my preaching gifts by contrasting them with my husband, became problematic. The years of bruising comparisons took their toll. What began as a vibrant pastoral team, what was a complementary union, began to deteriorate under the weight of the very calling that had blessed and defined our lives.

As the arc of my life begins to turn toward eternity, I have become increasingly conscious of leaving some record of my having lived, having preached, having served the Kingdom. I have lessened my role in the parish ministry, and concentrated on other areas of contribution. I have begun to write. My books *Coming Through the Darkness: Cancer and One Woman's Journey to Wholeness* (2000) and *Stories from Inner Space: Confessions of a Preacher Woman and Other Tales* (2003) have focused on the interior journey of the preacher woman. What does it mean in the sphere of humanity to operate effectively with a mandate from the Eternal? What is the "crushing" that turns the *olive* to pure *oil,* and which turns the *oil* to pure *light?*

Still on the Journey

As a pastor I have embraced all streams of the Christian church, despite my early days of circumscribed Pentecostal training. Simultaneously I found welcome in an ever-widening itinerancy; a circle of women's settings, conferences, worship contexts that validated my usefulness for kingdom work. From store-fronts to cathedrals, from prisons to universities, from tent revivals to mega-convention halls to the halls of government, I am still amazed at where the gospel has taken me. Some of these persons have become extended family, both nationally and internationally. The AME church, later the Baptists, and finally with mixed emotions, it seems, my Pentecostal brothers and sisters have embraced my ministry, claiming me as their own after I was validated in other popular settings.

Many of these way-making women have been, as Dr. Cecelia Williams-Bryant would term us, "co-journers" from the early days of seminary; we have lifted one another as we have climbed. We have each served as interpreters: the men/pastors/fathers in our own respective lives have needed and benefit-ted from their exposure to us. We have used one another as teaching tools, entering as invited, teaching, preaching, and modeling to widen the circle of understanding among men who were underexposed and often suspicious of women in ministry, or who knew none except their own wives.

Handling the Hard Spots

I have intentionally maintained and nourished not just the ministerial al-liances, but the *friendships* of women. I have cultivated a circle of ten women who have been my "hope and stay." These thinking, spiritually discerning, bal-anced women have been my collaborators, counselors, confronters, and com-forters through the decades and changes of life and ministry. These constant relationships have given me grounding when there were terrible humiliations and rejections from male counterparts. They have celebrated with me in the triumphs and high points (like just flying in to support me when I was asked to preach before 80,000 women at a particular conference). They have been my nurses and intercessors when I was stricken with breast cancer in my thir-ties and endured a mastectomy, chemotherapy, and all that it entailed.

We discussed and created feminine alternatives to the "good old boy" ways of doing ministry. We demonstrated them in the conferences we hosted and the worship settings we constructed. We laughed together about our detrac-tors. We commiserated about the ways our own church members (women) loved our husbands more than they loved us, though we were the ones really pastoring them. We funded and financed each others' ministry efforts.

In essence, we learned early on to create and protect a psychological buffer zone for ourselves and for the daughters who will follow us. These constant women friends, coincidentally, are all in public ministry but fit into my private life each in their own unique ways. I would never have survived the journey of building a church, earning graduate degrees, surviving in marriage, or managing a life fraught with crisis and challenge without the gift of these friends.

They have been my most tangible signs of the goodness of the Lord, to me.

After years of being "all dressed up" these sisters ensure that I will have "somewhere to go." And I will be wanted, welcomed, and celebrated until my dying hour.

Sermon: *"Tamar's Torn Robe"*
2 Samuel 13:1–20

Claudette Anderson Copeland

Christian life calls us to make decisions. But life sometime has already *made some* decisions for us. The issue of family life, and its impact upon a woman's physical, emotional, and spiritual health, is one of these areas. Sometimes decisions have already been made for us—by the time we arrive at adulthood, by the time we reach awareness, some things have already been set in motion. But the Christian life calls us, invites us, demands of us that we risk, look, examine, peek beneath the veil and make new decisions about our own redemption.

Persons are about as healthy as the families we come from. There is a spiritual dynamic in all of Scripture of "family blessing" and "family influences" and the streams that flow from "generation to generation." God knew the problems of first families, the problems of Adam and Eve, or the problems of *your* "mama and daddy." That is why we are invited into the family of God; why we need a new family, a spiritual rebirth, an opportunity to redeem, repair, refashion, and yes, reuse the issues of the natural family.

Family constellations hold family secrets. Family units contain emotional maps about who is connected to whom, in love, in anger, in violation, or in care.

The first family can bequeath to us good genes, a strong sense of self, integrity, and identity. The first family can set our sights toward the stars, gives us models for living, road maps to our life mate, and the raw material for knitting together a soul. We will fight outsiders who say the things *we know are true* about our family insiders. ("Playing the dozens is dangerous.") Thank God, in so many ways for first families. But some of us can bear witness that a certain kind of "family past" can pollute a woman's present.

Family secrets can affect a woman's present sanity. Saved women. Spiritual women. Sanctified women. Scholarly women. But some women are

113

affected by a past that we did not bargain for, and one we need the Lord to undo. And when we hear *that* voice, we must make radical decisions about facing our own *desolation*, letting go our own *despair* and *deciding* to change our minds, our ways, and our mourning garments.

The widespread epidemic of depression in churchgoing women, modern women, economically well off, hardworking, educated women, can often be traced to the childhood devastations that have never been aired out.

The pollution of our emotional and yes, physical health, can sometimes be tied to the soul pollution that has never been healed. *Our robes have been torn.* Our beauty has been spoiled. Our souls have been bruised.

Jeremiah 8:11 echoes the reality of many church women: "You have healed the hurt of the daughter of my people slightly—superficially; dressed the wound of my people as though it was not serious." Preachers have paid attention to this "woman wound" to the point of our own comfort and convenience. We have shouted. We have sung songs. We have collected money and built buildings. We have offered programs and platforms. We have preached irrelevant sermons. And for their coming, Sunday after Sunday, women go away with "torn robes."

Sometimes for deep and permanent healing we must probe beyond the persona, past the veneer of church pews, and look into the legacy of family life. And it will probably hurt. I invite you, today, to participate in your own redemption.

Let us consider the text: 2 Samuel 13 tells us several things.

There is first of all:

The Created Intention for the woman who is the tutor for our text. Tamar is a daughter of David; *King* David. She owns a position by relationship and by privilege. The paradigm. The original purpose. "God created them male and female, and gave THEM dominion, and blessed THEM . . ." Your present trouble will make you forget God's *original intention* for your life. The tests of your past will try to make you forget that you are loved and valued, and that God's created intention for every one of God's daughters, is good and very good. God intends women to live fully and well. To create. To share in riding upon the high places of the earth.

Second, we see the **Collusion of Men**:

The text opens with Amnon. . . .He is the oldest of David's sons; according to 1 Chronicles 3, he is born to David at Hebron, during the time of his first elevation as king. Ahinoam was his mother.

There is his third son Absalom, whose mother was a princess, Maacah, daughter of Talmai, king of Geshur. And at the end of the 1 Chronicles chapter, almost as an afterthought, almost in the margin of verse 9, it states, "and Tamar was their sister."

In the Samuel text is Jonadab the shrewd cousin, the instigator, who reminds Amnon of his male entitlement to get what he wants. There is David, the older father who should be wiser, who should be a protector, who should care. There is the personal servant at the door, complicit; consenting to Amnon's deed.

In society and in families, there is a certain kind of man in collusion with the destruction of our daughters. Not all men want to harm you, not all men are without honor or boundaries; not all men will fail to protect you or your children, abandon you emotionally or financially, or take advantage of your vulnerability. We love the brethren and desire their partnership. But there is a certain kind of man who must be exposed in our thinking. A certain kind of man that our daughters must be taught to recognize, and that good, strong *honorable men* must speak truth to behind closed doors or in public platforms.

A certain kind of man who thinks it is his privilege to use women; who believes in his own entitlement simply because he is a male.

A certain kind of police officer, who refuses to take the domestic violence call seriously; a certain kind of judge who will never institute or reinforce the child support; a certain kind of professor who will barter with female students for grades or who will ignore the presence of female students because he believes they have trespassed by being there in his classroom. Trust me, there is a certain kind of preacher man who believes that women exist as property and as playmates, a certain kind of husband who is insulted by the notion that his wife is an equal human being to be loved; who has dreams and goals; who deserves to be talked with and honored.

In the text, there is a collusion among these men: a silent agreement; a mutual consent . . . not to interfere.

We must remind our daughters to watch out for a certain kind of man (the man who won't meet your pastor, won't meet your parents, won't speak up to protect you; the man who will use marriage to you to mask his own lifestyle of sexual alternatives). We must teach *our sons* not to yield to the pressure to be that certain kind of man in order to become acceptable in the clubs that validate a certain kind of manhood. God give them strength to avoid the collusion!

Third, there is the **Confusion** between *love and lust* (v. 4).

How does this impact the health and wholeness of women? We are confused as women, because we learn secret *confusions* as little girls. One in three women will be *forced* into sexual activity in her lifetime, by someone who is supposed to love her. Some statistics say that one in five *men* will at some point be sexually molested, fondled, or raped; probably by someone they thought they could trust: the priest, the coach, the scout leader, Mama's boyfriend who paraded as a father. . . . Love gets confused with lust, and violation is three to four times more likely to be a family member, friend, or someone who *claimed to like you or love you* than a stranger. And in 50 to 90 percent of the cases, it will remain a secret and go unreported.

When lust is confused with love, women who are its victims are three to four times as likely to suffer from major depression; three to four times as likely to contemplate or attempt suicide; twice as likely as the general population to abuse drugs and alcohol; and almost certain to misuse food in some way.

When lust gets confused with love early in life, women get saved, have their sins forgiven, love God, come to church, and get *ready for heaven*, but too often, they don't go on to get healed, healthy, or whole and get ready for *life abundantly* right down here.

Lust is a physical force, demanding to satisfy itself, at all costs.

Love is a spiritual force, determined to satisfy you at all cost.

Lust is a blinding force that consumes the reason, overrides the will, and silences the conscience. It makes one vexed, upset, agitated if it can't get its own way. Lust uses. Listen to the heart of Amnon. "It was hard to do anything *to* her. . . ." Lust manipulates. Lust lies.

Love, on the other hand, is health producing; it sacrifices its own immediate desire, for your long-range good. Love protects; love provides; love does not keep score of wrongs; love does without so you can have . . . and never mentions it. Love is thou-centered, not I-centered. When lust is confused with love inside the family system we silence Tamar's voice; we keep her quiet in the brother's house; and she loves the guilty enough to protect them with her confused love.

Incest is a soul pollution. Sexual violation is a vandalizing of the spirit. *It tears up something.*

"Tamar tore the richly ornamented robe, the kind that kings daughters wore . . ." Her created purpose is damaged. The collusion. The confusion.

Fourth, there is the **Convenience**—In the entire text, we have no "mother-voice." There is opportunity for daughters to be spoiled when mothers are silent or absent from the daughters and sons in their own lives. The older brother requests: "Let Tamar come and dress the meat in my sight, as my sister." Some things, traditionally, a mother must do, in order for children to grow well. Mother is absent. Mother is busy. Contemporary mother is leaving our daughter's stuff in sight of the enemy. Are you that mother, who is consumed with your own agenda of being cute, and in competition with your daughters? We cannot blame women for what men do, but we must remind each woman to do what *we can* do.

Be present for your daughters and your sons.
Be alert to see what you see.
Be vocal enough to tell the truth.
Be strong enough to cover, correct, counsel.
Be whole enough not to need a man at the expense of the safety of your
    children's need for you.

We must not make the spoiling of our children *convenient to* their enemy.

Finally, there is **the Cry and the Consequence**—Tamar is one of the few women in Scripture who have a voice: "I do not want *this*." "I *do* want honor." "Ask the king for me." But she is thrown away. . . . Amnon violates her, then the text says he hates her; discards her; despised her. And she internalizes the shame.

Guilt is what I am legitimately responsible for. When I am guilty I can take responsibility, repent and seek forgiveness; make retribution and hope for restoration. That is guilt. But shame is trickier. Shame is stickier.

Shame makes me become one with the event. Identifies me, engraves upon me, excludes me from the embrace of possibilities ever again. Shame makes me feel defective. . . . Shame makes me shrivel, and act out and try to be what I am not because I do not like what I am. Shame makes me eat, trying to fill a void that I can't touch. Shame makes me take chemicals to silence the accusing voices in my heart. Shame makes me attach to whomever comes along for the moment as a distraction from my own unspoken horror. This old shame makes my boundaries fuzzy, letting the wrong folks in and wandering into places I should not be, because I never learned to discern the difference. And worst of all, this old *shame silences my voice and stops up my cry.*

But this is the good news of the gospel! When I cry out, God stops in God's tracks! The eyes of the Lord run to and fro in the earth, looking for someone to be strong for. The broken-hearted, to bind up. The captive to set free. The prisoner to bring out of darkness. *This is the good news*: that whosoever calls upon the name of the Lord shall be delivered. This is the good news!

David declares it thus: "Hear my cry, O God; attend unto my prayer. From the end of the earth will I cry unto thee, when my heart is overwhelmed; lead me to the rock [that] is higher than I" (Ps. 61:1–2 KJV). "This poor man cried, and the LORD heard [him], and saved him out of all his troubles." (Ps. 34:6 KJV)

Cry until a thousand poison rivers empty out. God is coming!

Cry until the rage gives way. God is listening.

Cry in prayer. God is about to restore.

Cry in therapy. God is sending help.

Cry at the altar. God will come with arms and a mighty embrace.

Cry until the confrontation arises. God will walk with you into a fearful past.

Cry until the truth makes you stronger than all your violators. Silence has protected the guilty too long.

Cry until you know the ear of the Lord has inclined toward you.

Cry out . . . there will be an answer. A healing answer. A restoring answer. An empowering answer. There will be someone to hear, someone to protect, someone to recover you of your affliction.

Do not miss the redemption when it comes. Tamar comes out! Damage has been done, we have been sinned against, some things have been torn. . . . But as Tamar, we can come out. She comes out of Absalom's house *with her robe.* Torn, but hers. The testimony of her survival.

Life can take many things. Some losses we did not deserve:

Poor parenting, betraying friends, financial reversals; dead children; dying marriages; failing health or faded dreams.

But every person is left with something . . . something with which to start again. Broken pieces but start again!

Fragments of bread in the basket, but start again!

A memory of how it was supposed to be, but start again!

She comes out with her robe. Torn, but a reminder that Satan did not get it all, that evil does not prevail ultimately; that there is a door of escape no matter how hard the trial. There is a past she can trade in for a future. Redeemable.

Your life, my life, may be used; may have high mileage on it; may have sustained some accidents and the frame may be bent. Men and women may judge us totally useless—"totaled," and relegate us to the junk pile of life.

But the spirit of the Lord is upon me to proclaim . . . grab your robe, hold it high, give voice to your testimony that the secrets are over! Put on the garment of praise; the truth sets you free!!

Grab your torn-up robe. You are about to trade it in! Put on the garment of gladness.

Try the knob of Absalom's door; leave your despair.

God through Jesus Christ bids you to come! Pain is not your permanent address! Start walking! Amen.

8

From the Driver's Seat to the Passenger's Seat

LaVerne M. Gill

In 1999, at the age of fifty-one, I was called to pastor my first church—Webster United Church of Christ in Dexter, Michigan. The previous year, I had received a Master of Theology (ThM) degree from Princeton Theological Seminary following the Master of Divinity (MDiv) that was bestowed in 1997. Webster is a rural/suburban church west of Ann Arbor, the home of the University of Michigan. For the then 168-year-old church, I was the first African American and the first woman to serve as pastor. As of this writing, the church has a membership of approximately 210, seven percent of whom are people of color, the remainder of whom are Euro-American. The average Sunday worship is about 160.

A former abolitionist and a temperance church, Webster is considered a liberal leader in this small rural township, even though most of its members are populous Republicans. Its past pastors have included a founder of Taledega College, a founder of Eastern Michigan University, and the first professor of American history to teach at Cornell University. The congregation is diverse in terms of religious backgrounds and theological perspective. A former farming community, Webster Church is perched on a grassy knoll surrounded by a cemetery and 110 acres of farmland. It is a bucolic scene that is soon to change as farmers are forced to sell nonproducing farmland to developers specializing in building $300,000 homes on three-acre lots.

The membership of Webster includes many of the local farmers whose families still occupy homesteads that date back to the era of the frontier, when the federal government gave once Native American–owned land to European immigrants to farm. Others are a part of the professional classes who moved

to the "country," purchased acreage and became weekend farmers. I often say
that I was brought into this Norman Rockwell painting with all of my Romare
Bearden sensibilities intact. There was no way for me to know that the journey of thirteen years of seeking would lead to this intercultural ministry.

THE JOURNEY

> Just then a Canaanite woman from that region came out and started
> shouting, "Have mercy on me, Lord, Son of David; my daughter is
> tormented by a demon." But he did not answer her at all. And his dis-
> ciples came and urged him, saying, "Send her away, for she keeps
> shouting after us." He answered, "I was sent only to the lost sheep of
> the house of Israel." (Matt. 15:22–24)

I think that God began laughing right away when I received the call from
the Webster UCC Pastoral Search Committee. To begin with the day of the
visit, the largest snowfall in twenty-five years was in progress. To my aston-
ishment people were riding around as if nothing had happened. My husband
Tepper accompanied me at the request of the committee. Tepper, a native of
Detroit, had lived in Ann Arbor during his doctoral studies at Wayne State
University in the 1970s. The traffic was not an obstacle to him. I think, however, that God's sense of humor came from knowing that I had spent much of
my seminary training planning to become a leader of "my people" and here I
was about to interview to pastor a church described, at that time, as "99 percent white." As an urban/suburban dweller all of my life, the thought of moving to a rural Midwestern community was sure to bring about culture shock.
Just entertaining the offer was a sign that transformation was in progress.

Seminary had provided time for me to be more receptive to God's call wherever it might lead. When I think back on it, my acceptance of Webster's invitation was another manifestation of surrendering to God. Surrendering came
gradually, but peace was somewhat quicker. Those close to me could tell. My
husband noticed it before I did. Tepper was very supportive throughout my
seminary education. Part of the reason was because it was the first time that
he felt I had found the cause and purpose for my life. Throughout our twenty-
some years together, my many careers—university teacher, corporate trainer,
Senate legislative aide, real estate broker, Federal Reserve budget analyst,
newspaper publisher, television and radio producer, author, and news com-
mentator—resulted in his labeling me an intellectual dilettante. My mother's
comments about the ministry were more succinct; "I was wondering when you
would try Jesus," she said. Despite these comments, or because of them, I knew
that the "call" to the ministry was authentic.

I experienced what is known as the "call" nine years before entering the seminary. It was in Easter of 1985—a few years after the six-month period in which both my brother and grandmother died—that I announced to my family that I was going to go into the ministry. None of us knew what that would mean, or how long the journey would take. I certainly did not know. I often define the "call" as a feeling of restlessness in a search for purposeful and faithful living. That feeling was readily evident during the time preceding the Easter announcement.

What followed were years of discernment during which I had long talks with my then pastor, friend, and mentor, Dr. Evans Crawford, the dean of the historic Howard University Andrew Rankin Memorial Chapel. We spent long hours in his study adjacent to what was then called the "little chapel," on Howard's main campus. It was the same chapel in which Tepper and I had been married in 1977. Dean Crawford would indulge me in my musings about religion, faith, and the significance of what life meant. Afterwards, he would provide words of wisdom and gentle nudging. There I was going on forty, married, with children, a home, and a career, yet still feeling that something was missing. And so, in the late 1980s, I applied to the Howard University School of Divinity. But my application was one recommendation short, and I procrastinated and never turned in the paperwork. I decided that perhaps it was something else that was driving me, not the ministry.

About a year later, I quit my "good government job" as a budget analyst for the Federal Reserve Board of Governors, and began editing and publishing a weekly newspaper. The newspaper was begun in protest to the lack of positive images and important commentary on issues that concerned African Americans in the Washington, DC, area. It also provided an outlet for frustrations with the Fairfax County School System and its racial attitudes toward African American students. My two sons were in the system and I became involved— both through the paper and local organizations—in making the system more responsive to their needs as African American males.

The paper, the *Metro Chronicle*, and later renamed *The National Chronicle*, became a popular alternative newspaper in the Washington metropolitan area. Alternative media outlets owned by African Americans were becoming more visible as the area grappled with the arrest and subsequent trial of Washington Mayor Marion Barry. This popularity led to a weekly radio program, a weekly guest commentary slot on WETA Public Television, and memberships in the Congressional Press Gallery and the National Press Club. Along the way, I produced radio and television programs, one of which—*Straight Talk: Sex, Teens and the '90s*—was nominated for a Washington-area Emmy Award.

Later on I produced another program that became a significant part of my faith journey. It was a public television special titled "He Never Sent Women:

The Ordination of a Female *Priest.*" This documentary on the black Catholic church movement of Bishop George Stallings brought me in contact with Rev. Dr. Delores Carpenter and Rev. Dr. Kelley Brown Douglas. Both were a part of the program's panel discussion. They will never know the impact they had on my later plans. Their brilliant minds, knowledge of Scripture, and their strong faith seemed to radiate before the cameras, inspiring me in a very profound way. At the time, I was convinced that my actual "calling" had been fulfilled by the production of this documentary. That was what the "calling" was, I concluded.

A year later, I was in Germany on a journalistic study tour and cut short the trip in order to attend the Emmy Award ceremony. I attended the ceremony, went home, and collapsed. My son took me to the hospital emergency room, where I found out that I was anemic, my blood pressure and sugar were both high, and I had fibroid tumors. I was scheduled for a hysterectomy.

Women who are as active as I was—trying to burn the candle at both ends and in the middle by being a mother, wife, professional, and a hopelessly addicted workaholic—are pretty much guaranteed such wake-up calls. I stopped everything—the newspaper, the radio, the television, speaking engagements— and returned to a period of discernment. What was God telling me to do? What was I doing wrong? Why did God put the brakes on this roller coaster? The metaphor that I used was that God had taken me out of the driver's seat and gently placed me in the passenger's seat. I was not in charge of the journey anymore. The waiting and the questioning were all going on in the midst of other turmoil in my family life.

I entered the hospital in late October 1992 and I assumed that I would be out in time to vote in the November presidential election for George Bush, Bill Clinton, Ross Perot, or some protest candidate. I took three books into the hospital with me—Alice Walker's *Possessing the Secrets of Joy* (about female circumcision—a cause of great concern to me); Machiavelli's *The Prince*; and the Bible. I knew that one of these books would be the key to the rest of my life. Either I would return to the media business and be a ruthless businesswoman, or I would continue on various quixotic missions of justice; or I would work for transformation through the gospel model of discipleship. I "knew" that my life was about to change, even though I was trying to keep from surrendering.

Even so, God's hand was still rearranging the pieces of my life. So even though I thought that I was finished with the hospital stay and was ready to leave and go to the polls and vote, God stopped me in my tracks again. Just as I was about to leave the hospital I experienced a night of absolute desperation caused by an infection resulting from the operation. This would bring me to my second encounter with Tony, who had been an unexpected presence during this core faith experience.

Tony was the orderly who rolled me into the operating room the first time. But he turned out to be more than an orderly. Tony had been described by one of the nurses as a person with a great sense of humor and a ready smile, and deemed to be quite a character. However, I never saw that side of Tony. When Tony approached my room, this tall, very robust African American man began wheeling me to the operating room—he was on one side and my husband was on the other side. Tears rolled down my cheeks. Tony bent over the bed and said to me, "Don't worry, you are one of God's children. Who is your doctor?"

I told him. "Oh she's good. She's one of God's daughters, too." As we approached the preparation room, Tony told Tepper, "This is as far as you can go, but I am going to go in there, put on a surgical mask, and stay with her until she falls asleep." All the while Tony was talking and prayerfully attending to me. I looked up at the clock on the wall and it was 1:30 p.m. Tony gave me a small pamphlet with the Lord's Prayer on it. I went peacefully to sleep. After the operation, my mother called the hospital. In the course of her conversation, she asked, "What time did they operate on you?"

"I think about 1:30. Why?"

"I thought so. At 1:30, I went into the bathroom (that is where my mother does her serious praying) and knelt down and said, 'Lord, you take her, she's in your hands now.'" I concluded that Tony had been transformed into one of God's temporary human agents summoned up by my mother's prayer.

I did not see Tony again, until the morning they were going to take me back into the operating room to perform a minor procedure to get rid of the infection. The journey had begun the night before when I was grappling with the effects of the infection. My temperature was so high that it caused me to have to be changed about five times during the night into dry nightgowns. I remember knowing that God was in the room that night. I know now that I was wrestling with God all night long. The nurses kept coming in trying to appease me, but nothing worked. They admitted their helplessness and tried to wait out the night with me.

Finally after wrestling all night and hearing from God, Tony appeared to wheel me into the operating room again. Once again he gave words of encouragement and ministered to me until I fell off to sleep. It would be easy to dismiss that night as one in which I was in a state of delirium due to the fever, but even now I am overcome with the feeling of God's presence even as I write about that night. I made a decision that night about which book would govern the rest of my life.

After leaving the hospital I did not go back to my media work right away. About six months later, my radio producer called to ask when I planned to return to the air. "I am sick," I told him.

"You can't still be sick, LaVerne," he said incredulously.

"I am sick. I will be sick until I get well," I told him. I was stalling.

Tepper was having a difficult time with his research institute at the university, and I started helping him while trying to figure out what was happening in my life.

In December 1993, Tepper and I went to Senegal, West Africa, to a technology conference for which he was one of the keynote speakers. While there, we met Adrian Backus, a Howard Law School graduate who was working for Africare. The three of us talked into the night about religion, life, and commitment. Adrian had considered going to seminary at one time. As a matter of fact, he had enrolled at Princeton Theological Seminary but decided against attending. I had ordered a catalog from Princeton at one time but put it aside.

When Tepper and I returned to the States, I returned to radio production and produced a radio program on African American Women in the 103rd Congress. It was a time when everything I put my hand to seemed to work, as if to create doubt in my mind as to whether or not this "calling" was authentic. I produced the program with a generous grant from International Public Radio and it aired on over 100 stations—a success, by some standards. Even with this "success," the work was not the same and my passion for it had subsided.

Still restless and seeking, I told Tepper in March 1994 that I was going to go to Princeton Theological Seminary for a weekend exploratory seminar. I called him after the second day and said, "I think I am ready."

"Well, I can't get in the way of God," he said.

Nine years after acknowledging the "call" to the ministry, I was ready to enter seminary and say "yes" to God. I applied and was accepted that fall. In the meantime, my oldest son, Dylan, was planning his "coming of age" trip to Africa. He was going to Senegal. I called the only person that I had made contact with—Adrian Backus—to ask if he would look out for Dylan.

"I would," he said, "but I am heading for Princeton in the fall. My family is already there."

"I am too," I replied.

At the age of forty-six, with the blessings of my family, I entered Princeton Theological Seminary, with young people the age of my oldest son. My youngest son Tepper decided to come with me to spend his last year in high school in Princeton. In September, I received a call from my agent that I had a contract with Rutgers University Press to write a book based on the radio program on African American Women in Congress. I hesitated because I thought that this would throw me off the track of the "call" to the ministry. Before accepting the call, I would have given my eyeteeth to have a book contract, but now it was different. After procrastinating, I decided that this would put closure to my pre-call life. I started writing the book and finished it before I graduated.

Seminary was one of those wonderful experiences that is rare in later life. Although many young people found it trying, it was the easiest job I ever had. It was a time to think, pray, read, write, and prepare for this new life—this calling.

In October 1997, I remember thinking on my fiftieth birthday how very happy I was. I had graduated from seminary, with a Master of Divinity degree and was embarking on the Master of Theology. My first book was out and I was working on a second book proposal. Tepper joined me in Princeton, after receiving a membership in the Institute for Advanced Study. We spent the year together in Princeton. My sons seemed to be headed toward their adult lives— Dylan was in the dot.com revolution and Tepper was in college. All seemed well.

While I had acknowledged the call, I was still not ready to embrace it. As long as I could stay in school, I did not have to face the fact that I was "called" to do something for God. Quite frankly, I did not see myself going into a church as a pastor. During internships throughout my seminary training, I had done ministry in various other settings. I interned for a year as a chaplain at the Garden State Correctional Facility, and I assisted my United Church of Christ in-care advisor in her role as UCC Chaplain for Princeton University.

During the summer of one year, I returned to Reston, Virginia (home), and interned at the United Christian Parish (UCP)—an interdenominational church. There I started a ministry called "Works Sunday." It is an interfaith, interracial, intercultural ministry that encourages people to leave their place of worship for a Sunday and go out into the community and become a part of some form of social justice or faith-based activity. This ministry designed for lay leadership continued for over five years. At times over two dozen faith communities participated. Under the name of Women's Radical Discipleship, I began doing a number of religious retreats, preaching, and speaking engagements. I was in no hurry to pursue congregational ministry. Part of this was due to the experience I had in my home church.

THE OBSTACLES

And he said, "Truly I tell you, no prophet is accepted in the prophet's hometown." . . . they got up, drove him out of the town and led him to the brow of the hill on which their town was built, so that they might hurl him off the cliff. (Luke 4:24, 29)

Of course, for every silver lining there is a cloud. My United Church of Christ home church was in the midst of turmoil. The United Methodist "interim" minister decided to stay. In his quest to stay, he took no prisoners. He saw me as a possible threat, and each time I returned home, the sermons invariably turned to some variation on the theme of "those educated people who go to big schools to learn about God." The pew became a hot seat. On the other hand, he would try to lure me into the contentiousness by asking if I wanted to "be in the pulpit" or would I like to preach. It was like a dysfunctional family.

I finally consented to preach. The Sunday that he scheduled me to preach, he was gone. The choir was on "vacation," and I was forbidden to ask anyone to provide music. A bell choir from UCP wanted to play for the service. They came and set up the bell tables, but the chair of the Board of Deacons came in on Saturday, dismantled the bell tables, and hid them somewhere in the church. Later he called with instructions from the pastor to tell me that the bell choir could not perform. For this sermon, my first in my home church, the choir, the pianist, the pastor, and most of the deacons were absent. Luckily for me the Holy Spirit was present.

While I can look back on this with amusement, that was not the feeling I had during the time. I was distressed about the turn of events, about the behavior of the church and the pastor. I was not a novice. I had been around politics for most of my professional life, so I was not naive about political maneuvering, but I found myself to be unschooled in the politics of the "church." The duplicity, the power struggles, the pettiness, the misogynist church leadership, and the mean-spiritedness just made me want to do something else. I did not leave the secular world to become a part of this kind of reality. I questioned my call and the time spent preparing for it. While I received assurances from other women clergy (primarily white women clergy) and from family members, and some friends, I was not convinced that I had done the right thing.

As I moved toward my ecclesiastical council—the UCC's preordination examination process—the pastor's constituency continued to attempt to place obstacles in my way. They refused to provide a mailing list for notification regarding the ecclesiastical council—which requires a quorum for voting purposes. I ended up having the council at United Christian Parish. The vote of support for my future in the UCC ministry was unanimous. Once again the presence of the Holy Spirit brought victory to the moment.

I eventually met with the "interim" pastor to clear the air. I told him that my ambition was not to be the pastor of my home church. That did not deter him. For whatever reason he was not convinced. As the church began to polarize around the issue of an interim becoming the pastor, my presence became one of the lightning rods for the various factions. Letters were written to members of the congregation alluding to people who wanted me to become the pastor. There was no truth to it, but truth was not an issue. Strategically creating an "enemy" was one way to galvanize a constituency to support the "interim" pastor's quest.

Perhaps the most disappointing aspect of this part of the journey was the fact that most of my detractors were African American male clergy and male lay leadership. Needless to say, support for my ministry did not come from my home church. Most of my support came from predominately white congregations such as UCP, where Rev. Suzanne Rudiselle, a second-career pastor and a Princeton graduate, was one of my most ardent supporters and able mentors. Another was Rev. Hazel Staats-Westover, my in-care supervisor—a feminist and UCC Chaplain at Princeton University. The lack of support from the African American male clergy is not a fact that I relish talking about. Whenever I think about my home church, I am reminded of Jesus' experience in Nazareth. At least they did not literally run me out of town—but they did figuratively.

THE CALL FROM WEBSTER UNITED CHURCH OF CHRIST

As a result of my home church experience, I was disenchanted with the prospect of parish ministry. Webster changed all that. Webster Church obtained my profile from the UCC's national database of eligible candidates for church openings. I was one of twenty-seven candidates considered for the job. The invitation came based on the profile alone. The search committee turned out to be a good cross section of the church membership—a longtime member of the church and the farming community; a corporate attorney and gentleman farmer; a University of Michigan professor and bee farmer; a populous Republican, veteran, and retired automobile plant foreman; a retired mechanical engineer; a former welfare recipient who had just finished an online degree program; a former staff person in the law school who had been a part of the legal proceedings for the University of Michigan Affirmative Action lawsuit; a librarian; and one of the grand dames of the church.

The church is an historic landmark because it is the oldest church still in operation in the same building in the county. Built in 1834 with a gift from the statesman Daniel Webster, the church is a plain white clapboard sanctuary with a bell tower and office space that resulted from the razing of the one-room schoolhouse and attaching it to the sanctuary. A wall leading to the pastor's office is lined with pictures of previous ministers of the church, all white and all male.

One of the members of the search committee wanted to know if I described myself as a "conservative" or "liberal" Christian. My response was that I was neither, but I considered myself to be a "radical" Christian in the same way that Jesus was radical. Another wanted to know whether I would find it difficult to minister to Euro-Americans, especially since most of my work and writings dealt with African Americans. I gave the response by reminding them of the story of the Canaanite woman and Jesus' response to her. I also spoke of race and ethnicity being one of the major growing edges of Christianity. During my time with the committee, the husband of a Search Committee member was entertaining Tepper. He is an applied physicist and Tepper is a theoretical physicist. The bridges were being built.

As Tepper and I headed home, I told him about the question concerning my being a conservative or liberal Christian. When I told him my response, he said something to the effect, "That's the end of that, you'll never get hired."

A few weeks later, I received a letter from the search committee asking me to come back for a trial sermon. This time they wanted me to spend several days with them—before giving my trial sermon—meeting with various committees, getting to know a little bit about the area, and meeting and greeting members. Sunday came and I was scheduled to preach at both the 8:30 and the 10:30 services. Preaching on the "wilderness experience" and its message to us, I received eighty-five out of ninety votes. One very precocious ten-year-old came up to me and said, "Pastor Gill, I prayed that we would have an African American woman preacher and God answered my prayer."

We toured the parsonage—a centennial farmhouse on a 100-acre farm. May was the earliest starting date because I had two manuscripts to complete and retreats to conduct. During that four-month period, the members of the congregation completely renovated the parsonage—putting in new carpet, restoring the woodwork, putting in a new bathroom and a new kitchen. It was an overwhelming show of support.

In between accepting the call and starting the ministry, UCC polity required that I be ordained. My ordination was scheduled for April. Normally such an event is held in one's home church. I decided that it would be best for me to have mine elsewhere—Andrew Rankin Memorial Chapel on Howard University's campus. Aside from the home church tragedy, Rankin was an appropriate venue for me. We went to Rankin during the early years of our sons' lives. We were founding members of the Friends of Rankin Chapel. I served as the historian for the program to install a stained-glass window featuring the former deans of the chapel, who included Howard Thurman and Evans Crawford. All of Tepper's professional academic life was on Howard's campus; it was my undergraduate alma mater; my husband and I were married on campus; and many of our special times of joy and grief had been ministered to in that chapel.

Some members of the search committee attended the ordination, and Dean Crawford preached from my favorite Psalm, 8. Nearly three hundred people attended. The congregation was interracial, intergenerational, and interfaith. For some of our Muslim friends, it was their first time in a Christian chapel. The laying on of hands was one of the most powerful, spirit-filled moments in my life.

In the meantime, my home church was in the throes of rallying people around the idea of disrupting the ordination ceremony because they felt that they were not involved in the process. I personally invited the pastor, but he did not come. Nothing ever came of the threat.

THE MINISTRY AT WEBSTER UCC

On May 1, when I officially came on board at Webster, the home going of the oldest woman in the church was being held in the township hall. The next day, I was asked to co-officiate at an infant funeral. Two days later, a member from the search committee had a car accident right outside of the church. That same week, one of the members had emergency surgery. I mention all of this to show how I was dropped into the middle of ministry at Webster. There was never any time to adjust to what it was like to minister to a predominately white congregation. I moved right into it without my usual analytical deliberations.

Intercultural ministry has its challenges, but it represents to me one of the most intense opportunities for seeing God work in the lives of the people and the pastor. My position on race is not the same today as it was when I walked into Webster in 1999. If one were to describe me in Harlem Renaissance terms, I could easily be called a "race woman"—like Zora Neale Hurston was a "race woman." In ministering at Webster, I have had an opportunity to see how God makes it possible to create community across cultural lines, even with someone as race conscious as I am. In the areas of preaching, music, and liturgy, I have become profoundly mindful of the cultural distinctions and the opportunities for celebration of them. This was not readily apparent when I started.

For example, I never considered clapping to be "an issue" in the church. The length of service beyond an hour was an "issue" in the church. The "call" and "response" was an "issue" in the church. These were never "issues" to me. It posed a dilemma for me, one that needed to be resolved if I intended to stay. How could I minister and maintain my integrity as an African American with a different church cultural experience and still provide ministry open to and welcoming of all? That was solved after my first year and my first evaluation. In that evaluation, while the pluses far outweighed the minuses, I could not ignore the fact that the concern about length of service, clapping, and spirit-filled responses to the service were problematic for some.

I approached it from the pulpit by continuing to reinforce that this was a church that had within its walls many different denominational backgrounds and many different worship experiences. The church, though small, included former Lutherans, Church of the Brethren, Quakers, Southern Baptist, Catholics, Methodist, African Methodist Episcopal, Unitarians, Evangelical

Reform, Dutch Reform, Buddhists, and previously unchurched people. All had come together to be at Webster for different reasons. What I wanted to impart, and what I continued to say, was that all of these denominations notwithstanding, this was a church where the Holy Spirit moved throughout the course of worship. Freedom to worship belonged to anyone who walked through the door. If some people wanted and felt the spirit move them to clap, they should clap. If it moved them to say "Amen," they should say "Amen." If they just wanted to sit and be quiet, they could just sit and be quiet. The only thing that was not allowed was for anyone to look askance at the person next to them because the spirit moved differently for them.

Over the years, I have been able to convince the members of the church that God is in the place doing work on Sunday morning and that we have no right to try and stop that work of the spirit. Celebrating diversity meant being open to the vitality of the spirit. By and large, I believe that the people of Webster have embraced much of that vision for the church.

I would say that four areas are probably the most characteristic of our shared vision for the church at this point:

1. *Enriching the worship experience*: Liturgy and music have become more eclectic since I arrived. The church engages in and celebrates the diverse backgrounds of the congregation and of the pastor. The coming together across cultural lines continues to be a growing edge in the church, but it is also the place where we have become more intentional, insightful, and prayerful.

2. *Deepening individual spiritual formation*: The proclamation from the pulpit serves the congregation's need for collective reassurance of God's grace, challenges, and mercy, but I found that it does not feed the individual thirst for intimate relationships with God. As a consequence, I have sought to expand opportunities for spiritual formation on an individual level. We started an outdoor ministry that includes a fellowship garden, a meditation trail, and a labyrinth. (Each project was constructed by an Eagle Scout under the supervision of the Boy Scout leader who did not want me to come to breakfast.) This outdoor ministry has as its focus an opportunity to create space for personal spiritual enrichment through meditation and spiritual reflection. As a consequence of my studies in spiritual direction, I have been able to expand my ministry to include one-on-one spiritual formation sessions with members who desire it.

Biblical literacy is another area of growth. In 2002, I began editing a monthly devotional, which consists of reflections and prayers written by members and friends of the church. This has been an opportunity to get people to read their Bibles and spend time in Bible study on such issues as the poor, love, the miracles of Jesus, the prayers of Scripture, as well as other topics and books of the

Bible. Even though we have Bible study and adult Sunday school, for Webster the monthly devotional is a better way to work toward biblical literacy.

3. *Broadening the church's concept of mission*: In 2003, the church's second delegation went to West Africa. The previous year a delegation of twelve visited Ghana, West Africa, and established a relationship with the Krisan-Sanzule Refugee camp in Sekondi, Ghana. One result of this relationship was the establishment of an economic base for women in the camp through the development and funding of a women's sewing circle. The women make dresses and other products, and Webster sells them in the States, thereby providing the women with an outside market for their goods and a source of income for their time in the camp. This income allows them to provide for their families in an honorable manner. The African experience continues to transform the delegation members and the church culture.

4. *Expanding outreach to a more diverse community:* In 2000, the Bailey Youth Forum was initiated. Mr. and Mrs. Bailey had been one of the few African American families in Webster Township. During the course of their lives they took in over 250 foster children. While they were not members of the church, they left money for the church to provide youth programs. The money had gone unused for over five years.

The first forum was televised on Michigan Public Television and was titled "Creating Peace." The daylong, multimedia program drew youth from around the county. This interracial, interdenominational, and interfaith gathering was the first of its kind in Webster Township. Over three hundred youth participated. The second youth forum, titled "The American Stew," was equally as successful and provocative. The story of America's many ethnic groups was told through the lens of the history of jazz.

In 2002, we started the First Friday series. This quarterly gathering of members and friends lifts up issues of concern to the community and to many of the members of the church. Topics such as mental illness, posttraumatic stress syndrome, land use, refugee issues, and others have been explored through this venue.

During my years at Webster, the church has had to face some difficult moments of discernment—September 11, the war in Iraq, the University of Michigan Affirmative Action lawsuits, a downturn in the economy, land use in this once farming community, and navigating the changing racial dynamics in the church. This, of course, is all viewed as a backdrop to the basic issues of the faithful—depression, grief, doubt, marriage, family divisions, divorce, and addictions of various kinds, just to name a few. I add to these my own particular challenges—movement from the East Coast urban/suburban community to a Midwest rural/suburban environment; having a long-distance commuter marriage (my husband remained at Howard as a professor); and a few setbacks with my sons' movements into adulthood.

Through all of this it has been a wonderful spiritually rewarding experience for me to minister at Webster United Church of Christ. It is good to be in this part of God's vineyard and grow in faith. The challenges continue daily, but the gifts of the Spirit guide and enlighten. I would be remiss if I did not say that as much as the Holy Spirit was pulling me toward God, an unequal force was trying to test my call. The struggle did not end when I began the ministry; it intensified.

My daily prayer is that I might walk close enough with God to stay on the right track and that I might be quiet enough to hear God's voice and that I might be humble enough to heed it.

Sermon: "The Day God Ripped Open the Skies"
Psalm 29; Acts 19:1–7; Mark 1:4–11

LaVerne M. Gill

This is the day that we talk about baptism, a controversial subject in the early church and I would say a controversial subject in today's church as well. It could be said that baptism prepares us to accept the work of God in our world. Baptism gives us common language to talk about our faith. Baptism places us in the community of the faithful. We open this Sunday with the baptism of Jesus coming out of a week in which we celebrated the Epiphany. We remember Epiphany as a kind of revealing of something divine in our presence. We have a "knowing." It is a revelatory manifestation of a divine sense of being. And so on the sixth day of this week it was the Epiphany that we celebrated as a part of the Christian tradition.

Although Epiphany is a sacred act, we sometimes use the word in secular discourse. Every once in a while, we get a sense of knowing that there is a divine and hidden presence in something that manifests itself in our lives. I had that happen. In preparing this sermon, I had an epiphany of my own. A sudden shining through of a hidden truth. In other words, a lightbulb went on in my head. I began thinking about Toni Morrison's Pulitzer Prize–winning novel, *Beloved*.

In the Scripture that I have before me, when Jesus comes out of the water, God speaks: "You are my Son, the Beloved; with you I am well pleased" (Mark 1:11). That's when Morrison's book came to mind. I tried reading it four times and now I think that I might have a handle on some of it. Perhaps Morrison was writing an allegory, where she takes a look at the concept of sacred water, of redemption, and of reconciliation in this very strange story. It is a haunting story. The kind of story that makes you think you are really there. You can't move anyplace. I picked it up and put it down, shaking my head, until I finally just read it. When I read *Beloved*, I think about baptism and

133

water, this sense of renewal. There is a child called "Beloved" and you may know the story.

Beloved is killed by her mother to keep from being taken into slavery—a slavery from which her mother escaped. The murder is a sacrifice, but also a consequence of Sethe, the mother's, despair of having endured horrific experiences during her own enslavement. The child comes back as a kind of spirit of sorts, an ethereal spirit that returns to the family. She comes out of the water—but she doesn't just come out of the water, she emerges from the water and makes herself known gradually. She returns into the life of her mother, and there Beloved hovers over the family. All kinds of changes take place in this household because of this spirit. There is renewal, redemption, and reconciliation. This presence has made itself felt for some reason. So as the story unfolds, Denver, the younger daughter in the story, evolves as a new creature. She is the hidden sign of hope, made manifest through the presence of Beloved.

Now that is a very clumsy way of looking at the story, but when you look through a theological lens, a connection can be made. And of course, even though Morrison is a wonderful storyteller, her story does not have the grandeur and the glory of the Christian narrative. So Morrison has the elements but not the ethos for this grand story of ours.

There is a sacrifice, renewal, and the cleansing water. We come into this understanding of reconciliation through the sacrifice of Jesus. Our Scriptures today give us a starting point for telling the baptismal story in all its grandeur and in all its grace.

We start in Psalm 29, where the power of God is explored: "Ascribe to the LORD glory and strength," (v. 1b); "The voice of the LORD is over the waters; the God of glory thunders, the LORD, over mighty waters" (v. 3).

The water, the words, and the seas. The kind of doxology the psalmist writes about shows the power and the sovereignty of God. The psalmist marvels at God's power and divinity. God who came and opened up the waters, who opened up the skies and created the majesty of the mountains and nature, is the same God who tore open the clouds on the day of Jesus' baptism.

With this image, this foundation, this vision we watch John baptize Jesus in the Jordan. We watch as Jesus comes out of the water—the earth sees a powerful God tearing open the sky and bestowing the spirit on him. As God breaks through he proclaims, "You are my Son, the Beloved; with you I am well pleased" (Mark 1:11).

We are given a divine manifestation of who Jesus is. Yet, through the rest of Mark we are given to believe that there is a mystery about who Jesus is. We ought not lose sight, however, of this picture of Jesus emerging from the water—this moment of grandeur, glory, and proclamation.

That is why this is such a powerful day—when we talk about John and Jesus in the Jordan. It expresses the very essence of our belief—that Jesus is the Son of God. Jesus comes out of baptism and the spirit of the Lord is made manifest in a dove that symbolizes for us the majesty of the God we serve. The God that is in charge of winds, mountains, and the seas. His Beloved is in our midst.

The magnificent moment when John baptizes Jesus is significant to all Christians. And yet as we go along in the history of the Christian faith, we get confused about baptism. In the Acts of the Apostles, Paul encounters Apollos, an Egyptian Jew. Apollos has a following all his own in Alexandria. He approaches Paul and Paul asks, "Have you been baptized?" He replies, "Yes, I was baptized by John." Paul asks, "Were you baptized in the name of the Holy Spirit?" and Apollos responds—here he reminds me of us when he says, "What is the Holy Spirit? I don't know anything about that." (I know that is not true in this church.)

Watch this next scene. Paul baptizes him in the name of the Father, Son, and Holy Spirit. He emerges ecstatic—speaking in tongues. The power is still there. Having two baptisms was a controversy of the early church, not so much the church today. We are concerned with other things such as whether people should be doused, sprinkled, or dumped, and whether infants should be baptized.

We still have these problems. I get it every time I baptize an infant. Should a baby be baptized? Infants can't commit to Christ, so why baptize them? These questions are raised. Our response here at Webster, and in most of the United Church of Christ, is that we ask the community of faith to take responsibility for the spiritual life of infants until they are able to make a decision for themselves through the confirmation process. That is what confirmation is all about.

I was baptized in the Baptist church at age thirteen, because they believed that you should not be baptized until you "knew for yourself" that you wanted to follow Jesus. I was not sprinkled or doused; I was dumped. I can remember it and feel that cold water even today. I went under, thrown back into the water; there was no mercy. I was baptized.

So even today there are those who cannot decide whether being sprinkled, doused, or dumped is the best way. This is what you call majoring in the minors. What is important is knowing what the commitment is. Baptism is a commitment. It is a defining moment. A moment of expectations. A moment of identification. It is a chance for renewal. A chance to start all over again. There is a newness that Christ gives. It truly is an opportunity to be born again. But it is not a Richard Pryor moment when you find yourself walking down the alley with a tuna-fish sandwich and hearing God call you. It is an authentic connection to God.

Then there is the grace that comes with it. If you were baptized long ago and you have resorted to your old ways, you can turn around. Every time you take Communion, it is a time when you can renew yourself, reinvent yourself, reconcile with your neighbor. You can become a new creature in Christ.

It is a reaffirmation.

Let me let you in on my joy today. This evening I will participate in the baptism of twenty young men at the Maxey Boys School. I am excited about what they are about to do. I know that there are skeptics who may say that this is just a jailhouse conversion. Well, who am I or you to say what it is for each of them? All I know is that twenty young men who took the wrong road have decided to turn their lives around through accepting Christ as their savior. That may not sound like a courageous act to you, but in some prisons, it can mean abuse and even death.

But the message of baptism is what is making me excited about this event. These young men know that even if the world has locked them up, God has not locked them out. They know that they can turn around and that they are an equal part of the kingdom of God. It is life giving for them to know that they belong to God, as you do and as I do. They now have a common bond, a common family, a common story. Just like us. They will be able to avail themselves of God's grace, and recommit each time they partake of the bread and the wine. Recommit and change their lives.

It makes all the difference in the world being a Christian. Always renewing—every day can be a new day. We are no different than they:

Were you sick yesterday? This is a new day.

Were you on drugs yesterday? This is a new day.

Did you beat your wife yesterday? This is a new day.

Were you drunk yesterday? This is a new day.

This is a new day to rejuvenate, reimagine, recover, renew, reconcile, recommit, reenergize, reinvigorate, reclaim, redefine, reidentify, and remember.

It doesn't matter how you got here; it doesn't matter whether you were sprinkled, doused, or dumped—whether you got a little bit of water and a lot of Jesus, we are all a part of that same grace. We are all believers in that Jesus who emerged from the water, and heard the voice of God say, "You are my Son, my Beloved; with you I am well pleased." This baptism, this water, this renewal belongs to all of us.

Praise God, praise God.

9

"Tensions, Tears, and Triumphs"

ALISON P. GISE JOHNSON

When I am asked to preach or lecture at churches I usually send a bio that outlines the notable accomplishments of an African American woman born the sixth of seven children into family from the south side of Chicago. The statement lists academic accomplishments of attaining a Bachelor of Science degree in chemical engineering from Northwestern University, a Master of Divinity degree from the School of Theology at Virginia Union University, and a Doctor of Philosophy in religion from Temple University. It also summarizes official ministerial validations of being licensed by Rev. Dr. Earl F. Miller and Pilgrim Baptist Church, St. Paul, Minnesota, and ordained by Rev. Dr. Earl M. Brown and the Fifth Baptist Church family of Richmond, Virginia.

As these accomplishments are read, there are times that I tear up with thanksgiving, but most often I sit, as I hear congregations respond in awe with a sense of being uncomfortably distant from those to whom I am sent. My concern is that the reading of accomplishments points only to the romantic. Presentations of credentials, taken out of context, represent the exceptional life of one called to the ministry as opposed to way-markers of a faith journey. They give a soft lens perspective without exposing the texture of a journey filled with tensions, tears, and triumphs. Nameless and faceless are congregations and men and women mentors who became angels making the rough places smooth, the crooked straight, the valleys high, and the mountains low.

Through my life I have learned many things, but two have been most sobering and centering. The first is that we overcome not only by the blood of the lamb but also by the words of our testimonies. The second, which is a product of my doctoral journey, is that it is important to share interpretations of the past for the sake of forging a powerfully faithful future.

For most of our lives people ask us to make choices based on false dichotomies and Enlightenment demarcations of discipline and vocation. Such a posture is even exemplified in the response my father gave as I told him that I was called to the ministry, leaving my chemical engineering job and going to seminary. "Al," he said, "there are enough black preachers. There are not enough black engineers." In being overtly disobedient to my father's requests, it is only through honoring all of our desires and the leading from within that we, our families, and our communities can appreciate the integrative power of God. So, though not without tension it is neither without apology that I love the academics of science and theology and find fertile places to plant and be fed in church, community, and classroom.

This posture is quite funny to me, now, because most of my life I have neither liked school nor church, and here I find myself continually defined in both. My students laugh because I am very honest about the fact that I have hated school since I was a four-year-old child in Head Start. I had nightmares the whole time that I attended Burnside elementary school on the south side of Chicago. I dreamed, seemingly every night, that a monster chased me through the third-floor corridors, and every August, I began to feel ill as the beginning of school drew near. More than occasionally I faked illness by chewing toast, mixing it in my mouth with orange juice, and heaving it over the side of the bunk beds that my sisters and I shared.

For church, I always felt myself participating in vacillating observations. There was something about it that seemed sacred, but most often it was scary. I felt as if church was full of an indescribable presence and at the same time full of strange superficial rituals that were a memorial to tradition that had lost its truth and overtly distant to the experiences of a child.

My memories of formal church are of attending St. Mark United Methodist, where I was carted off to Sunday school to color pictures of Jesus in the pasture petting lambs. One particular day when I was four years old, I remember feeling lifted up and hearing a voice from within. But I never told anyone mostly because I do not remember occasions when my family talked about personal spiritual encounters.

The only other spiritual encounters I remember were quite scary. Those came as I attended an Apostolic Pentecostal Church with my Aunt Chick, and my understanding of church took a sharp turn. Christianity, when seeking to be relevant, only judged people and sent them to hell. Church was a place where boys and girls were morally tutored to consider one another suspect.

Early in my life, my family stopped attending church, but a different kind of fellowship and formation continued every Sunday at the home of my grandparents, Nanny and Paw Paw. In the summer, Paw Paw barbecued, invited all of his friends, and moved his three-feet-tall speakers into the backyard. The air was filled with the sounds of Marvin Gaye, the smell of barbecue, and intergenerational laughter. Such an environment seemed as ripe a worship service as any that I had ever experienced.

However strange, sacred, and scary, it has been the intersection of both of these institutions that has given birth, given power, and been the site of fear. Ultimately, and most important, both are where I am able to hear the voice of God and have been given people who mentor me into holiness. This holiness for me is the process of excavating understandings of self and call that translate into unapologetic investments in community, love, and social justice.

I became conscious of this process in high school. For all of my life I had internalized a kind of rage that precipitated into a sense of insecurity. As a child growing up, it was difficult being light-skinned. Throughout my life in school and at home, I was called by the worst title that could be imagined—"white." Through elementary school I found myself having to justify my complexion and fight as a process of demystifying two myths; that light-skinned people thought they were better than others, and that they could not fight.

My observed, insecure life shifted into experiences filled first with feelings of hate, exercises of prerogative, and an unfolding sense of God and self. It was at Lindblom Technical High School that I felt I was becoming my own person. I enjoyed being distant enough from the vulnerabilities of childhood and close enough to adulthood in order not to internalize or interpret the world through the wounds of pigmentocracy. Specific to my junior year is my memory of taking an expository writing course with Mrs. Betty Jean Miller. During one of our class meetings, each student was required to go to Mrs. Miller's desk, to receive drafts of their paper and endure comments. I went up and got good feedback, I guess, but I can' t remember what she said to me because as I was on my way back to my desk, Mrs. Miller loudly exclaimed, "You people think you can just hand anything in to me." Everybody turned around to see to whom she was referring, and there stood Phyllis Chan. We were all shocked because in our recollection we never remember any of the Chinese students being so overtly chided. In our teenage minds we asked, what manner of woman is this?

Needless to say, until I finished her course, I wanted to stay out of Mrs. Miller's way, but after that, I wanted to be around her as much as I could. At the time, I did not know why. I just hoped I was not being an ultra-weird teenager. Now, I realize that my soul appreciated her because she acted like no other women that I knew. She walked through the classroom large and in charge. She said whatever came to her mind. She laughed without reservation and corrected people intentionally and unapologetically. I was free enough to talk to her about everything from disappointing friendships to boys I was dating. More important than her allowing me to talk, she allowed me to sit in her presence and the circle of other black women as they talked, laughed, and smoked in the English teachers' lounge.

The possibilities of those moments were almost tarnished by a run-in that I had with Mr. Rumlinski, who himself taught English but also acted as the advisor for the yearbook staff. I used to harass Mr. Rumlinski, almost daily, partly jokingly while at the same time serious, about his smoking in the yearbook office. Though I occasionally smoked Tiparillos with my grandfather and Pall Mall cigarettes with my grandmother, as a child, I hated smoke. One particular day, my interaction with Mr. Rumlinski shifted. I was sitting with Mrs. Miller and the other teachers, as they talked, laughed, and smoked. Mr. Rumlinski came in, looked at me, and said, "So you can stand their smoke but not mine?" Fortunately or unfortunately, I had at that time become quite witty and I responded, "Maybe it's not the smoke." He turned and left the room. I thought nothing more of the exchange, until he sent a friend to talk with me about the incident. I was incensed. I had never felt such overt, externalized, identifiable rage and deep hate in my life.

The weeks that followed were difficult. I felt sick. Because I could not understand the reaction, I was unable to make sense of what had happened. Had I been disrespectful? Should I have apologized? I didn't even know what to do with these newly found feelings and the battery of questions. Then I began to write my healing. This encounter reminded me of my introduction to geometry. Geometry, because it was like no other course in math, seemed to be the most difficult subject that I had ever encountered. There was no other course that overtly prepared me for it or gave me a glimpse of it. It was frustrating. The postulates and theorems seemed valueless. Then something happened as the illusive interplay between words and images was demystified. Theory and practical application converged and a line separating ignorance and knowledge was crossed, never again to be a boundary.

On that day with my teacher, a different line was crossed—from internalized racial innocence to social conscience. For some reason it seemed as if I understood the adult conversations on which I had eavesdropped all my life. I was not only conscious of racism but I was no longer thrown by its seeming chaotic presentations. The colorism of the black community made sense, the government that allowed an organization to have painted for all to see "STOP THE NIGGER" on the side of its building made sense. The tears my mother cried and I collected as a four-year-old girl as she watched the funeral march of Rev. Dr. Martin Luther King Jr. were now interpretable. The powerful preaching of Rev. Jeremiah A Wright Jr. that yanked Jesus out of the pasture petting lambs into the center of fights for social justice with fist raised and an unwaivering commitment to black people was understood.

This one interaction with Mr. Rumlinski made me realize the greatest cost of white racism was that it stood in the way of black people and all of humanity fulfilling God-ordained potential. Living in our racialized society demanded the building of altars and daily sacrifices to rage, hate, and insecurity. Racism unchecked and operative in this white man commanded that he be given attention and value above anyone else in the room, even well-educated women who were invested in the students they taught. In those moments, the greatest potential cost was to a black girl trying to name herself based on powerful models in front of her in a space that her soul deemed sacred.

This was the first time that I refused to exert all of my energy toward the maintenance of insecurity, which kept me on the margins of life looking in, afraid of being hurt. Instead I started a spiritual transition with investments in loving myself, regardless. And God honored those desires continually by providing people in my life who ushered me into holiness defined by self-discovery, openness to intimacy with God and others, and an undying refusal to let anyone who could not love me have any say in defining me.

As I left high school and began matriculation at Northwestern University, my newly found operating principles were the only things that sustained me. Northwestern was a very difficult time for me. All of my life, though I hated school, I had been defined as being very gifted. Within two semesters all seemed to collapse. I had my famous "3D" semester (receiving D's in three of four courses). It was devastating, not because of my grades, but because I did not know how to stop the slide. I studied. I even taught classmates the material, but by the end of the courses, for the large part of three years not only did I find myself on academic probation, but I had to sit across the desk from my advisor, Professor Mah. During one meeting, he looked at my records, looked at me, and questioned whether I was intellectually gifted enough to be at Northwestern. Though my grades were poor, as I got up from that meeting, I remember hearing from within, "I have known that I would go to Northwestern and major in engineering since I was twelve years old. I'll be damned if I allow this man to overturn my dreams and undo all that my family and community has inspired and entrusted in me in ten minutes."

My moment of empowerment did not keep me from becoming deeply depressed, however. I cried myself to sleep every night for several months. And one day I stood in the shower wishing I would just die, only to wake up on the shower floor, look at my nakedness, and change my mind. I was in a place that I had never been before. Gone were the black women who walked around with confidence who loved us in ways that gave birth to confidence. They were my guideposts. Northwestern was a wilderness experience in that all symbols of what was familiar were obviously absent and so I met God and self in different ways.

Perhaps the most pivotal and sustaining aspect of my life was being a part of the Northwestern Community Ensemble, which was a student-run choir that served as family. We traveled together, entertained one another, and prayed for one another. It was a very powerful group. Our repertoire consisted of hymns, anthems, and gospel music. No matter the genre, when we sang, even in rehearsal it seemed as if God filled the room. I experienced a spirituality that could not be contrived or forced in a "prayer circle." In those days, I realized that the voice that I heard as a four-year-old child was back. It was a voice that guided me, and one that I was continually learning to trust.

It was at Northwestern that my conscious sense of gifts for ministry became operative. I was elected as the chaplain of the choir, and though course work was difficult, I began to love to study the word of God especially as I heard the voice of God helping me to understand that which I studied. And though others actually relied on me to share counsel with them, I had no vocabulary that would ever define this as ministry. I just did what was in my heart to do.

It wasn't until I successfully completed my degree in chemical engineering and moved to St. Paul Minnesota as project engineer for 3M Company that an official call to ministry came. By then, I had become very social and rarely did I spend time at home by myself. But one particular night, I think it was in August, I lay on my living room floor not in humility, but because I never bought any furniture. As I lay there trying to figure out whom I would hang out with, I got the deep sense that I needed to stay in and study. So I pulled out my Bible and began to read the Psalms and the voice that was becoming more familiar guided me to Jeremiah. I thought to myself, Jeremiah is cool, but I want to read Isaiah, and the voice led me back to Jeremiah. After going back and forth a couple of times, I realized I needed to read the book of Jeremiah. And I began to read, "Before I formed you in the womb I knew you, and before you were born I consecrated you; I appointed you a prophet to the nations . . ." At that point the voice within said, "Stop reading. I have called you to be a prophet." The image that ran through my mind made me apprehensive. It was the memory of an old black woman who stood on the 87th Street elevated train platform on a frigid winter day and who pointed at me and said, "The Lord said put on a dress or you will go to hell." After attending a church that wanted to send people to hell for not speaking in tongues as evidence of a relationship with God, for boys and girls wanting to date and experience the bodies of one another, and for wearing makeup, my teenage disrespectful response was "It's cold out here. If your Lord requires that I put on a dress, then you and your God can go to hell."

During those moments of receiving my call, I imagined having to be that woman that I so disrespected. A woman having to stand on a street corner holding in my mind a four-foot by six-foot Bible telling people they were going to hell. The image frightened me because just like my response to Mr. Rumlinski, I did not need anyone to invite me to focus on hell and block my view of a possible heaven where I would be loved. However, as soon as the image passed, I asked God, "What does it mean to be a prophet?" and the response of God was, "I will teach you."

It was customary at my church, Pilgrim Baptist, that as soon as you professed your call you began a process that ended with you selling all and being shipped to Virginia Union University (VUU), the alma mater of the pastor, Dr. Earl F. Miller. Needless to say, I did not share my call with anyone, until I was instructed to four years later. In that time, God sent women who guided me into developing spiritual integrity who taught me it was not an abomination to be a woman, or to cry in the presence of God. They taught me to embrace spiritual gifts that had in my mind been the sole property of holiness denominations. These women encouraged me to see visions and speak in tongues and believe in healing—many of the things that had become covert operations within our "respectable" black church.

There came a day, however, when I did profess my call, and shortly after that I knew that I needed to go to seminary. I knew VUU was an option but I also considered Luther Northwestern and United Seminary in the Twin Cities, for if I stayed in the Twin Cities I could continue to work full-time and go to school part-time. The decision was made however, one day as I went home to Chicago, to the very familiar place of Trinity United Church of Christ. There I sat as men and women ministered and the people responded. The voice came again and said, "You can choose to go where you want, but look around; these are the people you will minister to." I knew what that meant.

So, in the autumn of 1990, I left my engineering career and enrolled in the Master of Divinity program at Virginia Union University. There I found the best and worst. The best was being returned to an academic environment that did not devalue the power of the spirit and love as essential to scholarship. Again I found intellectual mentors committed to teaching and speaking the truth and who demanded that we inform our investments in religion with intimacy with God.

Essential to that intimacy was learning what would be the foundation for me in ministry. This lesson came in the form of serving Fifth Baptist Church as the youth minister. As with most experiences that have become valuable in my life, ministering to youth did not rate highly at first. As a matter of fact, I did not particularly like children. But as I committed to be with those youth, they taught me something about ministry for which I will always be grateful. They taught me to love. They taught me that love was the ability to see potential and that intimacy demanded participating in the fulfillment thereof without devaluing and violation.

What they taught me helped me navigate what I considered the worst or perhaps the most shocking dimension of being in seminary—my introduction into the black culture of who is to preach and who is not. For all of my life I had never had to consider what I could and could not do based on my God-given gender. In seminary, however, it seemed that day by day for three years the men in the class argued about whether women should preach while the women raised eyebrows, studied hard, and simply tried to love the brothers in spite of their attitudes concerning the validity of our calls.

The strange thing was that although the brothers were having this discussion about us, I often felt more freedom to be authentic in my call than they. As women we did not have to force-fit our reality to give ascent to images that others created for us because our presence in ministry was rarely expected. On the other hand, the men seemed burdened by an illusion of access. They wore the right suits, they practiced their whoops, they married the right women; they connected with the right churches and influential pastors, and yet, their efforts seemed frustrated. The expectations that they strove to live up to rendered them unable to fulfill the calls on their lives with integrity. Their predicament seemed similar to the recollections of ex-slaves concerning poor white people. The enslaved Africans were well aware of their condition, but upon further assessment they were glad they were not poor whites—who for all practical purposes according to superficial delineation of race should have been free but they frustratingly were less free than the enslaved Africans.

So since as a woman I was never expected to preach or pastor, it gave me the freedom to pursue what I loved: study. In lieu of serving a church, I felt called to engage in doctoral studies. I went about the process all wrong. I evaluated programs based on proximity to Philadelphia. I never researched the schools or the interests of the faculty. So, I found myself at Temple University focusing on Hebrew Bible. After submitting my first paper to the Hebrew Bible scholar, I was told I needed help with my writing. He encouraged me to go talk to Dr. Katie Cannon. At the time, I had no idea of her contributions to scholarship. Instead of proofreading my work she asked me three pivotal questions. First she asked, "What is your project?" I replied that I wanted to develop a restorative ethic of community based on the Hebrew text. She then asked, "How long do you want to be here?" I responded not long, and explained that people were dying in my community and I needed to get back as soon as possible. Finally, she asked if I thought a degree in ethics was of less value than one in Hebrew Bible. My response was that my study was not for validation or status but preparation.

From that moment Dr. Cannon helped me to fulfill the present dimension of my call by handing me a vessel called womanism. She encouraged me to be conscious of the systemic evil around me, but never paralyzed by it. She ushered me through political war zones and only demanded that I do my work. She celebrated me as I emerged committed to work for paradigms of social justice, unapologetically predicated on love and adamantly refusing violence. She, along with those who held me before, helped me to understand what it meant to be a prophet.

As I reflect on this journey, I am continually reminded that the call does not begin with the internal audible, nor is it fulfilled in isolation. But the call is continually changing and being refined. It is accountable to God and community. And God never calls us to accomplish kingdom building by ourselves. For me there have been many men and women who have walked with me and protected me on my journey. To them I am grateful. Strangely enough, I have recently become aware that I will one day have to pastor. I have never wanted that. But having at various times neither liked school nor been that fond of church, I know that my dislikes have served as thresholds to greatness and invitations to be ushered in by mentoring angels.

Sermon: *"When the Miraculous Happens"*
Luke 7:36–8:3

ALISON P. GISE JOHNSON

For many years I have bypassed this text because this woman's interpreted reality seemed incongruent with my own. What could a prostitute teach me? In fact, why does her story even have to be in the text? Don't women have to fight enough such that the whole of our reality is not sexualized into limited confines of which we can be? Don't we have enough trouble trying to convince people that we were not the initiators of the constant raping of body, mind, spirit, and potential? And here is this woman lying down, pouring oil on Jesus' feet, and wiping it so erotically with her hair. Why doesn't she get up so that the rest of us can be seen in ways that don't reduce us to prostitutes?

After many years of silent bantering, one day, it became evident that the story of this woman had much more to say than I had given it credit. Many times we miss God's way-markers of the faith because we are invested in moral tutoring that assigns value based on appearance. We spend a lot of time fighting being associated with people who our socioreligious traditions deem as compromising to our reputations. And in those moments we lose the opportunity to be mentored into a sense of the miraculous that is predicated on intimacy with God and not investments in voyeuristic observations that reduce our concern to constructing a particular image.

This understanding came as I was listening to "Alabaster Box," when CeCe Winans sings in the voice of this woman, that we don't know the cost of the oil in her alabaster box. For unexplained reasons that I can only suggest were the movement of God, I realized that oil was not payment from clients uninvested in intimacy. And letting down her hair to wipe Jesus' feet was not a sign of an erotic past, but the response of a woman who had spent much of her life paying the cost of being what everyone thought she should be. Like many of us who have lost sight of dreams in exchange for lucrative careers

in occupations we no longer love, we pay a price. She, like many of us, esti-
mated it to be less painful to be loyal to our assigned places in religious traditions in spite of the fact that our souls have desired something deeper. We
pay a price.

But there comes a time when we are aware of the fact that we are paying
too high a price, and in that moment the miraculous happens. The miraculous happens when we recognize the presence of God in human form in our
midst. And for once we do not run, or give more reverence to traditions lost
of truth or expectations limited by labels. The miraculous happens when our
desire for deliverance, a glimpse of the possible, and stamina of courage force
our legs to move and our hearts to invest in a process that is not totally known
but deeply and unexplainably desired.

This is what our sister in the text does. She recognizes the power of God
on earth. As she bows at the feet of Jesus, in overt contrast to those who
exegete her life suggesting the erotic, she recognizes that the eternal has met
with the temporal in the form of a moving altar. The bronze feet of God's altar
are in her midst, and without delay she sacrifices her all such that the possibility of transformation may occur. She pours out on to the altar her oil, a
highly sought-after commodity, a symbol of wealth.

She revalues her assets in the ways that she refuses to invest in a world economy based on subordination and exploitation. She refuses to equate the blessings of God with giving ascent to a superficial, death- and debt-dealing
delineation of prosperity that fills closets and garages while desires go unfulfilled. She revalues her wealth, not to become impoverished but to usher in a
gospel propagated and underwritten by philanthropy. She revalues her wealth.

She lets down her hair on the altar in contradiction to a tradition that has
gotten so convoluted that it has lost the power of truth. Traditions of religion
and society and even family that value allegiance to their own stagnant sense
of self more than faithfulness to the Almighty. Traditions that are invested in
their continuance more than propagating a gospel that sets the captives free
from the unmitigated violence that the world demands, violence that is physical, moral, spiritual, sexual, and intellectual. She lets down her hair on the
altar, not to throw away traditions that have formed her, but she lets down
her hair to reclaim that which has been deformed.

Traditions that leave preachers invested in pharisaic adherence to law while
unfamiliar with and afraid of living water. Traditions that have exchanged cultivating the religion of Jesus for efforts focused on developing exclusive clubs
of who gets to preach, who gets to speak in tongues, who gets to be most intellectual, who lays claim on the spiritual, and who has access to God and blessings and wealth. She lays her tradition down at the feet of the altar not to leave
it but to demand its loyalty to love, its commitment to equity, and its reliance

on righteousness. She reclaims a faith tradition that has the power to recompass her path and make straight her journey.

And in those moments when the unanticipated miraculous happens, she weeps and kisses not as a sign of weakness but in restoration of that which is essential to being human; an uninterrupted connection with the Eternal often forged through the power of emotions. It is a connection that makes us lean less on external authorities that demand the reabsorption of our tears, the dainty navigation of our rage, and distrust of the voices of ancestors who shout in still small voices trustworthy directions to the throne of God.

In the person of this woman, God invites us to participate in the miraculous.

The miracle of repentance that comes as we recognize that without question we have participated in a society that demands that we lay aside our God-given dreams. When the miraculous happens, God instigates the miracle of forgiveness by inviting us to refuse to make daily sacrifices to emotionless living and loving. When prostitution is taken from our eyes, then God points to the promises of miraculous. Wealth is not lost but revalued. Traditions are not left but reclaimed. And emotions are not devalued but restored. When the miraculous happens, we are ushered past religion into healthy relationships with ourselves, our communities, and our God.

10

Dancing to the Tune of Life

CYNTHIA L. HALE

Before I formed you in the womb I knew you, and before you were born I consecrated you; I appointed you a prophet to the nations. (*Jer. 1:5*)

My life began in Roanoke, Virginia, on October 27, 1952. I was born the oldest of four children to Harrison and Janice Hale. My parents named me Cynthia, which means "a bringer of life." Little did they know that they were naming me for my destiny. I had what some would consider a pretty normal upbringing, in a Christian home, attending church every Sunday. I love to talk about the fact that I am a good mixture of the sacred and the profane. It was my mother who was the faithful one.

My father wasn't really profane; he was a man who had a passion for life and he gave it to me. He loved to party and have a good time. My father is the one who showed me how to embrace what has become my philosophy of life, "dancing to the tune of life and not missing a beat." It was my earliest introduction to what I believe Jesus meant when he said, as recorded in John 10:10, "I came that they may have life, and have it abundantly."

It was my mother who first introduced me to the Christ. At an early age she taught me how to pray and would make sure that I attended Sunday school and church every Sunday. It wasn't until I was nine years old when a neighbor invited me to a child evangelism program that I accepted Jesus Christ as my personal Lord and Savior. I remember it as if it were only yesterday.

Every Monday afternoon, we attended a class where they taught us a Bible story and gave us a Bible verse to memorize. The Bible verse that week was

John 3:16: "For God so loved the world that he gave his only Son." The teacher, a woman named Mrs. Long, explained that God loved us and wanted to be in relationship with us. She then invited me to give my life to him. I wanted to be sure about what I was doing, and so I asked if God was anything like my Daddy. When she answered, "Yes," I then said, "I want to know him."

The first thing I did when I became a Christian was to tell everyone I could tell. I remember meeting a man in the Laundromat and asking him if he had a personal relationship with Christ. The next person I confronted was my father. When I talked to my father, he listened but was not all that impressed, especially since I told him that if he did not give his life to Christ, he was going to hell. I was a bit zealous in those days, to say the least.

Another way of looking at it is I was excited about my new life in Christ and wanted to know everything there was to know about him. I wanted to see the world saved. I became active at my school with the Bible Club. My mother and I began to study the Bible together, and before long we were hosting Bible studies in our home taught by my junior high English teacher. There was one for adults and another for teens. It was through this class that I introduced a lot of my friends to Christ. It was this class, along with the teachings from the Child Evangelism Program, that laid a solid foundation of biblical knowledge and shaped my theology of life and ministry at an early age. I still live by and teach the importance of lifestyle evangelism and loving God with all your heart, mind, and soul.

Though a faithful Christian, I enjoyed life to the fullest as a teenager, participating in every extracurricular activity available. While in school, I "majored in the minors," winning every nonacademic award the school offered, spending every weekend night at some game or party, hanging out with my friends. I studied enough to get by. I was also the resident "student pastor" on my campus, leading a Bible study before school and counseling students when they were in trouble or in pain. I had never seen or heard of a woman in ministry, so I would never say that I was in ministry or admit that I would ever be, even though the folks in my church and in the community said otherwise. I ignored them. I had no intention of being a preacher.

During my senior year of high school, I led a young man named Richard to Christ. After Richard got a few Bible verses under his belt (1 Timothy 2:11–12, in particular, where Paul says, "Let a woman learn in silence with full submission. I permit no woman to teach or to have authority over a man; she is to keep silent"), he announced to the group that I would no longer be permitted to teach Bible study. The Bible said that as a woman I could not teach or have authority over a man. I quickly reminded him that I wasn't a woman yet and he was not a man. Nevertheless, I stepped down and became Richard's student, even though I was the one who had been studying the Bible for about eight years and him only about eight weeks. Little did I realize that all of this was preparing me for many future confrontations with men, and women too, who did not believe that women should preach.

After high school, I attended Hollins College, where I majored in music. I soon learned that I was not at Hollins College by accident; it was by divine appointment. Hollins was the place where I received and answered my call. It was all a setup. In my tenth year of high school, Alvord Beardslee, the chaplain at Hollins and one of the leaders of the National Conference of Christians and Jews in the city, invited me to accompany him to an antiracism conference in Asheville, North Carolina. My parents agreed to my going, and Alvord spent the entire trip recruiting me for Hollins College.

After I enrolled at Hollins, Rev. Beardslee told me that I had the gifts and graces for ministry. I paid him no attention. But I was very interested in religion still, so I became active in the chapel program, pursuing a degree in music education.

Hollins was where I grew up. Hollins was where I faced the real world of racism and discovered that I had to be better than the best as an African American woman. It was at Hollins that I discovered that I would never make it majoring in the minors. I needed to become academically and intellectually strong—and I did. It was at Hollins that I came into my own and discovered the power of being a gifted African American woman who believed in her God and herself.

I learned that lesson in the classroom as professors helped me to develop and sharpen the tools that I needed to gain the knowledge that would catapult me into my destiny. I also learned that lesson as I struggled with low self-esteem, that caused me to be insecure and question my self-worth at every turn. I had never felt so unsure of myself before. Perhaps it was because I had never had to defend myself and my reason for being, as I had to explain every day at Hollins as an African American woman.

It was in prayer as I wrestled with God about my destiny and my demons of insecurity and low self-esteem that God made clear to me in the words of the psalmist David (Ps. 139) that "I am fearfully and wonderfully made. Wonderful are your works" and that I had to know. Furthermore, "In your book were written all the days that were formed for me, when none of them as yet existed."

I thought I was destined to be an opera singer. Music and singing were my passion. I was preparing to stand on a stage and perform. It was clear in my own mind that opera was my goal, even though the chaplain said I had the gifts and graces for ministry and the pastor of my home church, Alvin Jackson, agreed with him. In all honesty, I did feel some rumblings in my mind and heart. Already God was speaking to me. But I ignored God and everyone else.

I had good reason to ignore them. I didn't believe that women were called to preach. I had never seen a woman in ministry or heard one preach.

It was my sophomore year when Alvord Beardslee announced that he was going on sabbatical. A committee was established, of which I was a part, to choose his replacement. When a woman's name was suggested, I was vehemently opposed to it, saying no woman will ever preach to me. A year later, I received my call in an undeniable way. I knew that God was speaking to me. It was confirmed by my roommate on "100th night," a Hollins tradition where seniors dressed up as their roommate's heart's desire. I dressed up as Johnny Morrison, my roommate's boyfriend. When I saw her, she was dressed in a black ministerial robe looking like a preacher. I asked her what in the world she was doing, and she told me to be honest with myself; everyone else knew that this was my heart's desire.

I continued to struggle with this "call" thing. The first thing that I asked God was if I became a preacher whether I could still wear pink. I was a girl and I wanted to maintain my femininity. Could I preach like a woman? Would people accept me as a female preacher? The next thing I wanted to know was whether or not I could still be married and have children.

God made it clear that I could be myself as a woman, but he said nothing at all about being married and having children. There was something inside of me that knew that even though there are lots of successful female pastors and preachers who are married with children, I would not be one of them. Today, at fifty-one and celebrating twenty-five years in ministry, I am unmarried and childless and still at times wondering "Why?"

Nevertheless, I said "yes" to God and "no" to a potential husband, who I knew was not the man for me. I went to seminary at Duke and fell in love with ministry. I was surrounded by some of the most dynamic men and women in ministry, who had a heart for God and a heart for God's people. In that place, we studied and prayed, dialogued, and sharpened one another for the task of ministry.

At Duke, I settled once and for all the question of whether or not I was called to preach. Not all of the men believed that I had been called to preach and told me so on a regular basis. I must admit, the constant putdown and questions caused me to doubt the call, but I would not give up. God continually sent sweet confirmations. My father—who had thought I'd lost my mind when I told him that I was going to seminary and had claimed he would never support me—gave his life to Christ after I preached my first sermon.

I had no money to attend seminary, but I trusted that God would provide and God did, beyond my wildest imaginations. Gardner C. Taylor came to the campus to preach and invited the students to have breakfast with him. He asked us all if indeed God had called us to preach. The men replied for me, saying that I had claimed that God had called me to preach, but that God didn't call women, did he? Being the gracious man that he is, Dr. Taylor did not bother to correct the brothers; he just looked at me and said, "Miss Cynthia, did God call you to preach?" When I said, "Yes," he replied, "Then don't worry about what anyone else thinks. God never wastes his material."

I learned from that encounter that I did not need to fight or try to defend my call. I just needed to know that God had called me and would use me. My gifts would make room for me and they did.

Not long after that, John Borens, the pastor of a small Christian Methodist Episcopal church in Pittsboro, North Carolina, asked me to come to Pittsboro and work with him. This was my second time in a congregational setting serving as an associate to the senior pastor. The first time was an internship during my first summer in seminary. Both experiences helped me to see that pastoral ministry was my call, and it also became clear that I was not called to be a youth pastor, an associate, or any other staff position. I was called to be a senior pastor.

It became clear to me that I am a visionary; I am a pacesetter. I have the gift of administration and I love people. I knew that I would never make it taking orders from others and promoting their vision. I had visions of my own about how ministry should be. I wanted to pastor a church so that I could establish the kingdom of God on Earth. In these ministries, I also discovered that I am a team player and enjoyed building partnerships with others. I just need to be in charge.

As I was completing seminary, I applied to a small Disciples of Christ church whose pastor had been there for over thirty years and had died. They were interested enough to invite me to preach and to be interviewed. The interview was interesting in that they asked a lot of questions about my personal life, who I was dating and the nature of the relationships. They were trying to see if I was sexually active. I wasn't sure that this line of questioning was appropriate. I wondered if they asked these same questions of men.

They interviewed me, but they didn't hire me. They were honest with me. They didn't want a woman, even though they loved my preaching and the fact that I was seminary trained. Instead they chose a man who was a barber and was attending seminary on Saturdays. I was disappointed but not devastated, because I believed that God had other plans for me. Later, they called to say they were sorry, but it didn't matter at this point because it was clear that God had something else in mind for me. I have the uncanny ability of moving on and letting go of disappointment without harboring anger, so that I am not hindered from going to the next level. I decided early in my life that no matter what I experienced in ministry, I would not be an angry black woman.

One of my classmates invited me to preach at the federal men's prison in Butner, North Carolina. The day that I went to the prison, the head chaplain,

a Catholic priest, asked if I would take the position of protestant chaplain. I
agreed and worked there for eighteen months. When I graduated from seminary, the head chaplain resigned and I was given his position, making me the
first female to serve as chaplain in an all-male federal prison.

Being a female in an all-male prison was quite an experience. I was all things
to all men, at least in their minds: pastor, preacher, counselor, mother, sister,
and girlfriend—whatever they needed me to be. What I sought to do was to
bring a sense of balance and normalcy in a place where dysfunctionality and
human frailty were so evident. I learned in that prison about loving unconditionally, treating all persons with dignity and respect, being present with persons in their lowest and weakest hour, knowing that I represent God. I love to
say that I learned how to be a pastor in prison.

I served in the prison for five years, before being reassigned to the Federal
Law Enforcement Center in Brunswick, Georgia, as a staff instructor. The
intention of the prison administration was to transition me into an associate
warden position because of my strong gifts in administration, but I was clear
that ministry was what I was called to do.

The general minister and president of Christian Church Disciples of Christ
called to ask if I would consider being one of his deputies. My position would
include being the general secretary of the national convocation, the black fellowship of our church. There was a merger agreement that stated that the
leaders of the national convocation were to be consulted as to who they wanted
to see in that position. Dr. Humbert, without consulting them, offered me the
position. Not a good move, because at the General Assembly where he was to
be elected and his deputies confirmed, the brothers and sisters protested my
appointment, saying that I wasn't qualified to lead them. They said I was too
young. I had never served as a pastor, so how could I serve pastors? They even
went on to say in an article in the Des Moines paper that I could not pastor a
black church. I didn't have what it took.

They never said that they couldn't accept my nomination because I was a
woman. But many believe that was the real issue, despite the fact that I had
just completed a term as the youngest person and first female to serve as president of the national convocation. Needless to say, this was the most painful
and humiliating experience that I have ever had. I often refer to that as my
"Calvary experience." I felt like my colleagues had crucified me. That experience taught me the reality of church politics, racism, and sexism in the church.
I know that my brothers and sisters meant me no personal harm. They felt violated by the system. I felt violated, too.

Time healed my hurt and also helped me to see that God does indeed "work
together in all things for the good of those who love him and are called according to his good pleasure." During the time that I was being interviewed by the

General Office, I also received a call to become a pastor developer of a new church in Atlanta. In all honesty, that was not nearly as exciting to me as the deputy general ministry position, but I wasn't looking at it from God's perspective. God sees the end from the beginning and had awesome plans for me in Georgia. I instead was dealing with what appeared to be the most attractive and prosperous offer at the moment.

Starting a church was not exactly what I had in mind. I just knew that God would give me a ready-made situation. But what God gave me was an opportunity to develop a ministry that had my design and his on it. So, after Calvary came the resurrection and the ascension. I did rise again. The woman that they said could not pastor a black church became the founding pastor of the Ray of Hope Christian Church in January 1986.

The Ray began with four persons meeting for Bible study in my apartment. After seventeen years, some 7,500 persons have joined our church. We presently have an active membership of 3,500, with an average of 2,000 in worship on Sunday mornings. The world would say that we are a success. But quite frankly, I felt like we were a success the day those four persons showed up for Bible study. In two months' time, we had outgrown my apartment and so twenty-five persons moved to Wesley Chapel United Methodist Church, and then in June of 1986, eighty-five persons worshiped for the first time in the cafeteria of Columbia High School, another success.

When I started Ray of Hope, I didn't know what I was doing. God's vision and direction for this church has been revealed in a progressive way over the last seventeen years. All that was clear at the very beginning was that I was to go after young or older unchurched, unsaved persons. Ray of Hope was to be a nontraditional, cutting-edge ministry.

And that it has been. In eighteen months, our church grew to eighty members and those eighty members purchased a $650,000 building. The church grew by about one hundred members the first four years! In the fifth year of our ministry, major changes had to be made. I realized that we needed to become more intentional about who we were and what we were about. The mission needed to be more clearly defined. So we adopted a fivefold mission statement. The result of this strategic move was that the people became excited, energized, and focused on mission and ministry, and 550 persons joined our church that year.

The Ray of Hope Christian Church is a church that has been established on the biblical principles of the early church, as recorded in Acts 2. We are a "Word" church. We are also a church that believes in the power of prayer. Prayer is the reason Ray of Hope has enjoyed the successes that it has. We pray and God answers. In 2000, having outgrown our first facility, we were blessed to relocate to the former New Birth Missionary Baptist Campus, which includes a sanctuary that seats 3,300. We are also a church that focuses on the needs of persons both in the House and in the World.

Being a female senior pastor has been rewarding and challenging. There is still this question about whether or not a woman should preach and pastor a church, especially in the Bible Belt. While the persons who join the church for the most part have been tremendously supportive and respectful of my leadership, some have felt free to question my leadership. Some have questioned the decisions that I make, the posture that I take in preaching or teaching, in ways that I am clear they would never challenge a man.

I am also aware that my style of interacting with people—the fact that I am open and inviting, allowing others to freely dialogue with me, and my desire for partnership and team ministry—has opened the door to familiarity and the taking of liberties with me that they would not otherwise take with persons in position of authority. But I dare not change who I am, what makes me uniquely me. I am constantly learning to professionally distance myself and set appropriate boundaries to encourage a healthy and respectful appreciation of who I am.

My ministry has always been and continues to be one that seeks to liberate women to discover and walk into their destiny in healthy and wholesome partnership with men. I preach and teach that we are both created in God's image and likeness and called by God into relationship with him to establish the kingdom of God on Earth. In my personal and professional relationships and my style of ministry, I seek to model how this is done as a strong, confident woman who is on her way somewhere and is called to take her brothers and sisters with her.

Sermon: "Celebrated, Not Just Tolerated!"
Genesis 1:26–27

CYNTHIA L. HALE

Then God said, "Let us make humankind in our image, according to our likeness; and let them have dominion over the fish of the sea, and over the birds of the air, and over the cattle, and over all the wild animals of the earth, and over every creeping thing that creeps upon the earth."

So God created humankind in his image,
in the image of God he created them;
male and female he created them"
(Gen. 1:26–27).

I want to celebrate women. No disrespect to the men, the fathers, the brothers, the beautiful men that God created in his image and likeness. But allow me to celebrate women who, too, were created in God's image.

Women are to be celebrated for their uniqueness, their beauty, their ingenuity, and creativity. Women are to be celebrated for their sassiness, their mystique, their quiet and demure way, their boldness and brassiness. Women are to be celebrated for their companionship and their compassion, for the special way they always seem to know what you need and when you need it; for how they make sure that their loved ones are taken care of no matter what is going on in their lives. Our world can be falling apart, as women, and yet, we have enough love and strength to hold someone else's together. Women always need to be celebrated and not just tolerated.

I use the word "tolerated" in the sense that women are not taken as seriously as we should be. In what some have called the "Century of the Woman," when women are making greater strides and enjoy greater privileges than we ever have in history, we are still struggling with the ugly vestiges of sexism and gender inequality.

Though there are female bishops, pastors, and ministers scattered throughout major mainline denominations and nondenominational churches as well; though women make up 75 to 80 percent of most of our churches and provide major support for its operation, there is still this question about whether or not women should be in leadership—and in many instances they are not. There are still people who say a woman should be silent and not usurp authority over a man. A woman's place is . . .

Women are merely tolerated when given token positions but are not allowed to exercise their gifts and abilities to the fullest and speak their mind without being labeled too aggressive, too bossy, and too controlling. Women, particularly black women, are being tolerated when not only in the church but in corporate America and other settings, and though they are just as educated, experienced, and efficient as their male counterparts, they receive less compensation for the same jobs and are penalized in relationships for making more money than their spouse and significant others.

Women are being tolerated when their ideas are not taken seriously, their opinions are not respected, their proposals are pushed aside and they are not interviewed, hired, promoted first, when they are the most qualified. Women are merely tolerated when they are abused, misused, treated as objects of another's pleasure at will, raped, murdered and their bodies thrown into the ocean or stuffed into the trunk of a car because someone got tired of them and wanted to trade them in for a younger or more desirable model.

Women are tolerated or not taken seriously when as little girls they are kidnaped from their bedrooms or front yards, and can be held in captivity for months a few miles from their parents' homes and not even try to escape. Something is wrong with this picture. What are we teaching our daughters? What are we communicating to them about what they are to allow to happen to them without being indignant or defiant about it? Do we promote the idea among our girls that they cannot and should not protect themselves? That they are to be respected by everyone they come in contact with?

Young girls and older ones too are just tolerated when rappers rap about them using profanity to describe them and their body parts. Boyfriends and others can pull on them and touch them inappropriately in public or in private, talk to them any kind of way, and then expect them to go to bed with them or "be their woman." Women are merely being tolerated when their feelings are not taken seriously, when their emotions are labeled unnecessary, and all their attitudes and moods are attributed to PMS or menopause.

Women are too important to the world in general and to our lives in particular to be simply tolerated, not taken seriously and taken for granted! Women are to be celebrated every day!

Though we are in the most enlightened time in the history of the world, some of us still cling to and promote an antiquated and traditional view of women. Women are thought to be and treated as inferior and as second-class citizens both intentionally and unintentionally. Much of this can be attributed to what some would suggest is the biblical understanding of who women are created to be. I want to suggest that is a misunderstanding of what the Bible says about women and today I intend to set the record straight.

What folks don't seem to understand is that when the creation of man is told in the first chapter of Genesis, it is talking about man and woman, "male and female he created them." In the Scriptures, when we see the word "man," the Hebrew word used here is "Adam," and Adam is not just the title or name given to the man but it is used for the whole human race. The term "man," or "Adam," includes both male and female. When a distinction between the two needed to be made then "ish" was used for male human beings and "issah" is used to refer to "female human beings." So that when God said, "Let us make man in our image and likeness," he was referring to both man and woman; male and female.

While the Scriptures do not spell out what it means to be made in the image and likeness of God, the word "image" refers to being "representative of" and "likeness" talks about "being similar to." When God made humans, he made himself in human form, he took on flesh; he made a mirror image of himself. Like God, humans can think, reason, plan, distinguish right from wrong, relate to others, love, and feel.

There is also this misunderstanding of the biblical account of the creation of women, found in Genesis, chapter 2, which causes people to think that women are inferior to men. The passage in Genesis 2, where it talks about the creation of man from the dust of the ground and then God's assessment that it is not good for the man to be alone and that he will make a helper suitable for him, has led people to believe that women were created subordinate to men as their helpers.

When God said he would make a helper suitable for Adam, it is the word "helper" that folks zero in on and suggest that as "helper" women were created to be subservient to men and meet men's needs. The implication is that it is men who count and that a woman's needs are subordinate to a man's.

But the Hebrew phrase that is used here is best understood as "a helper comparable" or a helper corresponding to him. In Eve, God provides a suitable helper because she shared Adam's image and likeness of God—the image that permits men and women to relate on every dimension of personality (emotional, intellectual, spiritual, and physical). You see, only one like Eve, who like Adam shared the divine image and likeness, would be suitable. Only one who was equally intelligent, could think, reason, and had ideas of her own. Only one who had discernment, and could judge between right and wrong, good and bad, only one who could understand his feelings and moods, his joys and sorrows, his strengths and weaknesses, would be suitable.

All human beings are created in God's image and likeness; both men and women share the same essential identity. Despite some appreciable differences, men and women were created to be equal from the beginning. Men and women were created in the image and likeness of God to be able to relate to one another and to complement one another and enhance the life of one another.

In the second, more explicit account of creation, the man (ish) is formed first out of the dust of the ground and God breathed into his nostrils the breath of life and the man became a living soul. After God planted a garden in the east, in Eden, he put the man there to work it and take care of it. It was then that God noticed that something was not quite right. It was then that God said that it was not good, not good that the man should be alone and that he would make a helper suitable for him.

God made the man go to sleep, and while he was sleeping God took one of his ribs, closed up the place with flesh, and made a woman (issah). When he gave her to the man, the man said, "This is now bone of my bones and flesh of my flesh; she shall be called 'woman,' for she was taken out of man."

The man knew when he saw the woman that God had outdone himself. He had not created something ordinary but extraordinary. God had saved the best for last. Adam and the animals were all created from the dust of the ground; the woman was made, she was formed, fashioned, shaped from the living flesh of the man, his rib. When God brought the woman to the man, he said, "This is now bone of my bones and flesh of my flesh, one who shares my identity. She is everything that I am and I am everything that she is. We complement one another."

To say that woman is man's helper is correct in the sense that she complements him; she assists him. Woman is man's counterpart; the most essential to the completion to his being. What you should know is that this word "helper" is also used to talk about God and the help, the assistance, that he gives to his people. Verse 1 of Psalm 121:1–2 (KJV) says, "I will lift up mine eyes unto the hills, from whence cometh my help. My help [cometh] from the LORD." God is our helper, but we wouldn't say that he is inferior to us, would we?

Matthew Henry says,

> If man is the head, then woman is the crown, the crown of her
> Band, the crown of visible creation. The man was dust refined,
> But the woman was double refined. One further removed from
> The earth, the woman was made out of the side of Adam, not out
> Of his head to rule over him, nor out of his feet to be trampled
> Trampled upon by him, but out of his side to be equal with him,
> Under his arm to be protected and near his heart to be loved.

Women were created to be celebrated, not simply tolerated. Women have the ability to think great thoughts and make them a reality, to dream big dreams, and to make them come true.

Women contribute in significant ways to this society and this world. Despite having to contend with racism and sexism, African American women have beaten the odds to become groundbreaking pioneers in a variety of fields. Let me name a few.

Patricia Roberts Harris was appointed ambassador to Luxembourg by President Lyndon B. Johnson in 1965 and became the first black to head a U.S. Embassy. She was also the first black woman to head the School of Law at Howard University and the first black woman to be named to a presidential cabinet position, by President Jimmy Carter.

Mary McLeod Bethune was the first black woman to receive a major federal appointment when, on June 24, 1936, she was named director of the Negro division of the National Youth Administration by President Franklin D. Roosevelt.

Leontine T. C. Kelly became the first black female bishop of a major predominately white denomination when the United Methodist elected her to serve the San Francisco–area diocese.

In athletics and many other professions, black women have dazzled many with determination, desire, and dedication. During the 1948 Summer Olympics in London, Alice Coachman became the first black woman to win a gold medal. Jackie Joyner-Kersee was the first woman to win back-to-back gold medals in the intensely fierce heptathlon competition.

Rebecca Lee Crumpler became the first black woman to receive a medical degree from the New England Female Medical College in Boston. Maggie Lena Walker became the first woman bank president in 1903. Madame C. J. Walker began a black hair care products company and used its products to solidify her place in history as America's first self-made black woman millionaire, and Oprah Winfrey was listed in *Fortune* as the first black woman billionaire.

And strong, intelligent, women just keep on coming . . . discovering their destinies, living life on purpose, owning their own businesses, creating their own possibilities, making the world a better place for all of us.

Women in general and black women in particular are to be celebrated every day. The way that we celebrate women is to

Appreciate and affirm women for who they are and their achievements and contributions at every opportunity given.

Take issue with concepts and practices that relegate women to second-class citizenship or rob them of the opportunities they deserve.

Refrain from engaging in discussions or the practice of denigrating or putting women and young girls down. Do not patronize anyone who does, which means you may not be able to purchase certain rap CDs, or go to concerts, parties, or activities where women and girls will not be treated with the utmost respect.

Teach your daughters to love and respect themselves by loving and respecting them. Let them be Daddy's girls and treat them like queens so that they won't look for what they should be getting at home from some messed-up little boys trying to be men.

If you are her teacher, challenge her. If you are an employer, pay her and promote her. If you are a friend, encourage and support her, affirm and appreciate her.

11

Too Far
to Turn Back

CARLA A. JONES

It seems that here in seminary, we are often asked to introduce ourselves or to tell our story. We may find ourselves in the safe company of friends at the lunch table or in the crosshairs of critique from our somewhat distant class-mates. The context in which we tell our story certainly gives shape to the story. When in the confines of a classroom setting in which we are simply attempt-ing to break the ice with one another, the story tends to appear in its abridged format. In this setting, I feel as if I have the liberty given by the church moth-ers during testimony service when one stands to give her testimony and hears the phrase "Do speak!"

My learned strategy for dealing with discomfort is to find a way to see the humor in a situation. When asked to consider the conditions under which I embraced the ministry, I heard myself laugh out loud and ask in response, "Who said anything about embracing it?" I believe that this ministry that God has presented to me has embraced me and I am not restrained by it but feel-ing my way into it. I have found the comfortable places in this ministry, but the threshold of comfort seems to change each day. As soon as I think that I can relax and just do what I have learned to do, a still, small voice within reminds me that just when I think I've got it, that's when I will be sent the reminder that it is just out of reach and I have to rely on God to do what needs to be done.

Every day, I wonder why God did not see fit to leave me in the high school classroom where I did what I was "trained" to do. I wonder what makes God choose any of us for this grand task called ministry. Then I think about all of the people in my life who have helped me to make it through each day and each challenge that the days brought. Each of us has the challenge and the opportunity to hear a call from God. I believe that if we are willing to heed the call to live out our double mandate, "You shall love the Lord your God with all your heart, with all your soul, and with all your mind . . . and . . . you shall love your neighbor as yourself" (Matt. 22:37, 39 NKJV), then we will be able to participate in the multitudes of ministries that God presents to us on any given day.

Having grown up in a Baptist church, I have always been loved, cherished, rewarded, and punished by people who accepted a call to care for the youth of the church. I have few horror stories to tell about being shunned or turned away when I sought prayer, a listening ear, or a holy hug. This was my model for what it meant to be a Christian. My childhood church affirmed the full participation of youth in the Sunday service and the daily lived-out mission of the church. The church of my young adulthood was a loving church with an emphasis on teaching and learning the word. Second Baptist Church in Long Branch, New Jersey, has Bible study every day of the week, and every man, woman, boy, and girl can study the Word and find encouragement to live it out. The church has one pastor and several assistant ministers. Three of those, including myself, are female. This church affirmed my gifts, not as an aberration but as a part of the natural and normal ministry of the church as a whole. The two churches that shaped my Christian walk welcomed the varied gifts of both men and women of all ages. My faith was not strengthened or shaped by negative circumstances in either church, but that did not mean that tests and trials would not come.

When I arrived on the campus of Princeton Theological Seminary, I felt out of place among some of my colleagues because of the ways in which we discussed our call. Many of my African American colleagues had been called to preach at an early age. Some of them knew that they were called to pastor. Some knew that God had called them to a career in academia. All I knew was that God had called me to seminary. I was not clearly called to preach. I was certain that as a first-year seminarian, my task was to come to school, learn some valuable information from the professors, and go back home and work with the youth as I had before.

I had no exciting story of running from the call—or so I thought. What I had was a good rationale that had lulled me into a state of contentment with my work for the Lord. Some years ago in my "angry twenties," while employed as an academic advisor by the Rutgers College of Pharmacy, I often whined, complained, and railed against the inflexible administrators who seemed to have no heart for the concerns of the students. I was passionate in my struggle to fight for the rights of my students. One of my colleagues, also a Christian, explained to me that for some, their job was just a job but for me, it was my cross. He said that these situations that seemed so oppressive to me seemed to be so because this job was not a job, nor was it a career. He suggested that this was my call. This was my reasonable service to the Lord.

Well, no greater excuse was needed! This explanation allowed me to feel good about what I did and to think that I was living out God's will for my life. Little did I know that this was merely an entrance examination for the curriculum to come. I worked in higher education and then in secondary education for almost ten years. At the end of those ten years, I made some lifestyle changes that allowed—or forced—me to listen to the still, small voice that had been drowned out by my addiction to "busy-ness." Finally, I was willing to settle down and try to see if this was really what God had in store for me.

I worked with the youth in the church on weekends and during the week, I patrolled the halls of the high school as Miss Jones and "Mama Carla"—the church lady. Teaching had become my place for ministry to the unchurched children of my neighborhood. Then, it happened. I will never forget the Sunday that my pastor was preaching from the book of Jonah. I cannot remember anything that he preached, and it was as if someone had pressed the "mute" button on my remote control. I didn't hear a word that he said, but I did hear the word "seminary."

I was so disturbed by it that I looked around for my friend who worked up in the tape room with me because I thought he was playing with me—but he was not in the tape room at that moment. After service, I went home and was almost afraid to pray because I did not want to hear anymore from whomever was whispering in my ear that morning. I did, however, proceed to list all of the reasons why God would not possibly call me to do anything more than go to church, work with the youth, and represent my church when called to do so. I had not served in that church as an officer. I had no qualifications. I had not even memorized much Scripture. What in the world would God want with me?

I asked Rev. Sandra McLeod to pray with me the next time that I saw her in church. She held my hands, looked in my eyes, and told me that any time that you are called into service for the Lord, it must be of God. Satan has other job descriptions for us, and none of them includes a devoted life of service through ministry. She reassured me that I was doing the right thing by listening, questioning, and praying with others. She encouraged me and prayed with me and again, my experience with "the church" was an affirming experience.

I immediately made an appointment to talk to my pastor, Rev. Aaron N. Gibson Sr. As I remember it, during that meeting my paternal pastor—that man who had taught me so much about biblical principles and about the love of God; about the way in which such love manifests itself best in the love of one another; that loving man who took such good care of his congregation— smiled at me and said, "What took you so long?" His loving response suggested to me that I was the last to know that God was calling me to do something else in the church. He asked me to tell him the story and I did—complete with my self-imposed objections. We then launched into a conversation about choosing a seminary and planning to move forward. In hindsight, I now know that my experience of loving affirmation is not necessarily the norm among women in ministry.

As I considered my options, I knew that as the mother of a child whose father lived nearby I did not want to leave the state. The next factor was location—Drew was too close to my parents; New Brunswick Theological Seminary was too close to the life that I had lived as a student and then as an employee at Rutgers University. That left only one option in the state of New Jersey, and here I am now several years later looking back on the days when I was about to apply to Princeton Theological Seminary.

At this point in my life, I am convinced that I was called to seminary and not to preach or to pastor because it has been this life at seminary that has shown me the many obstacles that exist for women in ministry. If I had gone into the ministry without going to seminary—a common practice in many Baptist churches—I might have missed out on a great deal of the preparatory work that has come not from the classroom but from daily living.

Being a single parent in Long Branch, New Jersey, was not a big deal. Being a single parent in my home church, where people loved me and my daughter, was not a big deal. Being a single parent and living in "family" housing at Princeton became a big deal. I never knew that being an unmarried woman with a child was an obstacle. In fact, it was not an obstacle for me, but the reactions of those with uninformed definitions of "family" became the obstacle. I often found myself wondering why I felt so disconnected from some of my classmates. It wasn't until I took the time to talk to the director of professional studies that I was made aware that I had a greater responsibility than most of my fellow students.

There was no spouse to pick the baby up from day care when I had a late class. There was no spouse to sweep the floors and load the dishwasher when I needed to spend extra hours at the library. There was no alternate syllabus for those who had to read bedtime stories to their children instead of the suggested supplemental materials on reserve at the library. These were not the obstacles. My interpretation of what it meant to be successful was the obstacle. I was running myself ragged by competing with my old overachieving self and my younger classmates who had only themselves to care for. I was under the impression that my success as a person was marked by my ability to maintain stellar grades at all costs—including that of my child's happiness. I was my own biggest obstacle in that regard. Taking that pressure off of myself has allowed me to redefine what is of paramount importance in my life and to maintain that attitude as I go forward into the next phase of ministry.

Now, lest we begin to think that all obstacles are self-imposed and that all is right with the world of the black woman in ministry, let me continue to share my testimony. In addition to those who are paid to help students negotiate this journey, there are angels in place for those Gethsemane moments when we are in the garden thinking that we, like Jesus, are in one of our "nevertheless" moments. We may actually be more like the disciples who were too tired to even pray that God's will be done.

It was not until I worked at a church other than the one in which I had been nurtured that I learned some of the job hazards of being a female in ministry. I had no idea what inspired Ella Mitchell to produce the book *Those Preaching Women*. I did not know exactly why we women preachers and ministers needed to have *Daughters of Thunder* on our bookshelves or on our bedside tables. While I knew there were men who were opposed to women preachers, I did not know there were men who were so opposed that they did not have decency to sit through a worship service where a woman was preaching.

I did not know that there were men of the cloth who were so insecure in their work that they had to use the most primitive combative methods to make it clear that women just didn't belong on their turf—the pulpit. I had no idea just how insidious people could be when it came to tearing one another down personally and professionally. I was in for a rude awakening.

I had worked in many other settings where I would have been on guard against sexual harassment, but I never imagined that I would have to fight that battle in a church. I never knew just how ineffective sexual harassment policies were until I had to rely on one. I never imagined that my status as a single woman would be considered fair game in a battle for authority. Excuse my naïveté, but I thought that God had the final say in matters of authority within the church. I thought that we were to treat one another with love and respect, not as objects for review and rejection or as disposable objects of our own internalized self-hatred and insecurities.

Those of us who are from a church background that includes testimony service will probably agree that there is value in telling of the goodness of the Lord. But the time comes when we must tell the story as it unfolds and not after all is said and done. One huge obstacle to my ministry was the sense that there was no one to help me out of this particular situation because no one seemed to listen. If the man who had been grossly inappropriate was supposed to be a man of God, then how was I supposed to pray? Who was supposed to pray with me? What was I to make of the fact that when I told one woman, she said that it was just one of those things that men do.

When I told my male friends, they agreed that it was inappropriate, but that didn't bring me closer to the healing that I expected to find. When I went to the designated campus resource, my reluctance to quickly and clearly name

the experience as sexual harassment—for fear of being wrong—left me in the
bind of having to honor a covenant agreement. I wondered why God would
do this to me in the midst of my studies, my loneliness, my difficulties with a
highly intellectual and attention-starved four-year-old girl. What was I supposed to say in my prayer? How was I supposed to help broken people find the
loving strength of a God who had left me in this position? How do we minister in the midst of mess?

Finally, God showed me that sometimes, even those of us who are called
have to think differently and pray fervently—not fretfully. God had put the
right people in my life and had also led me to a course on womanist/feminist
theology that gave me the vocabulary and a framework for dealing with the
situation. It gave me new words to utter in prayer. Those prayers gave me the
strength to stop meddling in God's business and await the angel of mercy. I
hate to sound like such a Baptist, but did not our God send both Goodness
and Mercy? Not only did I find support and solace in a sister who worked at
Princeton University, but she helped me to be strong enough to approach a
seminary faculty member who graciously acknowledged the situation as sexual harassment without making me vomit up all of the details of these events.

This pair of professionals not only listened to me, but helped to nurse me
back to some semblance of a state of mind out of which I could at least keep
my head above water long enough to make it through this trying time. Their
prayers, e-mails, and smiles were what I needed, but success came with the support to make the system work for me. The covenant agreement was dissolved
and I was given time to recover, while maintaining a course load that would
permit me to graduate on time. And yes, for that, we give God the praise!

I have been asked to address the manner in which I am and have been able
to persevere in the face of obstacles and challenges encountered by women
called to a way of life traditionally dominated by males. I wonder how we can
continue to look at our churches and describe them as male dominated. It
seems to me that women have always been important to the life and survival
of our churches. Yes, it is clear that most of the positions of pastor are filled by
men, but who are their secretaries? Who are their Sunday school teachers and
youth program workers? Who cleans and cooks the chicken after service and
for the funerals? God has called all of us—men, women, and children—to be
the church. So, perhaps we need to look at the church differently and recon-
sider what we mean when we say that the field is dominated by males.

Despite the statistics that might point to ministry or the pastorate as a male-
dominated field, I see myself not as an underprivileged minority but as a part
of a legacy of church folk who have had to fight to build what we have—
whether it be schools, churches, leadership positions, and so forth. Would I
ever make that statement in a vacuum and lead those women who are coming

into church leadership to believe that responding to the call is a cakewalk? Absolutely not. I would also not allow my sisters (or my brothers) simply to look at this situation from one limited viewpoint.

Although God has called all of us, it may seem that some of us are privileged in that call. It seems that male mentors are more plentiful because they tend to have a somewhat privileged experience that leaves time for mentoring. Some of my female colleagues and I agree that the demands placed on us make it difficult for us to be available to one another in the ways that we would like to be. So, either we accept the people who help us along the way—regardless of age, experience, and gender—or we operate out of the anger and frustration that accompanies this often lonely life.

I am certain that as this journey continues, I will run into new and more fortified obstacles, but I have to hold fast to the belief that even when I'm not, God is still able. I would not trade the mixed blessing of being a female in ministry in the black church for the illusion of ease that categorizes the male domination of the field. Yes, God called me, and yes, God made me a woman and she is good (even if I don't always believe it)! I thank God for making me the woman that I am, and I thank God for the people who have held out their hands as we climbed the rough side of the mountain. I thank God for those who stop to ask the question "What is it like to be a woman in a male-dominated field?" Most important, I thank God for the people who stop to listen for the answer to that question and who continue to raise questions and potentially eliminate the need for the question.

Sermon: *"Forgiven"*
Luke 23:32–35

CARLA A. JONES

Come with me, walk into this story with me and hear the Word of God. Look around . . . off in the distance . . . sniff . . . wrinkle face. . . . That smell! That smell! My God! It smells like centuries of decay. And that wind on this hill just blows that smell. It's so hot up here. I can't escape it.

It is as if these stones, my God, these stones that I'm standing on just hold in the heat. It is so hot! It feels like death! It even looks like death. No grass, no life, just dirt and these stones and that cross and this crowd. Those soldiers who mocked him. I saw that one slap him. Those women—they keep crying out to him. Oh my God, that must be his mother.

My mouth is so dry . . . I wish I could just cry . . . it's too hot and dry . . . there's no room for life . . . only death. All I can do is stand here and look and see him. As horrible as this sight is, all I can do is look at him.

Hanging . . . exposed . . . naked . . . stripped of his clothes . . . nailed to the cross. I was there, I heard the sound of his bones being crushed when they drove those nails into his hands and feet. I heard it! I heard it! All I can do is see him. I see the sweat. I see his tears. I see his tears and I can't even cry. Oh my God, I see him looking at me! It is as if there is no one here but us. He sees me. I thought I saw him, but I saw him looking at me. I thought I saw him but I saw myself stretched out . . . stretched out in front of an angry crowd . . . naked . . . exposed . . . abused . . . embarrassed . . . labeled. They labeled him "King of the Jews." This is a shameful death but how does he hold his head high enough to see me . . . to look at me while I too see myself.

My God! I remember! I remember!

I remember—oh God, the stones,

I remember that house . . .

I remember that mob . . . that mob that took me out into the street, dragging me over those same stones that they would use to stone me . . .

I remember . . . being betrayed by the one closest to me . . .

I should have died that day . . . the day the crowd cried "stone her . . . stone her . . . that nasty woman!

"We caught her in the very act! She is guilty! Now, stone her!" They tossed me at his feet and accused me of adultery. Claimed that they caught *me* in the act—funny, they only caught *me* in the act . . . they didn't *catch* me . . . they *used* me. They wanted to use me to trap and trick him. They saw an opportunity to dispose of me and atone for their own sins—because they didn't hate me, they hated the way that they felt toward me in their own hearts. They challenged him with the law of Moses, saying, "Teacher, the law commands that she be stoned. What do you say???"

Then he did a peculiar thing. He merely bent down and stirred up the dirt next to me. . . . I was terrified. . . . I was trembling in a ball at his feet awaiting the sting of the first stone and he stood up and said, "He who is without sin among you, let him throw a stone at her first." *First?* That surely means that there would be another and then another and finally so many stones that my life would be extinguished!

Merciful God! I could only cower there in fear and pray for my life, and as he bent down for a second time, I trembled even harder, for fear that he would pick up that first stone, but he never did. I didn't even know that this man *was* without sin and *could* have thrown the first stone. He simply bent down again . . . and I heard in one ear the sound of his finger stirring up the dirt again.

In my other ear, I heard the sound of sand and small stones crunching under the sandals of those who had to turn and walk away convicted in their own hearts by this Teacher. I heard the footsteps of the elders accompanied by the thud of their walking sticks. I heard the quicker steps of the younger men turning in great haste, none wanting to be the last to leave.

Finally, we were all alone and he looked me in the eye—like he is doing right now—and asked, "Woman, where are your accusers? Has no one condemned you?"

I could barely answer him, and I whispered, "No one, Lord," but I remember my fear as I awaited his response. I was guilty and he could have condemned me. I will never forget what he said to me: "Neither do I condemn you. Go and sin no more." He knew that I was guilty, but he *saved* me that day.

Can't you see it?

They labeled me an adulteress when it was convenient (but I really was).

They labeled him "King of the Jews" when it was convenient (but he really was).

The crowd condemned me and they were ready to kill me, but he saved me.

Pilate did not condemn him—I heard him! He said, "In him I find no fault" but even the great Pilate couldn't save him.

I was guilty and now I am alive.

He was innocent and here he is dying my death.

That mob wanted to use me for evil, but merciful God, you meant it for good.

This crowd meant this crucifixion for evil. They thought they could destroy him, but you, merciful God, have a good plan!

They tried to use me for atonement, but I wasn't fit to atone for their sins! (Who ever heard of a sinner being fit to atone for another sinner's sins?)

He is my atonement . . . I see myself in his eyes.

We were both accused, naked, alone, and brought before a crowd, bruised for someone else's transgressions!

I was in fear, praying for my own life.

Here he is on this cross and prays for their lives, saying,

"Father, forgive them, for they know not what they do."

"Father, forgive them for they do not know what they do."

Merciful father, allow me to pray with him, "Father, forgive my accusers, for they do not know that what they do only condemns them of their own sins."

Father, forgive them even now as they attempt to murder this man who saved me and committed no sin.

Father, forgive them when they unknowingly sacrifice their own children for fear of having to atone for their own sins.

Father, forgive them when they misuse women to atone for their own sins and self-hatred.

Father, forgive them when they presume that their title entitles them to certain liberties to which they were never entitled.

Father, forgive them when love doesn't bring them home at night.

Father, forgive them when they hate people for the color of their skin instead of loving them for the content of their character.

Father, forgive them when they oppress people into the grounds of despair like they pressed that crown of thorns into his head.

Father, forgive them when they identify the enemy as the man or woman on the television screen, or the front page of the paper instead of as the man or woman in the mirror.

Father, forgive them.

Father, forgive them.

Father, forgive . . . forgive . . . forgive us!

Father, forgive us when we forget that *we are them*!

Father, forgive us when we *think* that we know exactly what we are doing and, in our wisdom, we become foolish.

Father, forgive us when we forget to let the ones who look, sound, or smell a little different from us come into this house and gather in your name to worship you!

And finally, Father, forgive us when we forget to pray the prayer that you taught us to pray, saying forgive us our trespasses as we forgive those who trespass against us.

12

Laughing and Dancing with God

CHERYL A. KIRK-DUGGAN

This Little light of mine
Jesus calls me to shine
Shine mightily
As the breath and love of God
Illumine my heart, my soul
My joy, my hope, my all.

This little light
Is the light of God
Incarnated in me
Spoken forth in Genesis
Where God pronounced us good.
So these lights of God
Shine forth, radiant
Glorifying God on earth and in heaven
As we dance and laugh with God.

This God sits and looks
High and low,
Is a God:
Of prayer and play
Of mystery and majesty
Of sex and sensuality
Of life and vitality:

A God who cares about me
And that care is the gift
Of that God shining through you and me.

Some form of ministry has always been a part of my life experience. My parents were deeply involved in church life even before I was born. The thought of ministry as a vocation for myself, however, was nowhere on my radar screen. I thought I could simply let my light shine for God through music and leadership in the Christian Methodist Episcopal Church—a church of predominantly African American persons founded in the Wesleyan tradition. I had several family members who were ministers and preachers of the Christian gospel. My dad was everything I thought a minister should be. He loved God and people and served his community tirelessly.

My mother supported him and his work and was totally committed to her work in her church and her community. Neither of them was formally ordained; thus ordination as an option for me never entered my mind. In fact, the first time God called me to the ministry I ignored God's command and I told God if this were a true call God would have to call me again. In this entire ordeal God has had the last laugh because when all was said and done, I did indeed accept God's call to ministry.

This chapter explores the dynamics of my ministerial journey, one which I describe as laughing and dancing with God. I reflect on my two ministerial call experiences: the ecclesial environment of the Christian Methodist Episcopal (CME) Church which shaped me, and the Presbyterian seminary that nurtured me. I examine the ministries that God has called me to pursue, and provide some analysis of how I have worked to achieve these goals. My homiletical example is a funeral sermon based on the twenty-first chapter of Genesis.

MY FIRST CALL EXPERIENCE

My first call to ministry came while I was pursuing an operatic career in New York City. I was jogging in a park near the Hudson River when I sensed the presence of God in a most unusual manner. Not ready to go from being a concert diva to being a divinity student, I discounted the experience, thinking I was delusional because I was just coming off an extended fast. Wanting to be sure about what I thought was happening to me, I told God that if God wanted me in ministry, God would have to give me a clear sign that it was indeed God calling. I then promptly put the whole experience out of my mind. After that encounter I ceased to ponder God's initial call to me. My life soon changed, however, and these changes were significant because a persistent God used my husband to reveal my second call experience.

After a brief courtship, I married a wonderful man named Mike Duggan. He told me of his love for me on his birthday and proposed to me the next evening. After three months of demurring, I finally said "yes" from Germany while on a concert tour. Not only has he become my life partner, but he has also been crucial to my ministerial call. He has been a willing vehicle for God's work through me. After our honeymoon, I moved back to New York and Mike returned to Texas, but it soon became clear to us that a commuter marriage simply would not work. After my last audition in New York, I joined Mike in Texas.

NEW DISCOVERIES IN TEXAS

I had lived in Austin while pursuing a Master of Music degree at the University of Texas, but I had not been able to find a CME church. So on my return to Austin I decided to attend mass with my husband, a lifelong practicing Roman Catholic. While it was nice to worship with him, being the thoughtful and insightful man that he is, Mike said to me, "You know, we really need to find a church of your denomination that would feed you and serve your needs."

We attended an African Methodist Episcopal (AME) Church the following Sunday. While reading the announcements in the church bulletin, I discovered that there was a CME church nearby. When visitors were acknowledged, Mike and I stood up and gave brief statements about our religious affiliations. And much to my surprise I learned after service that morning that the pastor of the CME church was also in the congregation that morning.

At the coffee hour a gentleman came up to me and asked, "Did I hear someone say they were CME?" I said, "Yes, I am." He said, "Well, I'm Rev. Cox, the pastor of Trinity CME Church." He gave us the address, and we promised him that we would be there the following Sunday. The following Sunday turned out to be Super Bowl Sunday, but the upset that day did not have to do with who won and who lost, but rather the major change that came to my life as a result of my second call experience.

MY SECOND CALL

We arrived at Trinity CME Church on Super Bowl Sunday, 1984, along with approximately thirty other people who were attending this mission congregation. We entered a little after 11:00 a.m., and the church service had not started. Since most African American Protestant churches services begin at 10:45 or 11:00 a.m. I finally asked one of the congregants, "Excuse me, why hasn't church started?" She said, "The preacher isn't here. He has car trouble, and is coming from San Antonio." Minutes later one of the parishioners said, "I guess we won't have church today." I stood up and said, "Of course we will. Wherever two or three are gathered together in God's name, we can have church."

I went forward and took charge, because although I did not know the congregants, I did know the CME order of service by memory. While we were going through the hymns, Scriptures, and the responsive readings, I was trying to thumb through the Bible to find the Scripture that states "God will never forsake you," for a Sunday morning service without a preacher evoked in me a sense of forsakenness. Looking in Isaiah, I could not find this passage because it was actually Deuteronomy 4:31.

Not to be outdone, I reasoned that everyone knew the Twenty-third Psalm so I selected it for my text and did an extemporaneous sermon on "The Lord Is My Shepherd." In the course of the sermon, I mentioned my earlier "call experience." We completed the service and people said that the sermon was wonderful and inspiring. I thanked them and said we would see them the following week.

Driving off, with Mike at the steering wheel, the revelation about what had just happened took place. Mike has this incredible sense of humor and loves to be cryptic. He said, "It all makes sense why a person as brilliant and as talented as you are did not have a vocal career in New York City." I was thinking that I did not have the vocal career I wanted because I left too soon; it takes about ten years to have a moderately successful career. I then said to Mike, "Would you please speak English?" Be careful what you ask for, because in that moment his answer changed the whole course of my life—of our lives together. Mike said, "Maybe you do have a call to ministry." I felt like three Mack trucks had just rolled over me and parked on my solar plexus (stomach). My jaws dropped and locked. I knew then that God had indeed called me, but denial continued to grip me like a corset. Mike laughed and said, "Aren't you glad you aren't driving?"

MY RESPONSE AND GOD'S REPLY

Stunned, I again wanted to disavow this twice-repeated revelation, so I phoned my mother when we returned home. She replied, "Darling, it's not something I would wish on you but it does run in the family." Dissatisfied, I phoned three trusted friends who knew me well, hoping they would help me to deny my call. Everyone was home and no one was surprised. I was the only one who was upset.

On the following Monday, still in denial, I immersed myself in exercise classes, phone calls, and housework. Prior to this newest call experience I had not decided what I was going to do now that I was a "big girl" back in Texas. Finally on the Tuesday before Mike left for his office at the University of Texas, I asked him to pray with me about this "thing" that was weighing so heavily on me. He prayed with me. After he left I realized that I still did not have peace. Getting a little perturbed, I said "Look, God, if you're calling me to ministry I want to know and I want to know now. No more waiting."

Only once before had I demanded such an immediate answer from God. It was when I was in Cologne, West Germany, asking God if I should marry Mike. God answered that time through a physical sensation like electricity that moved from the top of my head throughout my body—a powerful way to give a positive answer to a covenantal marriage. For us, our marriage is a call by God.

The reply to my question about this call experience was a verbal answer tinged with laughter. God said, "You already know the answer, why are you asking me again?" I asked, "What about my music?" I had been connected with music since I sang my first solo in church at age four. So to me, music was clearly my ministry. God said, "Your careers will be parallel." I asked, "When? How?" God said, "You've got to wait, I am not on your chronometer!" I phoned Mike at the office and he said, "Great, we've got to get you some education." That was the most brilliant thing he could have ever said because I shudder at where I would be and how I would do ministry had I not had seminary training.

SEMINARY BECKONS

After accepting my "second" call to ministry, I thumbed through the yellow pages and looked under "theological education," where I found listings for Austin Presbyterian Theological Seminary (APTS) and the Episcopal Seminary of the Southwest. I phoned both schools and shared with them my call experience. Both were gracious and promised to send me a catalog in the mail. Both catalogs arrived in the mail the next day. God was moving quickly. Wednesday evening I read the catalogs cover to cover and decided that I should attend the Presbyterian seminary because they required the study of Greek for the New Testament and Hebrew for the Hebrew Bible. Thursday I phoned APTS and expressed my interest in their program of study. The admissions clerk asked if I could come for an interview the next day.

Mike and I spoke with Ann Hoch, the admissions director, and told her about our courtship and year-old marriage, and also about my call experience. Joyfully she said, "Great, when can you start?" I did not want to begin at midterm or in the summer just in case God and I had to renegotiate some things. Before I could say September, Ann informed me that classes would begin the following Monday. I was stunned, because I did not know that seminaries had a January term.

Both she and Mike were smiling and I said, "Excuse me, this is my life we're talking about."

Before I could collect myself, Ann said "Don't worry about it, you can take up to a hundred hours without declaring if you want to get a degree or not." The next thing I knew, I was registered for two courses as a part-time student. Over the weekend I was really confused. I went back and forth contrasting my thoughts about the differences between a seminary and a monastery. Did I need to wear anything special, navy blue or black cassock? Needless to say, the Austin Seminary community was stimulating and interesting.

In the fall of 1984 I began as a full-time student. The following summer I was grieving my dad's death while taking intensive Greek. That was one of the times when I embraced my dad's mantra, "God provides." Mike and I also moved into seminary housing and began building community. These were often trying times because I began to have painful difficulty with my eyes. I learned that my prayers could help me, but ultimately God worked through a phenomenal ophthalmologist, Dr. George Thorne. With keratoconus or cone-shaped corneas, I was legally blind. Dr. Thorne and Mike were my rocks of Gibraltar. Between their love and support, and Dr. Thorne's expertise, I see well today with two cornea transplants in 1986 and 1987.

I rallied through Greek and Hebrew, and the other required and elective courses in Bible, the Reformed tradition, theology, philosophy, ethics, pastoral care, church history, Christian education, mission, and worship. My seminary career included several concerts, when Mother and my sister Dedurie came to support me, as well as a travel seminar to Central America; and it concluded with senior seminar and my senior sermon on Zaccheaus, Luke 19.

Austin was a wonderful experience for us. I learned a great deal and made the transition from diva to divinity student pretty quickly. I made many new friends and have remained close to several professors.

ORDINATION PROCESS

During the spring and summer of 1984, I began the CME denominational process toward ordination. I preached my trial sermon and received my local preacher's license by a vote of the church conference. My name was presented to the quarterly conference to be "admitted on trial." Rev. Cox presented me with my black clergy robe just before our annual conference session in Houston.

My name was submitted during the business session on ministerial concerns and subsequently I was ordained a deacon. Bishop C. D. Coleman, the presiding prelate for the Eighth Episcopal District (Texas), wanted me to have some authority to do ministry at Trinity in Austin. Thus I was granted a special dispensation called the "missionary rule." Usually it takes at least two years from the time of being admitted on trial before one is ordained a deacon. I received my second ordination, as an elder, in 1986 and was admitted to "full connection" in 1987. I now can pastor anywhere a bishop appoints me in the CME connectional church, in the United States and Africa. I have been an associate pastor in Austin, Texas; Durham, North Carolina; and now Berkeley, California.

SHIFTING GOALS

During my second or middler year, I realized that my call was not to parish ministry but to the ministry of training pastors and teachers, so I needed to get a PhD With Mike situated in Austin, I wanted to be near him, because my marriage was important to me.

As God would have it, I began my PhD studies at Baylor University in the fall of 1987. I was able to manage with scholarships and assistantships, and also much-needed assistance from the Fund for Theological Education. My degree is in religious studies with a focus on theology and ethics. I had other intense study in Bible, philosophy, and music. This was not a time of bliss and I had to face many challenges.

In addition to the institutional realities of having no women on the doctoral faculty of the religion department, unconscious institutional racism, sexism, and illness seemed never to be far away. Mike had to have surgery and could have died in 1988. A student colleague had to have major surgery in the summer of 1989. My mother was diagnosed with leukemia in June and died in October of 1989. My father had died six months after Mike and I were married in 1983. At that point, I asked God "to cut me some slack!" I had no more spiritual and emotional reserves. If anyone else died or became seriously ill before I completed my program I was not going to finish. No one else got sick or died at that point. Many months later, as I neared the end of writing my dissertation, one friend who was part of our interfaith prayer group died. That prayer group was, and remains, such a source of strength and support. Praying in the anointing of the Holy Spirit, with Bible study, music, and sharing resulted in great healing, joy, and peace.

Shortly thereafter, I graduated in December of 1992 with my dissertation entitled, "Theodicy and the Redacted African American Spirituals of the 1960s Civil Rights Movement." Called to serve in the Academy, we moved to North Carolina in fall 1993.

MY CALL TO PARTICULAR MINISTRIES
MEREDITH

My academic ministry in religious studies began in the department of religion at Meredith College in Raleigh, North Carolina. I taught courses in Bible, theology, ethics, and religion and culture. Meredith is an all women, Southern Baptist, liberal arts college affiliated with the Raleigh Consortium of Colleges. There I learned a lot about matters of concern to young women in a primarily undergraduate, parochial setting. Mike retired the year we moved to North Carolina.

We lived in Durham and I commuted the forty-mile trip daily to Raleigh. In late spring of 1996 I received a phone call recruiting me to become the first full-time director of the Center for Women and Religion at the Graduate Theological Union (GTU) in Berkeley. Now my ministry was about to shift from a liberal arts setting to a consortial setting of nine member seminaries, research centers, interfaith conversations, and master's and doctoral degree programs, requiring administrative and pedagogical skills. Each step of my ministry has involved a call to excellence; a call to a new and even more demanding context.

GRADUATE THEOLOGICAL UNION (GTU)

The Rev. Lori Pistor phoned me and asked if I would be the Christian voice in an interfaith service with Muslims, Bahais, and Jews in the spring of 1996. The other three faiths were represented by men and they wanted at least one woman. Although my plate was full, I consented and decided to play the professorial role. I spoke about the four different faiths, their prophets, origins, sacred texts, and their primary principles. Lori was good friends with the then president of the GTU, Dr. Glenn Bucher. Lori suggested that Glenn phone me. Realizing it was time for me to leave Meredith, we began the interview process. This position was largely an administrative one, new terrain for me. After an initial interview in Durham with the GTU president, I later flew to Berkeley for an on-campus interview.

During the time I was contemplating the move to California, I was also a visiting Coolidge Scholar with the ARIL (Association for Religion & Intellectual Life) Summer Colloquium, Yale University, New Haven, Connecticut. The program involved four weeks dedicated to a research project and a commitment to attend a religious service every day. My research project focused on women in gangs and women in sororities. One day I was asked to lead a walking meditation for our last contemplative time together that summer, so we walked up to the Memorial Gardens at Yale and meditated under a weep-ing birch tree. At the end of the thirty minutes I wanted to sing something rather than say "time's up," but of the several thousand tunes I knew, I could not think of a single one.

I thought, "God, this is not funny, I need a tune." God sent me the song with the chorus: "I'll go, I'll go, if the Lord wants somebody, here am I, send me, send me." As we were walking down this hill, I remarked, "You know, Jesus did a lot of meditating on hills." Then I "got it," and I laughed. The GTU is located on what is called "Holy Hill" in the center of Berkeley. Only my God would answer me through a song in a way that I could not deny. This was an affirmative answer to go to California and direct the center. This song was only sung when the bishop read ministerial appointments at the Annual Conference when I was a little girl. Thus, God called me to the GTU. After completing my work at Meredith and culminating that experience by helping to create a program that honored civil rights leaders from the 1960s, many of whom had not been recognized for thirty years, through song, poetry, dance, and proclamation, I began the post at the GTU in February 1997.

As director of the Center for Women and Religion, and in residence and core doctoral faculty member, I have had the opportunity to work with and witness monumental conferences, superb presentations, and tremendous interfaith dialogues between various schools, faiths, and community- and church-based organizations. I have sat on dissertation, theses, and faculty working committees. While at this post, I have also been an associate pastor at Phillips Temple CME Church, Berkeley, where I serve as pastoral support and work with womens' ministries and other departments in the church. This ministry has been foundational to my ministry where I laugh and dance with God.

A MINISTRY OF THE PEN, PULPIT, AND PODIUM

I wrote my first book, *African American Special Days: 15 Complete Worship Services*, (Abingdon) in 1996, and coauthored a book of poetry, *It's in the Blood: A Trilogy of Poetry Harvested from a Family Tree*, with my sister Dedurie and my cousin Alice Kirk Blackburn, in 1997. *Exorcising Evil: A Womanist Perspective on the Spirituals* (1997) is a rewrite of my doctoral dissertation. My other books include *Refiner's Fire: A Religious Engagement of Violence*, (Augsburg/Fortress, 2000), *The Undivided Soul: Helping Congregations Connect Body & Spirit* (Abingdon, 2001), *Misbegotten Anguish: A Theology and Ethics of Violence* (Chalice Press, 2001), *Soul Pearls: Worship Resources for the African American Congregation* (Abingdon, 2003), *Welcome Speeches* (Abingdon, 2003), and *Mary Had a Baby: Advent Study on the Spirituals* (Abingdon, 2003). God has blessed me to write countless articles, and to do numerous sermons, presentations, and special lectures in the academy and the church.

Writing and research concern my ministries of letters and thought. Research is a spiritual exercise where my mind and soul meld as one. Writing, as laughing and dancing with God, is a privilege, a joyous gift. I have edited several volumes of the *Journal for Women and Religion*, published by the Center, and am an associate editor for *Semeia: An Experimental Journal for Biblical Criticism*. My first volume, *Pregnant Passion: Sex, Gender, and Violence in the Bible*, is in press due out soon. My essay in *Pregnant Passion* is a comparative work on Othello and David. The other form of writing that is part of my called life is that of preaching.

TOWARD A TWENTY-FIRST CENTURY MINISTRY

Throughout my life, I have always listened for the leading of God, for directions where I am to "let my light shine," for the glory of God. The work of ministry as service has been an intimate part of my life, beginning at age four, when I sang my first solo. The steps I have taken usually have begun with a question as a way to begin discernment: "God, what are you calling me to?"; "What is your will for me?"; and "Please give me the power to do your will for me." The discernment process involves prayer and meditation and taking consul with trusted family and friends. I have always been blessed to have those with the patience and grace to walk with me through my various opportunities and challenges in life.

One phase of the discernment process involves writing down the pros and cons regarding the particular decision, doing research, and taking into consideration the wise counsel of others. Often I look for a sign or an indication of where God is leading me to go and the path God has chosen for me. Once a decision is made, I then set out to embrace the particular task of ministry with gusto. I study, prepare, then set up schedules to follow. I have also learned to delegate and let others join me in the process of attaining particular goals. The conferences and journals that I have been a part of have met the markers of excellence because of the deep levels of camaraderie, support, and shared participation.

Most recently, I have asked the ultimate question of wholeness. What is the purpose of a particular task or invitation to serve in my ministry and my life? Can I make a meaningful contribution? Will I grow through participating in such an activity or event? Will this event/opportunity be detrimental in any way? Is this how God would have me spend my time, creativity, and energy given to me by God? Is this truly God's will for me, or is it my will for God?

When I can say, "All is well with my soul," in the midst of and at the completion of a particular phase of ministry, then I know I am on the right track.

Epilogue

Preaching, pastoring, pedagogy, philosophy, and penning multiple *magnum opii* were not the categories dancing about in my dreams of what I would do when I was a young child. In my youthful imagination, I knew I would be a performer, an operatic singer. I was born to be a musician—that was my ministry, or so I thought. Incredibly supportive parents, a devoted husband, and extended and church families have nurtured and supported me every step of the way, in leadership and life preparing me for what has become my call to various ministries. Their love and support and my trust in God allowed me to be valedictorian of my high school graduating class, to pursue a double major in voice and piano performance in college, and to complete two master's degrees and a PhD. Throughout my life, the place from which I have proclaimed "Thus says the Lord" has been the concert stage, the classroom, the pulpit, and on bookshelves. When God first called me to ministry, I said, "No!" Today, I say, "Yes, Yes, Yes!" Wherever I go, I thank God for the opportunity to let the divine light of the universe shine through my thoughts and deeds: "To God be the glory!"

The Sermon

The sermon that follows is a funeral sermon. I wrestled with the Holy Spirit in discerning how to minister to family and friends when the life of a young man was snuffed out as he lay in prison. God calls me to radical, revolutionary acts and places. For this call and this ministry I am grateful. For the early care, encouragement, and love, for my life itself, I give thanks to my many families. For walking with me through numerous challenges and joy, and for being the witness to my preaching, pastoral, and professorial, call, I give my deepest heartfelt thanks to my beloved husband, Mike.

Sermon: "From the Wilderness to the Light"
Genesis 21:14–20

CHERYL A. KIRK-DUGGAN

Thesis: In the wilderness of the desert, in the depths of the valley, on the mountaintops with eagles, all there is, is the love of God; that love is relational.

INTRODUCTION

In his classic funeral sermon, "Go Down, Death," James Weldon Johnson begins:

> Weep not, weep not
> She is not dead;
> . . . . . .
> She's only just gone home.

THE SETTING

Kelly might also want us to know, heartbroken mother, weep no more; grief-stricken sister, weep no more; left-lonesome friends, weep no more; I've only just gone home. Yet life and death are a paradox; it is not so simple, for Kelly's death was not a simple death, one of natural causes. Kelly's life was not a simple life. He was a noble spirit with a zest for life, one who loved to play, and was an athlete par excellence. Here I depart from Johnson, as I say make room for your tears, though we know Kelly will suffer no more. Take the time to grieve, and as you grieve honor the good times. Remember Kelly in your heart. At the same time we recognize that the funeral and eulogy honors the deceased, and is primarily to give a good word to family and friends.

As I wrestled with what biblical text to preach from, I needed to put aside myself and listen to the Holy Spirit; for I too, am an extended part of this family. Particularly I love Faye as a true, soul sister and Hope like a favorite niece. I never met Kelly face to face, but I knew Kelly through his mother and sister. Over this last week I wondered, Lord, what would you have me say? Where I began to look in the Bible was not what came from on high. What came is what is most appropriate, a lesson from the book of beginnings, of Genesis. When we romanticize, we think that there has never been a time as bad as this, and surely in the good old days, life was better. We can know that life was simpler in many ways and more complex in others. We now live longer and have better living conditions, and there are more people. With more people, there is more chance for pain and suffering. Families have always been complex and complicated. Families have always been the center of greatest love and greatest pain. As you look into your heart today, you know where you stood in Kelly's life, if you were there for him, or if not. If you loved or injured him. This is an opportunity for us to celebrate the love and name the pain, so that all guilt and shame may be placed on the altar and those who remain on this side of Jordan can make confession, can know the need to ask for forgiveness, and can experience healing. In the wilderness of the desert, in the depths of the valley, on the mountaintops with eagles, all there is, is the love of God, of love in relation, the hallmark for all healthy relationships.

NAMING AND LOVING

First, the Hagar who named God,
is the Hagar who loved her boy-child.

Hagar had fled to the wilderness, to the desert after she and Sarai, Abram's wife, could not get along. There Hagar encountered an angel of the Lord. The angel of the Lord told Hagar to go back and submit to Sarai, to go back; that she was pregnant and that her son would meet with hostility. Moved by this encounter, Hagar gave the name of El Roi to the Lord who spoke to her: "You are the God who sees me." I have now seen the One who sees me. How amazing is it to see God, to know God. To know God is to know ourselves; to be embraced by love and light. As stated in John's Gospel, to know from the beginnings of the world was the Word, and the Word was with God, and the Word was God. From the beginnings were families, and families are the places where we have to face our greatest and worst selves. Families can stand, however, when love abounds. God created us out of love. Kelly was born to be loved. Hagar, who God loved, named her boy Ishmael. How many of you love your boy children? How many of you who are men love the boys within you? In the wilderness of the desert, in the depths of the valley, on the mountaintops with eagles, all there is, is the love of God, of love in relation; the hallmark for all healthy relationships.

THE QUESTION OF FORSAKENNESS

Second, since God never forsakes Hagar,
God will never forsake you.

How did Hagar feel out there in the desert, told to go back to being in a household where she would be disrespected? What kind of love for her boy and ultimately for herself did she have to go back and stand in the midst of jealousy, envy, and hostility? How many days are we in situations that feel hopeless? In walking this morning, initially I was disappointed that the normally radiantly blue sky was all gray and cloudy. The sky had a heaviness that's not there on bright clear days. Prayerfully I looked around and was reminded that like nature, not every day we experience is going to be one of light and apparent beauty. There are cloudy days in life. Days of rain, storms, hurricanes; cold, chill. Days that feel miserable. Yet, regardless of the time, temperature, or barometric pressure, God is still there.

God is there for Hagar, and promises never to leave her. God has promised time and time again, to never, never, no, never leave us alone. No, never alone. No, never alone. God promised never to leave us, never to leave us alone. We are but to wait on God and be of good courage. God is always there, on cloudy, rainy days. God is still there. God is present right now, if we but open up our hearts.

GOD FOR US

God created us, God the Son came to show us how to love and love unconditionally; God the Holy Spirit is here to comfort us and give us power. Remember, it is not flesh and blood that we must come up against daily, but its powers and principalities: the powers of hate, greed, and jealousy. The powers of low self-esteem, fear, and envy cause us to harm others. The powers of needing to be first at all costs, of needing to be superior to our neighbors, of needing fame and to be in the limelight sometimes causes us to compromise ourselves, and sell out our souls, our partners and spouses, our children. We sell them out for a brief moment of feeling good about ourselves, a brief, brief moment that does not last. As Scripture tells us, they that "wait for the LORD shall renew their strength, they shall mount up with wings like eagles, they shall run and not be weary, they shall walk and not faint" (Isa. 40:31). Wait, wait on the Lord. Don't be too quick to sell out your souls like Judas for thirty pieces of silver—whatever that thirty pieces of silver may be. In the wilderness of the desert, in the depths of the valley, on the mountaintops with eagles, all there is, is the love of God, of love in relation; the hallmark for all healthy relationships.

GOD OPENS OUR EYES

Third, God opens our eyes, that we might see
living water of love.

As we wait on God, we are able to be with God and God can open our eyes that we might truly see. Some of us look, but we don't see. We look but can't see because we have all of these issues weighing us down. We have on designer glasses with blue, red, pink, or polka-dot lens that skew our vision. We can't see what we're looking at because we look through lens, not tinted by grace and love, but lens tinted by pain, by cancerous thoughts, by evil deeds, by shame and guilt. If we but wait on God, we can begin to see the living water of love.

Beloveds, no matter what we do, where we go, who we know, the only thing that is enduring, that lasts, that has value is love. Some people have died and left extraordinary demands to be buried in their cars. Others have huge mausoleums constructed for their repose. Some people spend all of their lives accumulating stuff, accumulating false friends, accumulating wealth—and they are miserable. They play a good game, but anyone tuned into God can see that life for what it is; a farce.

FOR KELLY, THE EULOGIZED

One of the things I have learned about Kelly was that he was real. He told his mother, whom he fondly called Mim, for example, that he wasn't going to dress up or wear suits, because she dressed him up too much as a child. He loved life and I'm sure if I called up John or Tahj now, they would tell you, Kelly was a guy who was really real. He did not pretend to be anything he wasn't. Some of you appreciated Kelly for who he was. Some of you didn't. Kelly is at peace now, and we have to deal with what we did or did not do to support and love him. So I invite you in the coming days to be with your grief. To take an assessment of your own lives, while you yet have time.

Figure out what is really important. Figure out why you do what you do. Get support and therapy or spiritual counseling to help you come to grips with who you are, and what you need to let go of. If you already know who you are, and you have been willing for God to open your eyes, continue to praise. As Christians, we are called to let our lights so shine before men and women that they might look to God. We are to be a Christ presence here on Earth.

For our sisters and brothers of other faith traditions, you too are called to be the light, to be a vessel of the living waters of love. No sacred book of any tradition claims life is fair. Life is not fair. But these texts do teach about love, about the importance of community, the importance of family, and the sacredness of life.

Friends and family, remember Kelly is now free. As we continue to live, we will experience many a wilderness within the deserts of life, but God and love are there. We may be thrown down into the depths of the valleys of heartache, despair, and grief; the light of God and love are there. When we wait on God and we have those mountaintop experiences with eagles, God and love are there; therein lies that which endures: relational love.

"When I was a child, I talked like a child, I thought like a child, I reasoned like a child. When I became a man, I put childish ways behind me. Now we see but a poor reflection as in a mirror; then we shall see face to face. Now I know in part; then I shall know fully, even as I am fully known.

And now these three remain: faith, hope and love. But the greatest of these is love" (1 Cor. 13:11–13 NIV). Let us move through the wilderness into the light.

13

A Preaching Desire

CHARLOTTE
McSWINE-HARRIS

BEFORE I BECAME A PREACHER

Early preparations were being made, unknown to me, to help filter the frustrations of being a woman in ministry. Growing up in a city that was touted as the "Cotton Capital of the World," I had never heard of a woman preacher. However, I knew that it was taboo for women to even enter the pulpit unless they were helping with church decorum. In my little home church, which sat off of Money Road, directly in front of the Yazoo River where I was baptized, I learned the realities associated with being a Christian woman. Quite frankly, I enjoyed the music ministry of the church and I learned to appreciate the point of the sermon presentation where our pastor, the Rev. A. W. Williams, made what I can only describe as a "sweet" sound with his voice. This is what we called "tuning" in our congregation.

In retrospect, I guess I "enjoyed" that part of the sermon also because it was a signal that church service was coming to a close. Although not a lot of words were shared with me about the church's expectations of me, this is where I discerned that children and women were treated differently than men. I learned that there were duties we could perform, places we could not be, and things we should not do. In other words, what was emphasized in our church was more of what we couldn't do than what we could do. Based on my observations, I "played" church at home and as I "played" church, I felt comfortable singing and shouting and serving as an usher, which often included taking the pastor a glass of cold ice water.

I felt very comfortable beginning a prayer with "this mo'ning (morning) our heavenly Father, we come before you head bowed and body bent . . ." I was at ease presenting my welcome for the Easter program that began with "Mama fixed me up so neat and daddy said doesn't she look sweet . . ." As an elementary student, I remember that my role in the Sunday school class was to help my teacher pronounce the words that she and the other children were unable to articulate properly.

I have some amazing images sketched in my psyche regarding the church. For example, we were taught to be skeptical about the sincerity of the minister. This unspoken and unwritten rule was universally understood because it was our understanding that we had to protect our church from the pastor. If we didn't we were told he'd take the money and abuse the women. This myth permeated the church and had the effect of gospel truth. Near the chancel area to the left, lodged in the corner, was a group of men who served as deacons. They were mostly old men who had been in the church a long time. In the center of the pulpit area were two huge burgundy chairs made of leather with brass studs. A plastic plant on a stand separated the chairs. Children could not enter this holy pulpit area under any circumstances.

The choir loft was located to the rear of the church. If one were to remove the men who were in the "shot calling" seats, the rest of congregation would consist mostly of women and children. Then there were those church meetings where the details of the pastor's pay would be fine-tuned and the amount of church salary (the specified offering) that grownups would give was voted on. I also remember vividly that I couldn't wait to become an adult so that I could give a dollar. My thinking was that grown-ups gave one dollar and children gave change mostly—a silver dime, as we called it.

One of my worst experiences in church happened when I was a teenager trying to dialogue with the preacher and one of the sisters turned to me and told me "Children don't do that." I liked "conversating" with the preacher because it took the edge off boredom for me. Seemingly, the church put many of the same limitations on me that were reflected in secular society, but they were less of a hurdle at school and home than they were at church. By this I mean, when I got off the school bus in the morning the first thing I would do when the weather permitted was to join in a game of marbles. As I got older it was playing basketball after lunch. Shooting marbles was sort of benign, not because I was the only girl that "shot marbles," but because it was an individual kind of experience.

Basketball, on the other hand, was more problematic because it was a team sport. I loved the game and my dad even put a basketball rack on the house for me. However, at school the kids would pick the best male players and most of the time the best female player or players would go next, and after the girls were chosen the boys who couldn't play if their lives depended upon it were finally selected. Most of the time nobody would openly say that I could not play; they simply chose me last or not at all. From this, and similar experiences, I have been able to negotiate being discriminated against simply because I was female. This is a strange but all too familiar feeling when one is only being who God has made her. I have never said I wanted to be a man, nor have I said that I can't be what I want because I am female. As a female, it is often important to check one's stamina to see if one is up to the challenge that is sometimes posed for one just to be oneself.

For example, can I cut my hair because I want to and for its convenience? Do I need some kind of medical explanation? Will the chairman of the search committee call me to see if am I trying to be more "manly" so I can get the church that brothers can rightly have because of their gender? Naturally, one has to develop a wholesome sense of self if one will survive when people think like this and treat you like this. Apparently I have been inoculated with something that allows me to keep trying to get on the team; to keep collecting as many marbles as I can in order to win—and most importantly to be who I like being over against norms that I "should " follow.

This does not mean that my journey has been pain and stain free. Nevertheless, there have been many monumental positive influences in my life, starting with my parents. My parents didn't try to limit or confine me to "girl things." However, my mom made me wear dresses for every schoolday picture-taking ceremony, and I recalled that I hated that experience! On the other hand, my dad bought me a .410 shotgun as a Christmas gift. He would also wake me up some mornings with instructions to "take a look at" one of our vehicles that would not operate properly or not at all. This meant that he wanted me to repair the truck.

He would leave the checkbook with me and tell me to take a look at the car and fix it if I could. Of course, he would emphatically tell me not to spend any more money than what I needed for the parts. My freedom at home helped me make the necessary positive adjustments in church and secular society. It has always been incidents like these that have allowed me to keep my head above water. While growing up, H. D., an older gentleman who lived across the street from me, said that I was a peculiar girl because I cut hair, fished, hunted, manicured our lawn, detailed our vehicles, and worked on lawnmowers, go-carts, cars, trucks, and vans. I also worked in the cotton fields during the summer either chopping cotton or riding the spray rig. Although H. D. thought these activities were peculiar for a female they have been rewarding even until this day, and as the older folk would say, "I wouldn't take nothing for my journey."

I also trailed my dad as he frequented many of the local churches. He sang with an all-male gospel group called "Melody Kings," and they vowed not to include women in the group because they didn't want the challenge of relational issues. Anyway, I went to hear him sing and sat on the second pew where the music was loudest because I wanted to be near the instruments. I was fascinated with the music and wanted to play drums, but my mother didn't want the noise because she suffered from migraine headaches. However, at some point, my mom didn't mind my bringing both the lead and bass guitars into the house, and I would get to pluck on the bass. My parents never told me what I could not be. As a matter of fact, my dad told me I could be something as novel as an astronaut and he nicknamed me his little "Astro."

My great-grandmother was another powerful influence in my life. The fact is that she has been the most powerful and positive influence in my life. Most people addressed her as "Miss Lottie"—the exception being white people. This all had to do with the fact that we lived on the Whittington plantation near Greenwood, Mississippi, for the first years of my life. My parents, my sisters, and I and a group of other people lived with my maternal great-grandmother, whom we affectionately called Mama. Mama was an extraordinary woman in the African American community in which we lived. If one needed something to drink or eat, or if one needed to borrow money, hitch a ride into town, or simply have someone put in a good word for them, Mama was the one to see. She was either well respected or highly feared.

I first learned about having two faces from "Mama." On the one hand, "Mama" had some admirable qualities and on the other hand she had some despicable and ugly ways. Nevertheless, I always think of her as an amazing woman. She would wear torn and ragged clothes that didn't match. It would be nothing to see Mama with a short-sleeve dress on and a long-sleeve thermal undershirt, a long pair of pants, and an apron at the same time while smoking a Mississippi Crook cigar. She taught us about common sense or "mother wit," survival techniques, and integrity but she wouldn't say a mumbling word about slavery.

She came from the old school. She was born around 1896 and passed on to us the ways of what seemed to be long ago. I remember a heated exchange with her when I decided I would no longer say "mister" to the boss man if his children did not address her in a respectful way. It pained me to see this older woman well in her sixties being called by her first name by children younger than I. Mama explained to me that it was a survival tactic that I needed to learn so that I could live a long time. Although I did not like it, I went along with it because I believed that my "Mama" would never tell me anything that would bring me harm.

It was next door to Mama's house that I had my first encounter with racism. While playing with the boss's children our playtime was interrupted when some of their little white friends showed up. I learned that they only played with me if they didn't have access to their white friends. The day I learned this I was deeply troubled; nevertheless, it is a lesson that has paid off many times since. For example, one has to understand in ministry that there are people whose only purpose is to use you until the so-called "real deal" comes along. From this experience, I have learned how to survive in hostile environments, places that were developed to keep me down. It is fascinating to note that from childhood to adulthood these experiences have been launching pads. All of this happened before I became a preacher.

By the time I entered college I was no longer satisfied at my home church. I knew there had to be something more. My church met then, as they do now, only on the third Sunday of each month. I went to other churches seeking something better. I didn't really know what that looked or felt like, but I did realize that I had not found it in my home church. While looking all over Greenwood, Mississippi, I found nothing that was much different from my church.

The second Sunday after I graduated college, I arrived in Kansas City, Missouri, early in the morning. I took a little nap in the home of my cousins Diann and Sammie West, who'd allowed me to come and live with them so that I could become gainfully employed. Diann insisted that I go to church that morning in order to meet Sam Watson, an employment entrepreneur. I sat in on a Sunday school class that was designated for my age group. I felt comfortable enough to read and to make a few comments. Things went really well. The church was so huge (seating approximately a thousand people). It had running water and central air. The people were immaculately dressed.

When I entered the sanctuary my breath was almost taken away. I had never seen anything like this before in my life. For some strange reason, I sat near the back. The sanctuary was filled with people, and the man playing the piano could "really play" and read notes, unlike the people I had heard for years "bumping" on the piano. (By "bumping" I mean what was played could not be identified until the lyrics would come forth.) Everything was formal. We had hymnals and programs that directed us through the worship service.

All of that was okay, but when Reverend Dr. Mac Charles Jones, who is now deceased, read the Scripture, I was mesmerized because I had never heard Scripture read like that. He got my attention and that day I knew I had found something better. Rev. Jones preached a familiar text and what he said all the way through mattered. It meant something to me because I understood the gospel message as never before. He was smart and articulate, and he had traveled. I was introduced to Sam Watson, and he agreed to assist me with finding a job. That meeting, however, was not nearly as important as my hearing the preacher preach that morning.

I remember making this comment to my cousins when they questioned me about the worship service later that day. I said, "The preacher reminded of Martin Luther King Jr." Not that I knew a lot about Dr. King except that when he spoke I felt something positive inside me. In the same manner Dr. Jones's preaching helped me to realize that "tuning" the voice was not preaching and when "tuning" is used to replace substance it is only a good sound wasted. This guy spoke of concepts that I had never heard.

Liberation, justice, and peace seemed to be his forte. The manner in which he illumined the Scripture to teach those things was incredible. I became a member of the St. Stephen Baptist Church in July of 1985 after being in Kansas City for a couple of months. I went through the new member orientation program, and that was a blast. I took notes that I occasionally take a look at even now. When it came to church life, I was in heaven. I was learning so much. Church was so fulfilling and challenging to me that it helped overhaul my life. I began a journey right there. I learned that the gospel was portable and that I was obligated to take it everywhere. Nothing kept me from church on Sunday morning. I went to Sunday school. I joined the choir and went to choir rehearsal.

I went to the Baptist Training Union (BTU) on Sunday evenings and to outside engagements where our pastor was guest preacher. I took special classes offered at the church. I tutored youth at a group home and visited nursing homes. I was involved in the work of ministry, and I was overwhelmed in a good way by my new church life.

Of course some of the same atrocities perpetrated in the South took place in the Midwest; nevertheless, it was mostly enjoyable until I saw the politicking going on in the church. But while this ugly monster was raising its head, another monster was being raised on my job. I worked as an electronic technician at a company called Midland International, and while there, racism, sexism, and ageism tried to destroy me. I was distressed because I thought one went to college to get a job and work with nice people. I was introduced to yet another training ground. I had experienced home, school, play, church, and now work.

The first two weeks I was literally placed in a corner and given two thick manuals to read. Had I not asked my supervisor when was I going to start work, I may still be in that corner. I was finally placed with a teaching assistant who was white, probably in her mid- to late thirties, who had no prior experience working closely with a twenty-two-year old African American woman. She was on my left and to my immediate right was a young white male about my age who had attended a trade school. Because I was not prepared for the real world after college, the racism on the job had a major negative impact on me.

I didn't know about jealousy and racism on the job. I didn't realize that my race was going to be a problem. I thought I had left that in Mississippi until I found myself in the mall exiting through a door being held by a white man whose wife was on the floor tying one of her shoes. I said, "Excuse me," and passed through the open door. He said to me, "I was not holding that door for you." Once I learned that the playing field was not as friendly, I made the same adjustment that I made back home. I relied on being the "me" I liked rather than the "me" people wanted me to be. I had African Americans teasing me about my southern drawl and making fun of the fact that I wanted to "mash keys" and not potatoes and "cut off the lights" instead of turning them off. But the nurturing that I was getting at church—the constant reminder from Pastor Jones that you are somebody and that your color shouldn't matter, your gender shouldn't matter, and your age shouldn't matter—helped me scale the wall of oppression. I was so eager to live what the preacher talked about until it drove me to constantly ask myself, "What am I supposed be doing for God?"

Although I participated in a number of ministries at the church, I felt that there was still another work that God was calling me to do. While at my job as a technician I developed a rare lung disease that forced me to quit my job because the doctor said there was a 50 percent chance that my illness was due to my work, although he was unwilling to put that in writing. I took a job as a teacher's aid/substitute at an elementary school, and I did a good job with the kids. But I was very unfulfilled or I did not feel like this was the place for me. Upon saying yes to preach the gospel, it seemed as if the bumpy ride had changed to smooth. This, however, was more a wish dream than reality.

SINCE I HAVE BECOME A PREACHER

Upon answering the call to preach I was licensed by the St. Stephen Church on Super Bowl Sunday of 1990. On that night, my pastor made a profound statement that deeply affected how I handle myself as a preacher. He said to me, with a platform filled with mostly male preachers, "Charlotte, many of the doors that I and some of these other fellows can walk through will be closed to you, but the doors that God wants you to walk through will be opened."

That one statement has made my journey easier. Pastor Jones in those few words taught me a lesson that has stayed with me. He was really saying to me, "Don't go around using unnecessary energy to open doors. Don't walk around with your gloves on and laced all the time. Rest on your gift. Be confident and competent and you will get where you need to go." He wasn't saying don't fight and don't be prepared to fight, but be prepared to balance fighting with periods of restraint from fighting. Pastor Jones was teaching and training me long before I answered my call to the gospel ministry. I remember him saying that there was no sermon without kerygma. Because of who he was as a mentor, I have not had to endure as much as some other women in the field of ministry—or should I say, he prepared me to sidestep some of the stuff.

Dr. Jones told every preacher he licensed that preparation was required, and so I was ushered off to seminary. Robert Stephens, our evangelism minister, helped me make my initial contact with the Virginia Union University School of Theology. Dr. Stephens was instrumental in helping me believe in myself. He and others were paving the way and moving obstacles so that I could sail as smoothly as possible. Dr. Stephens also made arrangements for me to connect with the Rev. Dr. James Henry Harris, pastor-elect of the Second Baptist Church in Richmond, Virginia. Upon my arrival, I made myself known to Dr. Harris and he scheduled a meeting with me for a later date.

Dr. Harris embraced me and afforded me countless opportunities that women, or even other male classmates, were not given on a regular basis. I remember there was one hush-hush kind of situation with a deacon not wanting me to serve him Communion. In addition to being female, I was not yet ordained. For the most part, Dr. Harris made my tenure as pain free as possible, sometimes literally taking blows that were meant for me. I accomplished a lot of firsts at Second Baptist Church, and I know that without Dr. Harris's continued help and support there would be no way for me to be where I am today. The lesson is that women in ministry have to connect with a minister and ministry that is headed somewhere.

There are doors that God uses spiritual fathers and mothers to open for us, and if we are not connected and plugged in, they can't bless our lives. My point is that I learned that I could not do it by myself. From an internship to a part-time assistant to the pastor to a full-time minister of Christian education, loyalty to your mentor counts. Dr. Harris has never shown any hesitation or trepidation in recommending me for opportunities in ministry. All of the strides I have made since being in Virginia are in some way associated with his kindness.

One of the most trying times that I have experienced as a minister came during a very brief tenure as the pastor of a rural church in Charles City, Virginia. I was so happy to be chosen as pastor. I didn't doubt my ability or my competence to pastor, but because I am a woman I relied on previous experience in ministry. I had said if all things were equal then certainly I could pastor. But all things were not equal, so I didn't think pastoring would happen in a million years. I knew it would be possible if I changed denominations, but I never thought that was a necessity. I had always said that God would have to do something special before I would dare to think about pastoring because I have been very close to situations that were unfair, un-Christian, unjust, and unacceptable.

I knew that it took a special person to deal with people mistreating and abusing you simply because you wanted to usher in the will of God. I must say that it was difficult to see a dream go down the drain. There were so many people present at the "called meeting" to see if the church wanted to vote to vacate the pulpit. The consensus was to hold another meeting to declare the pulpit vacant or occupied. I never thought I would pastor as a Baptist woman, nor did I think I would be fired from a church. Even in 2004, some women are still fighting to either knock each other down or to keep each other down. The most vocal and vigilant opponents to my pastorate were other women.

While the church was about to vote on whether to keep me as pastor, a woman was heard saying these words: "Where is she? Point her out to me." Women were used to lead the way for me to be fired. I mention this because there is an illusion that females are going to stick together. I spent countless hours trying to convince people and win people over, but to my chagrin I learned a powerful lesson: work with the people who want to work. By following this rule, one will always get more accomplished than trying to convert folk.

I was voted out/fired or asked to leave Little Elam Baptist Church after an eight-month stay. From a pastoral perspective, I have learned to try to be a pastor in the midst of mess and not lose sight of the big picture. Moreover, I had a fine example in Dr. Mac Charles Jones, who promoted fighting fair with people who used underhanded tactics. I never heard any of my mentors say, "I am going to get back at these people for hindering the advancement of the kingdom of God." Again, it is important to be around positive people in ministry.

I often find myself saying that I have not had to fight as hard because of some wonderful male pastors. Among them are Mac Charles Jones, Robert Louis Stephens, James Henry Harris, John W. Kinney, Gregory Theodore Headen, Darryl Frederick Husband, A. Lincoln James, Nathaniel Douglas West, William Eric Jackson, and Dewayne Edwin Whitehead. Unfortunately, I have not named any female models in ministry. This is not to say that there are not any out there but rather that I have learned to benefit from where I find myself. Although I don't reference any women in particular, I do realize that I stand on the shoulders of all the women who led the way in ministry whether they were licensed or not.

Ultimately, I want to lead a conscientious Christian congregation; a congregation that is doing ministry person by person, one step at a time. A large following definitely would flex my ego, but I am much more interested in Christians making an impact on one another and the unchurched population. When my pastoral ministry is concluded, my desire is that people can say that I did just that.

I am keenly aware that I did not give equal time to my life before I was a preacher and my life after I became a preacher. That is because the life I lived before I became a preacher is informing the life I live as a preacher. "Mama" used to say, "You can't know where you are going if you don't know where you have been." I thank God for the before and after.

Sermon: *"At the Table"*
Mark 2: 13–17

CHARLOTTE McSWINE-HARRIS

We live in a time where it seems easy to dismiss and exclude people from an opportunity to sit at the table. We live in a time where exclusionary attitudes suggest that others are not "fit" to sit at the table. Consequently, persons are deliberately plotting and planning to keep some other people from the table. I have a feeling that some of us knowingly and unknowingly keep others from the table. We often think we have a right to keep people from the table because of how people look. We think we have a right to keep people from the table because of a person's past.

We think we have a right to push people from the table because of gender, sexual orientation, size, and color. The fact of the matter is that some of us have made decisions not to welcome persons to the table because they have injured our egos, rubbed us the wrong way, or crossed someone dear to us. No matter what our reason, fabricated or true, we do not have a right to keep people from the table. We do not have a right to keep anyone from the table because of the bold demonstration that Jesus makes in this text.

This language of fellowship "at the table" has to do with being in the presence of God. See and hear verse 15 (TEV) in our text: "Later on Jesus was having a meal in Levi's house. A large number of tax collectors and outcasts was following Jesus, and many of them joined him and his disciples at the table." Jesus shows us to be at table with humankind, even though he knows it's not kosher for him, a Jewish man, to mix and mingle at the table with sinners. His actions highlight his interest and desire for us to mix at the table.

The company Jesus is keeping is considered morally and ethically unacceptable; however, Jesus does not allow this rule to keep him from being with people who have "messed up." Jesus didn't just sit at a table designated for outcasts only for the benefit people back then. He was doing it for persons

200

today as well. Jesus' sitting at the table points backward as well as forward. Christians have a duty to follow Jesus' lead. Therefore it is incumbent upon us to tear down barriers and boundaries so that folk can get to the table.

If we don't do it, we will miss opportunities for reconciliation. If we don't do it, we will miss opportunities for redemption. If we don't do it, we will miss opportunities for restoration. If we don't do it, we will miss opportunities for forgiveness. Since we know what happens at the table, we have to be eager to invite folk to the table. We have to become fanatics about making room at the table for people who don't have it all together; people who may have been born on the other side of the tracks; people with gender issues that may not represent the status quo; people whose thinking may not be in sync with our own. If we want our tables to be Christlike we have to go out of our way to get folk to the table.

How do we get people to the table? How do we overcome the obstacles that often chase people from the table? Creating opportunities for the newly called to have center stage will get people to the table. In other words, when new people are called into the fold of Christ they can get a chance to shine without having to earn a place. Please seek to see and hear verse 14 (TEV): "As he walked along he saw a tax collector, Levi, the son of Alphaeus, sitting in his office, Jesus said to him, 'Follow me.' Levi got up and followed him."

Levi's resume does not include a long history of following Christ. It does not include him living in an extraordinarily righteous way. Nevertheless, we are at Levi's house where the table is spread. If we follow this example, the newly called will not have to worry about access through family ties. They will not have to worry about being too young to lead. We don't see Levi mentioned again in the Gospel of Mark, but for this moment he shines. If we follow this example, the newly called will not have to worry about a legacy. They will not be bogged down by gender issues because we are making room for them to "be."

All too often in our clubs, cliques, and churches the new people have to wait for the seniors to die before they can take center stage. Before new people can lead we demand that they clean up their acts. We insist that they quit smoking, drinking, fornicating, cheating, lying, or stealing. If we are to have a table that looks like the one Jesus sat—where people with issues sat—we have to give the newly called center stage. We can let the newly called have center stage via church school because it will give them a platform. It allows them a chance to know what their local church represents. It will keep new people from being lost in the crowd as well as lessening the use of the revolving door.

When we allow the newly called to have center stage we gain momentum in the area of soul winning for Christ because they come with families and coworkers to whom we might not have access; they travel in circles that may be very different from ours. That is why it is crucial that they get center stage. The young man with the baggy pants, the young lady whose stomach is swollen because she is pregnant, the father who has done nothing to take care of his children, and the mother who aborted her child without any consultation with the father—they all deserve center stage. Let's get them to the table where some cures and resolutions may be found for some of the atrocities that plague us today. Let's get them to the table because they count and because we will be doing the will of God.

Not only do we get people to the table by allowing the newly called to have center stage, but we can also get people to the table when we allow the table to become a symbol for inclusivity. In other words, the table represents a place for everybody. See and here verse 15 again as barriers come down: "Later on Jesus was having a meal in Levi's house. A large number of tax collectors and other outcasts was following Jesus, and many of them joined him and his disciples at the table."

The table must reflect inclusivity. Look around this table where Jesus and the rest sat. Look at Jesus' audience. There were persons there who were accused of overtaxing their own people for personal gain. Please, look around the table and notice it was not just a few people, but the text says, "a large number of tax collectors." Look around the table; outcasts were at the table. Consider some of our modern outcasts, for example, people who have been to jail, people who have bad habits—drug addicts, liars, backbiters, cheaters and beaters, overeaters, molesters, murderers, and so forth.

By all means, go ahead and put your sin on the list. If I have not named your indiscretion, just plug it in because the good news is that no matter what you may have done there is room at the table for you and me. Not only were the outcasts there. Not only were the tax collectors there, but the text says that the disciples were there. The Bible never says that in order for one to be called one has to have a flawless history. Just look around the table at persons who occupied the center of Jesus' circle. Judas would have been there, and we know what he did. Peter was there, and we know what he did. Thomas was there, and we know what he did. Levi was there, and we know what he did. None of them dotted every i and crossed every t.

Most importantly, Jesus was at the table. This is the table we need to emulate. Jesus allows them to sit at the table because being at the table really has nothing to do with our indiscretions. It has to do with Jesus' agenda and authority. Jesus calls and we follow. It's ironic, but during Jesus' day it was common for the disciple to approach the teacher and ask to study with him. Jesus reversed this scenario and he calls us—letting us know how much we are needed, letting us know how important we are to him, letting us know that past failures do not prevent a present relationship with him. It is not about how good we have been but rather how good he is to us.

The text says it much better: "People who are well do not need a doctor, but only those who are sick. I have not come to call the respectable people, but the outcasts" (vs. 17 TEV). Jesus' response is a call to inclusivity, and it is the key to getting people to the table. Nobody has a right to block us from the table. Ultimately, each person has to look at his or her life and make the call. Whether I am a respectable person or an outcast, the words of invitation are the same: Welcome to the table!